THE RAMSEYS AT SWAN POND

THE *Ramseys*

AT SWAN POND

*The Archaeology and History
of an East Tennessee Farm*

CHARLES H. FAULKNER

THE UNIVERSITY OF TENNESSEE PRESS / KNOXVILLE

Library of Congress Cataloging-in-Publication Data

Faulkner, Charles H.
The Ramseys at Swan Pond : the archaeology and history of an East Tennessee farm /
Charles H. Faulkner. — 1st ed.
    p. cm.
Includes bibliographical references and index.
ISBN-13: 978-1-62190-303-1
1. Knoxville Region (Tenn.)—Antiquities. 2. Tennessee, East—Antiquities.
3. Archaeology and history—Tennessee—Knoxville Region. 4. Excavations
(Archaeology)—Tennessee—Knoxville Region. 5. Ramsey, Francis A. (Francis
Alexander), 1764–1820—Homes and haunts—Tennessee—Knoxville Region.
6. Ramsey family—Homes and haunts—Tennessee—Knoxville Region. 7. Farm
life—Tennessee—Knoxville Region—History. 8. Material culture—Tennessee—
Knoxville Region—History. 9. Knoxville Region (Tenn.)—Biography. 10. Knoxville
Region (Tenn.)—History. I. Title.

F444.K7F38 2008
976.8'85—dc22   2007027436

*To my wife, Terry Faulkner, who inspired my interest
in Knoxville history and archaeology, and to our daughters,
Kelly and Stephanie, who (with their mom) long endured
my sometimes physical and mental absence while
I was digging and writing.*

CONTENTS

ILLUSTRATIONS

ACKNOWLEDGMENTS

My most memorable experience during the historical and archaeological research at Ramsey House was meeting and working with the wonderful people I met from 1985 to 2007. Despite the years, they have not faded in my memory, but if I forget someone who encouraged and helped me along the way, I am deeply sorry.

The Ramsey House archaeological project would not have gotten "into the ground" so to speak if it were not for the board of directors, executive directors, and staff of Ramsey House who encouraged the research and were so hospitable when we were excavating at the site. My sincere appreciation to members of the board of directors: David Duncan, Ruth Howe, Connie Hudgens, Kay Long, Janet Maynard, Anna Patterson, Max Ramsey, Mary Jane Sharp, Joe Spence, and Mary Jane Sharp, and Nancy Wagner; and to the executive directors: Lisa Allen Belleman, Marjorie Krull, Fiona McAnaly, and Helma Sickles; and the staff: April Almond, Leicle Cooper, Ben Frazier, Jim and Sara Frazier, and Tom Gass.

I wish to especially acknowledge the help of Robert Van Deventer, who since 1952 was instrumental in preserving the history of the Ramsey family and Ramsey House. Another valuable contribution was made by the descendants of the last Ramsey family to live in the house during interviews with my wife at the 1985 Ramsey Family Reunion: Jeanette Powell, Conrad Lam, and Claudialea Watts. I have also had the pleasure of meeting Fred R. Ramsey, who shared his knowledge of the family at the last family reunion.

I also wish to thank the descendents of the John Kinzel family, Amy Winter McCallum and Bob Winter, who contacted me about their family's connection to Ramsey House and shared their family history with me.

Another high point of this research was my interviews with former owners, residents, and neighbors, whose reminiscences about the "stone house" are a valuable part of this study. My appreciation to Mrs. James Armstrong;

Mrs. Walter Combs; Cas Cox; the Clyde Hickmans; Max Kreis and his parents, Mr. and Mrs. Sam Kreis; Sammie Lane; Lester Lane; the Ike Raders; the James Sands, and Edith Watson.

Obviously, this study would not have been possible without the hard work and dedication of my field school directors and assistants, undergraduate and graduate students enrolled in my field school courses, volunteers, and students in my historical archaeology laboratory at the University of Tennessee. The names of my field directors and assistants read like a who's who of my talented graduate students, most of whom have gone on to be professional archaeologists: Todd Ahlman, Valerie Altheizer, Susan Andrews, Jennifer Barber, Paul Avery, Tim Baumann, Phil Carr, Sean Coughlin, Ginny Ellenburg, Tanya Faberson, Mark Groover, Brooke Hamby, Alan Longmire, Dean Owens, Kim Pyszka, Wayne Roberts, and Amy Lambeck Young. Laboratory supervisors include graduate students Susan Andrews, Tanya Faberson, Brooke Hamby, Tommy Stinson, and Wendy Tanner.

I regret that space does not allow me to individually name all the field school students, field volunteers, and laboratory students. To give the reader some idea of the sheer numbers of these people to whom I owe a debt of gratitude, there were 30 volunteers, 77 field school students, and 67 lab students who learned the basics of historical archaeology during the Ramsey House project.

Much of the research at Ramsey House was funded by grants from the Tennessee Historical Commission. I wish to acknowledge the contributions of Cleva Marrow, who wrote the grant proposals for Ramsey House; Steve Rogers, who ably handled the grants at the Tennessee Historical Commission; Frank Sparkman, who assisted in the grant writing; and Pam Poe and Charlene Weaver, who kept track of the grants in the UT Department of Anthropology.

The preparation of the final reports to the Tennessee Historical Commission and the Association for the Preservation of Tennessee Antiquities, Knoxville Chapter, and the completion of this manuscript are the result of the assistance from a number of people, including Steve Cotham, McClung Collection; Sherry Turner Hermann and Doris Martinson, Knox County Archives; and Trent Hanner, Tennessee State Archives and Library. For cheerfully giving me professional advice about historical and archaeological questions that stumped me: Donald Ball, Elwood Christ, Steve Ferrell, Bernard Hermann, Victor Hood, James Hooper, and Amos Loveday answered my letters and e-mails promptly. For taking and developing many photographs used in this book: Nick Myers and Carla Sharp, UT Photo Services. For the use of some historic photographs in this book: Ms. James Dean, J. Bennett Graham, and Ms. Edith Watson. For typing the final reports: Cheryl Shope and especially computer guru Donna Griffin Patton, who also helped organize and reproduce this manuscript, and Carol Chamberlain, UT Graphic Arts, who took charge of printing the final reports on the Ramsey House Project to the Knoxville Chapter of the APTA and the Tennessee Historical Commission. And finally, I feel special appreciation for the help of my wife, Terry Faulkner, who drew the figures and shares my fascination with the history of Ramsey House.

Introduction

HISTORICAL ARCHAEOLOGY

Since the discovery of the ancient cities of the classical world in the eighteenth and nineteenth centuries, the American public has been fascinated with archaeology. Unfortunately, this fascination has sometimes resulted in the erroneous perception that archaeology is a treasure hunt, adventurous archaeologists like Indiana Jones discovering buried cities and snatching artifacts from ancient temples to display in museum cases. Archaeology is not the avocational collecting of ancient relics but a science that studies tangible material remains of any past human activity, using the scientific method to describe these activities and establish their meaning in the evolution of human culture.

Another false assumption about archaeology is that it only deals with the most ancient human cultures. While some subfields such as prehistoric archaeology are concerned with humans who lived before the time of written records, other archaeologists study American culture as recent as the Second World War. This subfield is historical archaeology, often defined as the study of both archaeological and historical data recovered on sites that date after the European discovery of America.

One might ask why we need historical archaeology in the United States; after all, we have been a literate society since the founding of our nation, and our libraries and homes seem replete with literature about our historical past. Sad to say, however, the record of our nation's exciting and colorful history is woefully incomplete and is often biased. It contains gaps due to inadequate documentation of the lives of ordinary people, and it is often biased because until recently it has focused on our political and economic history rather than social and cultural activities, concentrating on "great" events and the elite or "distinguished" persons. When American historical archaeology emerged as a viable discipline at famous historical sites such as Williamsburg and Jamestown in the 1940s, it merely complemented current histories by concentrating on memorable events and notable citizens of those places. Excluded from these "notable" citizens were nonwhite minorities, working-class whites, and women of all ethnic groups and social classes.

By the end of the twentieth century, historical archaeology in the United States no longer focused on the mansions of the rich and famous, as it had become increasingly associated with the study of cultural anthropology, revisionist history, and the civil rights movement. This shift in the focus of historical archaeology has been called "backyard archaeology," the study of the cultural remains of people who worked in the kitchen as well as the squires who were served in the manor parlor (Fairbanks 1977). It had become the archaeology of all Americans who have constituted our society, both the privileged and the disenfranchised, the highly visible and the practically invisible persons in our written history. By the 1970s, historical archaeology no longer merely supplemented what is often a subjective historical record of the past but focused on the objective study of material culture with a new emphasis on answering anthropological as well as historical questions about our nation's history. It is this combination of archaeological, anthropological, and historical inquiry that makes American historical archaeology such a unique, informative, and exciting field today.

The archaeological excavations at Ramsey House, the Ramsey family farm settled by Francis Alexander Ramsey in the late eighteenth century, referred to hereafter as Swan Pond[1] in Knox County, Tennessee, are an excellent example of this historical "backyard archaeology." While many of the important events and activities at this historic site are associated with the elite and prominent Ramsey family, residents representing other ethnic groups and socioeconomic strata who played important roles at Swan Pond were also revealed in this study. Primarily through archaeological research, we now know the Ramseys were just one family among numerous individuals and families who lived at the site. Swan Pond was visited by prehistoric Native Americans thousands

1. The names "Ramsey House" and "Swan Pond" will be used concurrently in this study, the former referring to the stone dwelling constructed in 1796–1797 and the latter to the property around it that was a part of the Ramsey family holdings in the late eighteenth and the nineteenth century. Swan Pond was a large body of water near which the house was located.

of years before Europeans set foot on this continent, and it was the home of enslaved African Americans and, later, white tenant farmers. Like so many other large farms and plantations in the antebellum South, Swan Pond was largely operated by enslaved African Americans whose presence is completely ignored in the historic record. And following the historic pattern of many large farms in East Tennessee, it was affected by the Civil War, when farmers often struggled to make ravaged farms productive again and large tracts were continually subdivided through the system of patrimony. The lifeways of later yeoman and tenant farmers are seldom mentioned in our local histories, and it has largely been through the recent archaeological study of southern farmsteads that their important place in our ever-changing rural social and economic systems of the past 200 years has been recorded.

Even the daily lifeways of the reasonably well-documented Ramsey family at Swan Pond are incompletely known. Letters between patriarch Francis Alexander Ramsey and his children relate interesting family matters, but virtually none describe what to them were mundane day-to-day activities. How did the landscape change during the historic occupation of the site? When, where, and how did daily activities take place in various areas of the farm? What did they eat? What kind of table did they set? What did they wear? How did they amuse themselves? These are questions that often only archaeology can answer, through the study of material culture such as fence lines and outbuildings, animal bones and sherds of pottery and glass, buttons and buckles, and marbles and doll parts. It is the study of these tangible clues from the past within the context of the archaeological record that tells the real human story, an ethnography of continuing human challenges and successes at Swan Pond from the prehistoric past into the mid-twentieth century.

Chapter 1

OVERVIEW OF EXCAVATIONS
AT SWAN POND

Viewed from the broader national perspective, the archaeological study of Swan Pond examines the place of East Tennessee in the dynamic economic and social milieu of the United States from the late eighteenth through the early twentieth century. One question still asked is did the southern Appalachian region, often characterized in the literature as isolated and backward in the past, fully participate in the vibrant economic and social dynamics of the past 200 years? Did East Tennesseans from the earliest period of settlement have access to the resounding and expanding economic prosperity of the past 200 years of this young nation?

The Ramsey House was built in 1797 for Francis Alexander Ramsey, a prominent early settler of East Tennessee. Purchased in 1952 by the Association for the Preservation of Tennessee Antiquities (APTA) to save this beautiful stone structure from certain destruction, through the years it has been developed into an outstanding house museum by the Knoxville Chapter of the APTA (Figure 1). Like many historic houses, however, it stands a lonely and silent vigil in East Knox County, the property robbed of the numerous outbuildings that once graced the grounds and where many of the daily household and farm activities took place from the late eighteenth through the early twentieth century. The outbuildings, so important in the interpretation of the lifeways at Swan Pond, were torn down long before the purchase of the property by the APTA, and very little documentary evidence remains as to their location or function. The landscape, too, has changed dramatically since

FIGURE 1. Ramsey House, photographed in 1985.

the Ramseys first settled the site in the late eighteenth century, transformed by the ax, the plow, and the bulldozer from an unspoiled Eden into today's bustling suburbia.

At the present time, three modern buildings stand at Swan Pond in the vicinity of historic Ramsey House. These include the modern log caretaker's house near the kitchen, a refurbished cement block and frame twentieth-century milking barn now serving as the visitors center, and a log shed to the rear of the visitors center that was recently moved onto the property. The restoration of the Ramsey House over the past 50 years, the construction and moving of these modern buildings onto the property, the building of driveways and parking lots, the cultivation of flower beds, and the installation of buried utility lines have compromised archaeologically sensitive areas and features that retain the imprint of the site's prehistoric and historic past.

In 1985, the Knoxville Chapter of the APTA contacted me at the University of Tennessee, Knoxville, Department of Anthropology about initiating a long-range, comprehensive archaeological project to locate the former outbuildings in the inner house yard and peripheral farmyard at Swan Pond to determine the function of these buildings and systematically collect artifacts used by the residents of this site during the prehistoric and historic periods. Two short-term archaeological excavations had been conducted previously at Ramsey House in 1973 and 1976, the former a test in front of the house to determine the construction of the original entrance (Dickson 1974) and the latter a follow-up test adjacent to the front doorway (Townsend 1976). Neither project, however, produced any definitive data on the original entrance, nor were they part of a long-range plan for establishing the cultural history of the site.

Comprehensive archaeological projects based on such a long-range research design were first carried out under my direction during eight field seasons between 1985 and 2001 with student crews and archaeological field schools funded through contracts and grants from the APTA and the Tennessee Historical Commission.

As previously mentioned, a distinguishing feature of historical archaeology is that it integrates data in documentary records with archaeological remains to reach a more objective and complete interpretation of a site's cultural history. Ideally, the historical archaeologist gleans information from the historic documents about who lived on the site, when they lived there, and what they did there that left an archaeological record that can be systematically recovered and interpreted. When archaeological investigations at Swan Pond began in 1985, I first undertook an archival and informant study of the property, publishing the data in a monograph entitled "A History of the Ramsey House and Its Occupants, 1797–1952" (1986). This study attempted to identify all the families who lived in the Ramsey House until the APTA purchased the property in 1952. I was immediately struck by the rarity in the documents examined of descriptions of the cultural landscape of the earlier Swan Pond farm and the daily activities that took place there.

The history of Ramsey House was originally divided into the Ramsey period (1793–1866), the Victorian period (1866–1912) and the Modern period (1912–1952) (Faulkner 1986). This chronology is modified in the present study and now includes the prehistoric period (ca. 10,000 B.C.–A.D. 1783), the early Ramsey period (1783–1820), the later Ramsey period (1820–1866), the Victorian period (1866–1912), and the Modern period (1912–1952). As is the case in most ongoing historical studies, additional documentation was revealed between 1985 and the present as previously unknown written records, photographs, and informants who had lived in the house or knew previously unrecorded oral histories were discovered.

PRELIMINARIES TO AN ARCHAEOLOGICAL INVESTIGATION AT SWAN POND

Scientific archaeology is grounded in the fact that tangible material remains— the artifacts (tools, ornaments, etc.) and features (foundations, trash pits, postholes, etc.)—found on an archaeological site are systemically related and largely result from human cultural behavior. This relationship is discovered by carefully and accurately observing and recording the horizontal (spatial) and vertical (chronological) relationship of artifacts and features in their archaeological context. Spatial relationships of these archaeological remains are determined with a grid designated by stakes, pins, or some other markers on the ground surface accurately tied with an engineer's transit by distance and direction to a permanent principal datum point. Vertical relationships are established with a permanent benchmark, either a known sea-level elevation point or more commonly an arbitrary elevation point that establishes depth (chronological) relationships of artifacts and features within the site.

Spatial and Chronological Controls at Swan Pond

The first priority upon commencement of excavation at Swan Pond in 1985 was the establishment of an overall grid system for the site so that accurate horizontal controls would continue to be maintained throughout the project and during any future excavation at the site. Unfortunately, no grid appears to have been established in the testing of the front door area in 1976 (Townsend 1976), and we could not relocate the datum for the 1973 excavation of the front porch area (Dickson 1974). Therefore, it was necessary to establish a new grid on the site.

The new grid provided maximum accuracy for the 1985 fieldwork and for the fieldwork through the 2001 season and beyond. The principal datum point is an iron rod placed at the northwest corner of the house and designated 100N110E. This location has not been disturbed for 200 years and should remain a permanent datum point as long as the Ramsey House stands. The designation 100N110E allows us to expand the grid in any direction across the entire site on north-south and east-west axes. Iron rods were also driven into the ground just below grade at 100N100E and 50N100E parallel to the orientation of the house. The 100E midline line was located so that there were no obstructions across the front, side, or rear areas of the yard or parallel to the Ramsey House orientation because the foundations of outbuildings, when located, would usually also run parallel with the house (and therefore the grid) and could be more easily traced and mapped (Roberts 1986:4). This has proven to be the case with the early outbuildings found thus far at Swan Pond. As fieldwork progressed beyond the northwest house yard after 1985, additional principal datums were placed on the property, mostly ¼-inch PVC pipe, so that excavation in these other areas of the property could be more easily tied to the overall site grid.

A principal benchmark for vertical control (elevation) was established in 1985 on the bottom stone step leading to the rear entrance of the house. This point could be seen from the entire rear yard area and was given an arbitrary elevation of 100 feet. When testing commenced in the east side yard in 1994, a second principal benchmark was tied to the original elevation point by the placement of a PVC pipe near the southeast corner of the caretaker's house.

ARCHAEOLOGICAL TESTING

The archaeological testing of the Swan Pond site began in 1985 and proceeded in successive years to primarily cover most of the area where both prehistoric and historic habitation was probable. This includes virtually all of the peninsula that originally protruded into Swan Pond and on which the Ramseys built their home, and the adjacent upland across the former pond to the east where a modern rental house now stands.

Archaeological testing is often accomplished by what is called "shovel testing," digging a small shovel-width hole on grid points to subsoil or a precultural soil horizon to locate buried features such as foundations and concentrations of artifacts. Such locations can then be further explored by excavating larger areas usually referred to as units or blocks. Shovel tests, however, can be dug with other tools besides the ordinary shovel. For example, the common two-handled posthole digger or a manual soil auger can also be employed to remove soil for examination. For very deeply buried archaeological soils even a power soil auger may be used. The choice of digging implements is based on a number of factors, which will not be covered here. At Swan Pond, a standard posthole digger, which can be centered over the grid point and removes a consistent volume of soil, was used.

1985 Testing

Testing in 1985 began in the northwest quadrant of the rear inner house yard where an unconfirmed oral tradition maintained Francis Alexander Ramsey's office was originally located. As was standard procedure throughout the testing phase in the inner house yard, the 181 posthole tests were dug on 3-foot centers. Throughout the testing phase from 1985 to 1996 soil was removed in ½-foot increments until subsoil clay was reached or the test could not continue due to an obstruction such as a large rock or large tree root. All soil was screened through ¼-inch hardware cloth. No evidence of Ramsey's office was found in this area of the yard, but this testing did reveal prehistoric and historic features (Roberts 1986).

Between February 1989 and June 1995, four areas in the peripheral rear yard and twentieth-century farmyard/barnyard areas were tested. In February 1989, 127 posthole tests on 3- foot centers were dug north of the concrete-block visitors center to explore this area in anticipation of an expansion of this building in that direction. No evidence of eighteenth- or nineteenth-century structures was found although numerous architectural remains of a former twentieth-century barn were recovered (Faulkner and Young 1989a). Emergency testing was initiated due to a change in construction plans in September 1989, with seven 1-foot by 1-foot shovel tests into a gravel parking area in front of the visitors center. Again only twentieth-century artifacts were found (Faulkner and Young 1989b). Testing of the rear barnyard area continued in April 1994, when 46 posthole tests were dug in the grassy parking lot east of the visitors center. Only 10 historic artifacts were found, the majority of modern age (Faulkner 1994a). Testing was finally completed around the rear barnyard area in June 1995, when the remaining untested areas around the visitors center were explored with 61 posthole tests on 6- and 12-foot centers (Faulkner and Owens 1995).

1994 Testing

A major testing project was conducted in the fall of 1994 (Faulkner 1995) (Figure 2). A total of 683 posthole tests were performed in two areas: the east inner side yard (402 tests) and the west inner side yard (281 tests). A heavy concentration of historic artifacts (2,973) and a significant number of prehistoric artifacts (225) were found in the east side yard, where 18 historic features were also recorded. Several of these features were possible structure foundations marked by concentrations of limestone marble/rock. The Ramsey House is constructed of a metamorphosed limestone called pink marble, still quarried nearby. Since it is difficult to distinguish this from other forms of the locally abundant limestone, the term limestone/marble will henceforth be used for this rock found abundantly on the site.

A brick walkway was encountered in five of these posthole tests (Figure 2, Features 14–16). Both handmade and machine-made brick fragments were found around the bricks, which could not be removed from the small postholes. The walkway appeared to curve toward the south doorway of the kitchen and can be seen in a 1931 photograph of the east side yard. The walkway appears to have been covered by a dirt driveway in an earlier photograph of the house taken after 1927 (Faulkner 1995:42). In his personal notes and in an interview Robert Van Deventer describes what he called a "depression" in the ground, 15–20 feet from the southeast corner of the front yard. He related that it was filled with bricks, plaster, cement, and other rubble and that the brick walkway led to it (Van Deventer 1985). The fall 1994 posthole testing of the east side yard did not encounter such a feature (Faulkner 1995). While

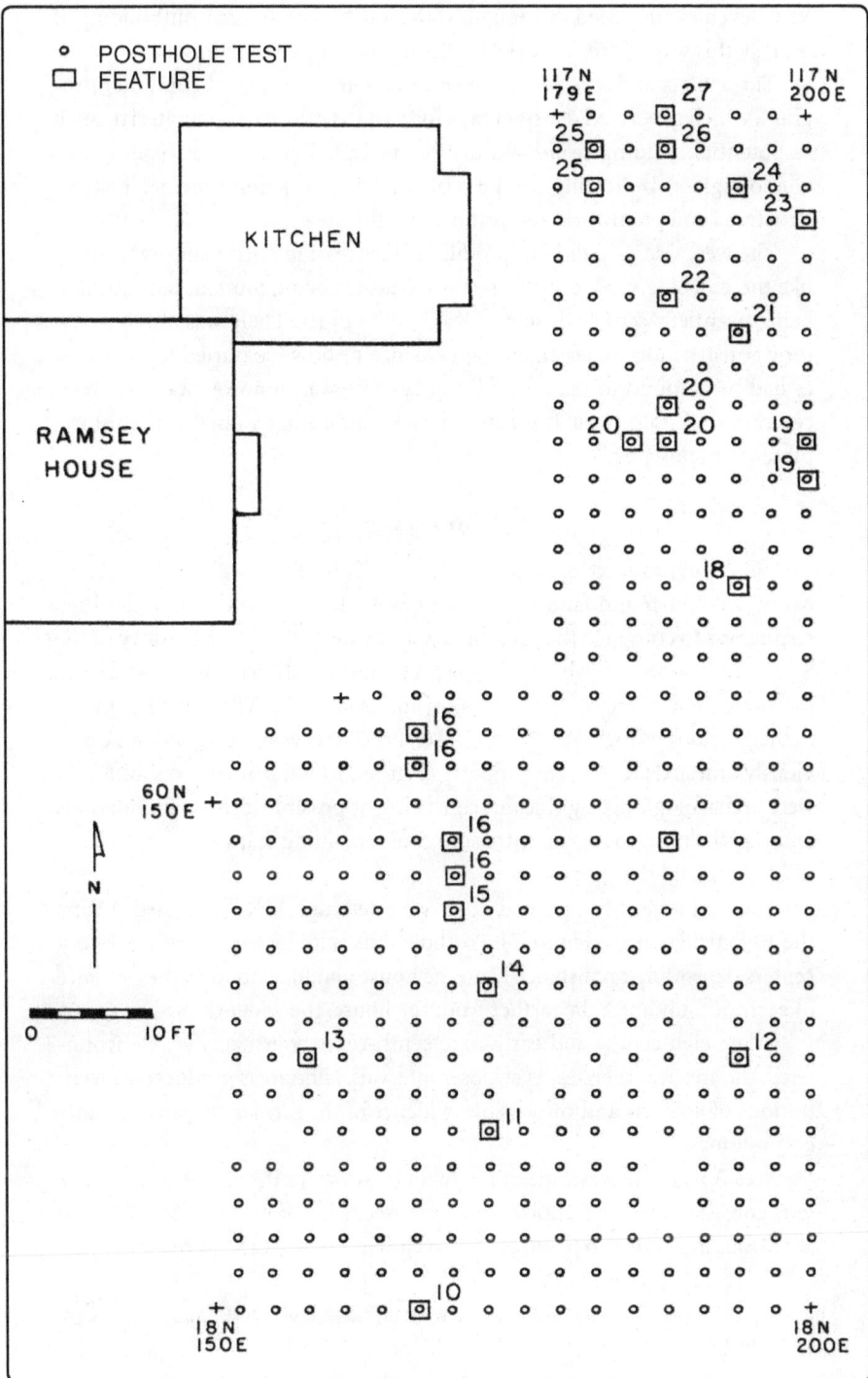

FIGURE 2. (Posthole) tests and feature locations, east inner side yard, 1994 season.

Van Deventer suggested this might be the location of an early outbuilding, it is likely this was fill from the post-1952 remodeling of the house.

The artifact and feature data were entered into an AXUM computer program, which generated density maps for various categories of materials such as potential building stone and distinctive functional artifact types (nails, window glass) indicating the possible location of several former historic structures and prehistoric and historic activity areas.

The west side yard did not produce evidence of intensive cultural activity like the east side yard, only 12 historic features being located, half of them being twentieth-century iron and PVC utility pipes. There was also less historic construction material and no evidence of possible buried foundations as had been found in the east side yard. There was, however, a denser concentration of prehistoric fire-cracked rock,[1] indicating a notable prehistoric presence in this area.

1996 Testing

The final and most extensive testing phase at Swan Pond was conducted between September and January 1996 (Avery et al. 1998). The goal of the 1996 testing was to complete the preliminary study of the landscape history of the Swan Pond property, which included locating additional former structure locations, activity areas, disturbed soils, and negative activity space not found in the previous testing projects. A total of 1,052 tests were excavated in 11 previously untested areas on the property (Figure 3). Of the 57 features found, 33 were archaeologically significant, consisting of possible historic foundations and a prehistoric rock concentration. The remaining features were modern utility lines and drainpipes.

The 11 previously untested areas were lettered A–K and tested during the 1996 field season (Figure 3). Posthole tests were located on 6- to 15-foot centers depending on distance from the house and likelihood of the presence of early outbuildings; the farther from the house, the wider the spacing was.

If late-eighteenth- and early-nineteenth-century artifacts were encountered, the area was then tested at closer intervals. Nine areas produced concentrations of artifacts and/or possible evidence of the former existence of early outbuildings.

Area A is on the west side of the main driveway to the visitors center. The tests consisted of a single north-south transect (line of posthole tests) spaced at 12-foot intervals. No features were recorded in the 12 excavated tests.

1. Fire-cracked rocks are heated and fractured rocks that were used by prehistoric native people for cooking and heating.

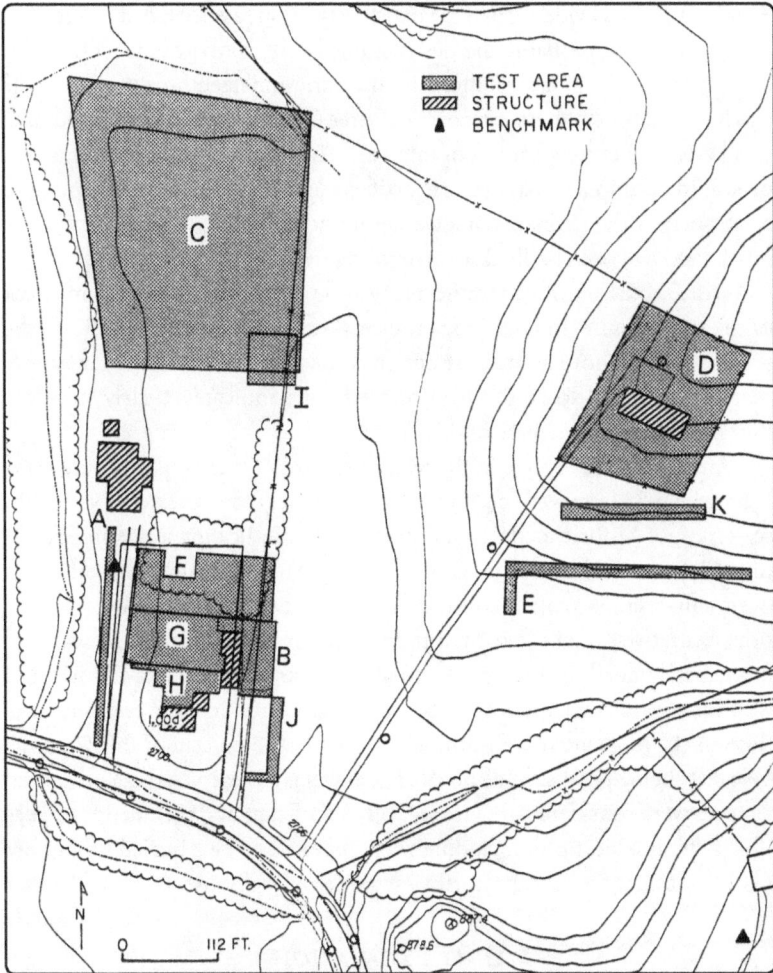

FIGURE 3. Excavations areas, 1996 season.

Area B is on the east and north sides of the caretaker's house in the east rear inner yard. The area on the east side of the building produced a moderate number of artifacts and the possible structural remains of at least two earlier buildings. North of the caretaker's house, however, in the present heritage garden area, few artifacts were recovered. One hundred and eight posthole tests were dug at 6-foot intervals in Area B.

Area C is in the rear peripheral yard or what was called the north field. Nine transects were excavated across this field, the tests being placed at 15-foot intervals. Two possible structure areas were located. The southwest corner of

Area C produced evidence of a former structure, but associated artifacts indicated that it was probably the destruction debris from a twentieth-century barn. A scattering of late-eighteenth- and early-nineteenth-century artifacts was found in the southeastern corner of Area C. This area was designated Area I and was further tested at 5-foot intervals. The 134 posthole tests in this area produced additional early historic artifacts and scattered limestone/marble rock, possibly the remnants of a former foundation. Soil strata indicated the north field had been badly disturbed for many years by plowing.

Area D consisted of two transects at 15-foot intervals in the front and back of the rental house. In addition, a transect was run in Areas E and K on the southern slope above a spring. A buried A soil horizon,[2] scattered limestone/marble rocks, and some early historic ceramics indicate an early structure may have stood somewhere in this vicinity.

Areas F, G, and H were in the rear inner yard of the Ramsey House. Area F, on which 89 tests were performed at 12-foot centers revealed a very light scattering of historic artifacts and buried rocks indicating a possible structure. Closer to the house, Area G produced light to moderate nineteenth- and twentieth-century artifact concentrations and two possible structure locations tentatively identified by buried limestone/marble rocks. Area H is immediately north of the house and attached kitchen and like the east and west inner yards was tested at 3-foot intervals. Other than the east side yard, this was the most intensively utilized area, with 98.5 percent of the 270 posthole tests being positive (i.e., producing artifacts). Eleven of the 32 recorded features were considered archaeologically significant and included four possible structure locations, including what appeared to be a buried limestone/marble foundation near the northwest corner of the house.

Unit Excavation

Excavation units, or blocks, are larger areas that are dug to expose features such as buried foundations and produce larger numbers of artifacts for study. Units are usually square and can be of various sizes depending on a number of factors such as research design, intensity of occupation, the number of features that might be encountered, and the depth of the deposits. The size of the excavation crew can also be a factor in unit size. The smaller the units, the more control one has over spatial relationships of artifacts and features. A rule of thumb, however, is that the corners of the units be designated by some kind of stake or pin and that this marker be accurately tied into the

---

2. The "A horizon" in soil formation is the humus zone.

grid system. At Swan Pond, corner grid markers were 6-inch gutter spikes. The southwest spike was the grid location designator for each unit; that is, it was used to determine how many feet north and east of the principal datum the unit was located.

Measurement of grid systems and shovel test and unit locations in archaeological excavations can be in either the English system or the metric system. While the metric system is frequently used in the United States today, my work on historic sites in the Knoxville area including the Swan Pond site has been done in the English system (feet and tenths of feet) because the people who lived on these sites measured distance in feet and constructed their buildings accordingly. I have found that a 3-foot-square unit works best for me. This is because a small unit can provide greater spatial control of the location of artifacts and features; a two-person team can work these units effectively, one digging and one screening; they are close in size to the popular one-meter square unit; and I have consistently used this size unit on other historic sites in the Knoxville area, allowing an easier comparison between sites.

Except for the 1985 field season, when arbitrary levels of .3 feet were removed in the excavation of units, soil was removed in natural/cultural strata that differed in soil color, consistency, or artifactual content. If a stratum was over .20 feet in thickness, the soil was removed in .20-foot arbitrary levels within the stratum. All soil was dry-screened through ¼-inch hardware mesh, and 2-liter soil samples were collected from each level or stratum below the recent humus and from all features.

A feature is any disturbance, construction, or artifact concentration resulting from human activity or natural processes on a site. Features are often the result of a single episode or event in the history of a site and are important for dating these events and establishing the specific activities that took place there. For this reason, features are recorded separately from the strata in which they are found; they are photographed and drawn to scale in plan view and vertical profile.

Unit excavation proceeded simultaneously with posthole testing based on the data collected from the testing and sometimes on historical information or even on intuitive reasoning as to where features might occur. The following is a summary of the unit excavations at Swan Pond from 1985 to 2001 and the major discoveries that were made during that time.

1985 Unit Excavation

Fifteen 3-foot by 3-foot units and one 3-foot by 1.5-foot unit were excavated in the 1985 field season based on features and artifact concentrations found in the posthole testing and on the presence of ground surface anomalies. Unit designation was based on the grid coordinate of the southwest corner pin. Eight consecutively numbered features were found in these units (Roberts 1986). Significant features included a concentration of historic window glass dating from the early nineteenth century, a rectangular brick foundation from a twentieth-century sweet potato slip bed, a prehistoric fire-cracked rock concentration, and a historic hearth or furnace containing two heavily fired clay flues. Artifacts around this unusual hearth dated from the late eighteenth to the early twentieth century, so the date of construction and function of this feature was unclear. At the time, this feature was believed to be either the remains of an eighteenth-century whiskey still house or a nineteenth-century sorghum furnace.

1995 Unit Excavation

The next excavation of units was in 1995, when 22 units were opened in the east inner side yard of the Ramsey House to define the size, construction technique, and function of outbuildings suggested by features and artifact distributions found in the 1994 testing of this area (Figure 2). While the official unit designation and locator continued to be the southwest corner pin, units from 1995 on were numbered in consecutive order for ease of recording. Unit numbers began with 17, since 16 units had been designated earlier by the southwest corner grid coordinate in the northwest yard area (Faulkner 1996a).

Six features found in the 1994 testing were considered historically significant enough to place excavation units over them. These units were opened in a north-south line in the east inner side yard with the placement of subsequent units based primarily on below-surface probing on 1-foot centers and an estimation of building size based on studies of standing early outbuildings on East Tennessee sites (Faulkner 1996b). Excavation of these units resulted in the discovery of the foundations/wall lines of three structures, an early fence line, and a large brick-lined cistern (Figure 4).

The structures were arranged in a linear pattern perpendicular to the long east-west axis of the house. Structure 1 had a foundation built of loosely stacked limestone/marble rocks along the east and west sides, this foundation extending under the caretaker's house (Figure 5). The base of a fired clay hearth from a log-and-clay chimney was centered on the gable end, and a fired clay basin hearth was located in the interior floor of the building. The floor and surrounding area were covered with a thick wood ash deposit containing a number of animal bones suggesting this was the early Ramsey smokehouse (Faulkner 1996a).

Structure 2 had been built over Structure 1 after the latter building was torn down (or moved?) in the later nineteenth century. Based on the three footers

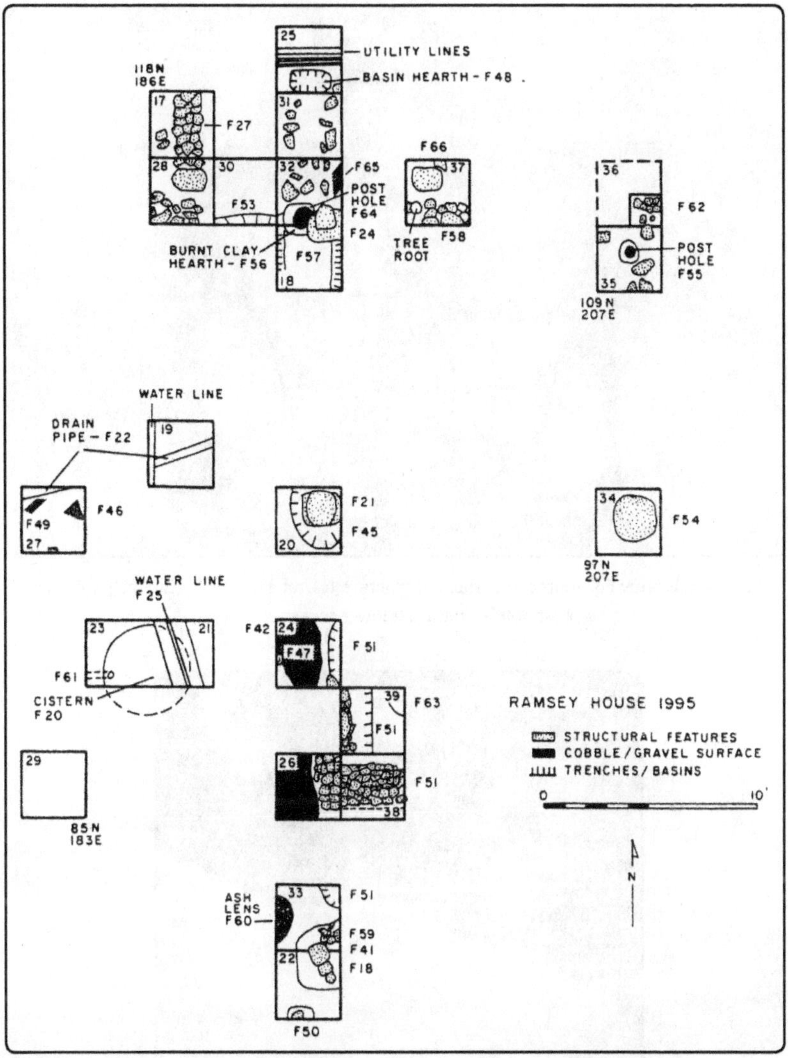

FIGURE 4. Features in east side yard excavation, 1995 season.

uncovered, this outbuilding was at least 16 feet wide on an east-west axis and extended under the caretaker's house. The sills of this building rested on large limestone/marble footers that had been set into deep builder's trenches (Figure 6). Horseshoes, tools, and other metal agricultural objects around this building indicated at the time that it might have been a barn or stable.

The west edge of a third structure was found just south of, and in alignment with, Structures 1 and 2. The west wall of Structure 3 appeared to be

FIGURE 5. Feature 66. Southeast corner of Structure 1, Unit 37. Note Feature 58 rock-filled post hole(s) in the left lower corner of unit.

FIGURE 6. Feature 21 footer. Note wedge rocks between the top and bottom rocks.

at least 18 feet long and was identified by a refuse-laden depression or shallow crawlspace under the building. Possible foundation stones were also present along the west edge of the depression. While a large number of late-nineteenth-century artifacts had been dumped into the depression under the building after it was razed, ceramics found at the base of the depression indicated Structure 3 might have been constructed in the early nineteenth century. Its function was unclear, however, at this early stage of excavation.

1997 Unit Excavation

After the completion of the fall 1996 testing season, the University of Tennessee, Knoxville (UTK), Department of Anthropology archaeological field school returned to Swan Pond in the summer of 1997 to follow up discoveries of features and activity areas found during the previous year's testing (Faulkner 1999). Twenty-five units were placed in the inner and peripheral house yards, with 25 new features being discovered. Eleven of these features were identified as late-eighteenth- to early-nineteenth-century installations, including two large overlapping postholes that tentatively identified a portion of an early defensive fence around the inner house yard (Area H).

An additional large dressed limestone/marble footer from Structure 2 was also found 18 feet east of the footer in Area B. This was believed to be a footer along the east wall of this possible barn or stable, which indicated this outbuilding was at least 36 feet wide on an east-west axis.

The most interesting features discovered during the 1997 field season were located near the northwest and southwest corners of the Ramsey House, consisting of what appeared to be dressed limestone/marble "pads" or "pavements." Only a single large slab of stone was exposed at the southwest corner of the house, but at the northwest corner a 4-foot-long pad/pavement consisting of several large flat stones (unfortunately badly damaged by a PVC water pipe) was completely excavated in a 54-square-foot area (Figure 7, Figure 26). This feature (70) was associated with a wide and deep builder's trench (Feature 76) along the north cellar wall of the house (Figure 8). The posthole and pad are believed to be part of a scaffold that was raised to build the stone walls of the two-story Ramsey House (Faulkner 1999).

Five units were excavated in Area I where late eighteenth-century artifacts were recovered in the 1996 testing phase. A unit was placed in Area K to determine if early historic artifacts were present in a buried humus stratum discovered in earlier testing. A unit was also dug at the southwest corner of the attached kitchen where it meets the wall of the main house to potentially date the construction of the kitchen. Although additional late-eighteenth- and early-nineteenth-century artifacts were found in the units

FIGURE 7. Excavation units showing Feature 70, view south.

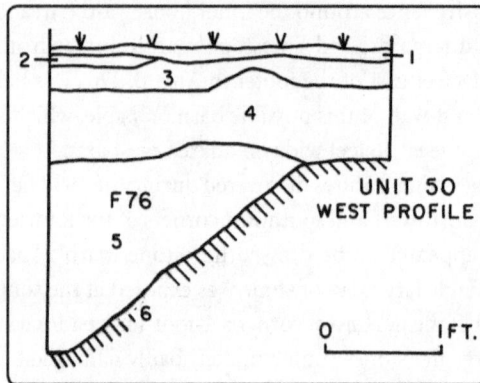

FIGURE 8. Unit 50, west profile: 1. Humus (10YR3/2).
2. Clay lens (10YR5/8). 3. Loam (10YR3/3). 4. Silty loam
(10YR3/4). 5. Mottled clay (10YR4/4, 7.5YR5/8).
6. Clay subsoil (10YR5/8).

of Area I, years of plowing this area apparently destroyed all traces of a foundation, and determination of an exact location of a former building was not possible. Few artifacts were found in the buried A horizon (humus) in Area K, and determination of the presence of an early structure here was also inconclusive. Unfortunately, the corner area between the house and kitchen was so badly disturbed by twentieth-century rebuilding of the bulkhead walls of the cellar entrance that the builder's trench of the kitchen in this area had been destroyed, thereby precluding determination of a construction date for this addition at this time.

1999 Unit Excavation

The UTK field school returned in the summer of 1999 with the goal of further defining the buildings and other features found in the previous field seasons and continuing to excavate around the kitchen walls to precisely determine when this building was constructed. Twenty-nine 3-foot by 3-foot units were opened in five areas of the east inner house yard, with 35 features being excavated, 17 dating from the late eighteenth to early nineteenth century (Faulkner 2000a).

The most extensive excavation was conducted in the east inner house yard over Structure 3. All four wall lines were located, indicating a structure 18–20 feet square, defined primarily by the shallow depression under this building and a parallel alignment of chinking rocks that had been placed under a large log, long since rotted away, that ran east-west down the center of the building. This was identified as a girder, a support that at the time was believed to have supported a sagging puncheon floor (Figure 9). Later excavation of Structure 3 indicated that this was a log skid that was left in place after the building was moved.

FIGURE 9. Structure 3, girder Feature 51A view to the east.

FIGURE 10. Feature 8 view east. Feature 120 is in the foreground.

Artifacts such as slate pencils and an inkwell suggested that this might have been Francis Alexander Ramsey's office, and the presence of blue glass beads[3] indicated it might have later served as a slave quarters after his death in 1820.

One of the most interesting features discovered in a unit in the east side yard was a large pit (Feature 115) exposed in the east profile of Unit 83. At the time it was believed that this pit was dug and filled while Structure 3 was still standing, suggesting it might have been a small root cellar under the building.

Units were also excavated on a north-south axis in the east side yard to locate additional footers of the large Structure 2. Unfortunately, all traces of at least two additional footers of this building were removed by later plowing and erosion, but a robber's trench marked the former location on this axis indicating it was at least 32 feet by 32 feet in size. It was also discovered that this building was superimposed over a late-nineteenth-century fence line, indicating it was not built until after the turn of the century.

The possible whiskey still or sorghum furnace in the west inner side yard was also further excavated in 1999. This excavation revealed that the east end of the fired trenches had been disturbed by a mid-twentieth-century trash pit and the west end by a large borrow pit (Feature 120) apparently dug when

---

3. Glass beads on East Tennessee historic sites are characteristic of African American occupation.

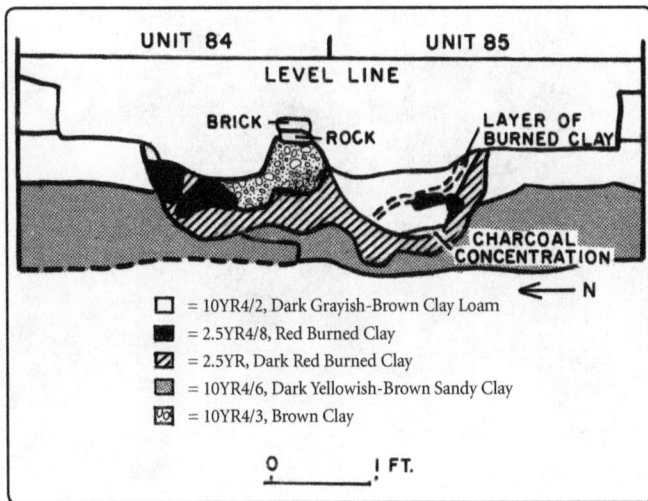

FIGURE 11. Feature 8, east profile.

the farm lane on the west edge of the yard was built in the later nineteenth century. No artifacts were found in the fired trenches, but the configuration of this feature indicates a sorghum furnace (Figures 10 and 11).

Further excavation was conducted in Area H, the inner rear house yard, to find additional postholes of what appeared to be an early defensive fence line discovered in the 1997 field season. Based on a common spacing of 6 feet for early fences, a unit was placed 6 feet east of the 1997 unit. Four large

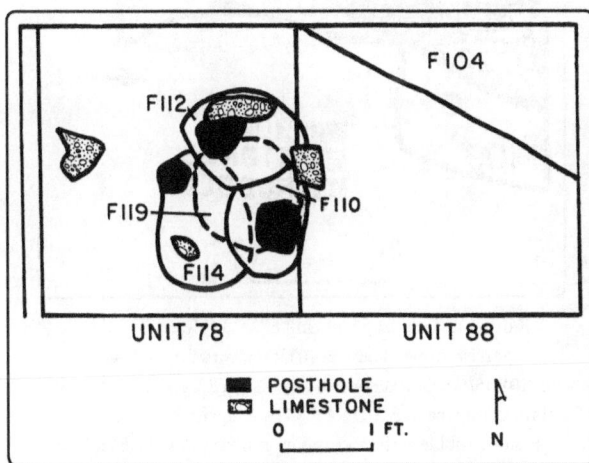

FIGURE 12. Plan view of postholes in Units 78 and 88.

FIGURE 13. Kitchen builder's trench, Feature 109, view north.

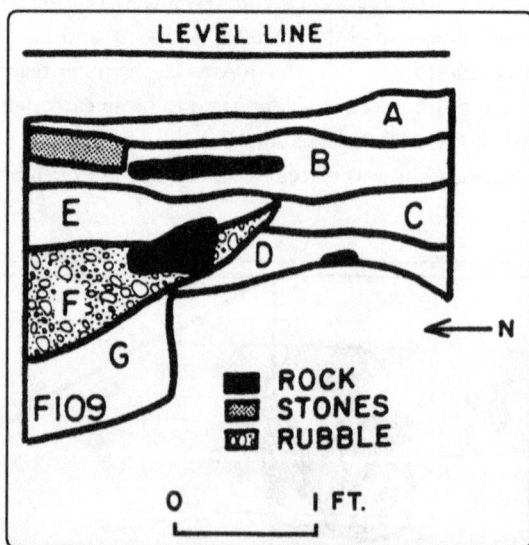

FIGURE 14. East profile of Unit 87. A. 10YR3/2, very dark
grayish-brown loam. B. 10YR3/3, dark brown loam.
C. 10YR5/6, yellowish brown clay. D. 10YR3/4, dark yellowish
brown silty loam. E. 10YR4/6, dark yellowish brown clay silt.
F. Stone rubble with sand and mortar mixed with 10YR4/6,
dark yellowish brown clay silt. G. Feature 109 builder's trench.
10YR4/4 dark yellowish brown clay mottled with 10YR3/4
dark yellowish brown silty clay.

superimposed postholes containing early historic artifacts were found 4 feet east of those found in 1997 (Figure 12).

One of the long-standing goals of the excavations at Swan Pond has been to date the construction of the attached kitchen, obviously built after the main house was constructed in 1797. Two more units placed along the south wall of the kitchen exposed an undisturbed section of the builder's trench. This section of the trench was devoid of artifacts, suggesting the kitchen was added very early, probably around 1800, before much trash had accumulated adjacent to the house (Figures 13 and 14).

2000 Unit Excavation

The summer 2000 archaeological field school at Swan Pond focused on completion of the excavation of Structure 3 and determining the alignment of the fence from the cluster of four large postholes at what was thought to be the southwest corner of the building. Twenty-one 3-foot by 3-foot units were excavated over Structure 3 during the 2000 field season. Additionally, units and features uncovered during the 1999 field season in Structure 3 were carefully cleaned, rephotographed and redrawn. Thirty-seven features were excavated in the Structure 3 area. By the end of the 2000 field season approximately 85 percent of Structure 3 was excavated (Faulkner 2001).

The final excavation of Structure 3 exposed additional postholes of the defensive fence(s), making it possible to determine the alignment of these fences through time. It also exposed the east half of Feature 115, the feature now measuring 3 feet by 3 feet in diameter and 1 foot deep. It had been covered by the rock-chinked girder, indicating it was filled before Structure 3 was moved over it.

Opening units to the east, west, and south of the southwest corner of Structure 3 where the cluster of large postholes was located in the 1995 field season indicated the defensive fence line extended east under this structure. When units were opened west of the posthole cluster, a mortared limestone/ marble feature 6 feet by 6 feet in size was uncovered, identified as the chimney of a previously unknown building on the west side of Structure 3. The discovery of this building, designated Structure 4, required a major revision of our interpretation of the function of adjacent Structure 3. It was now evident that this newly discovered building was the location of the office/slave quarters and that it was moved to the east sometime after the mid-nineteenth century to become what we had called Structure 3, and later converted into a shed used as a blacksmith shop. Structure 3 was eventually torn down before the turn of the century.

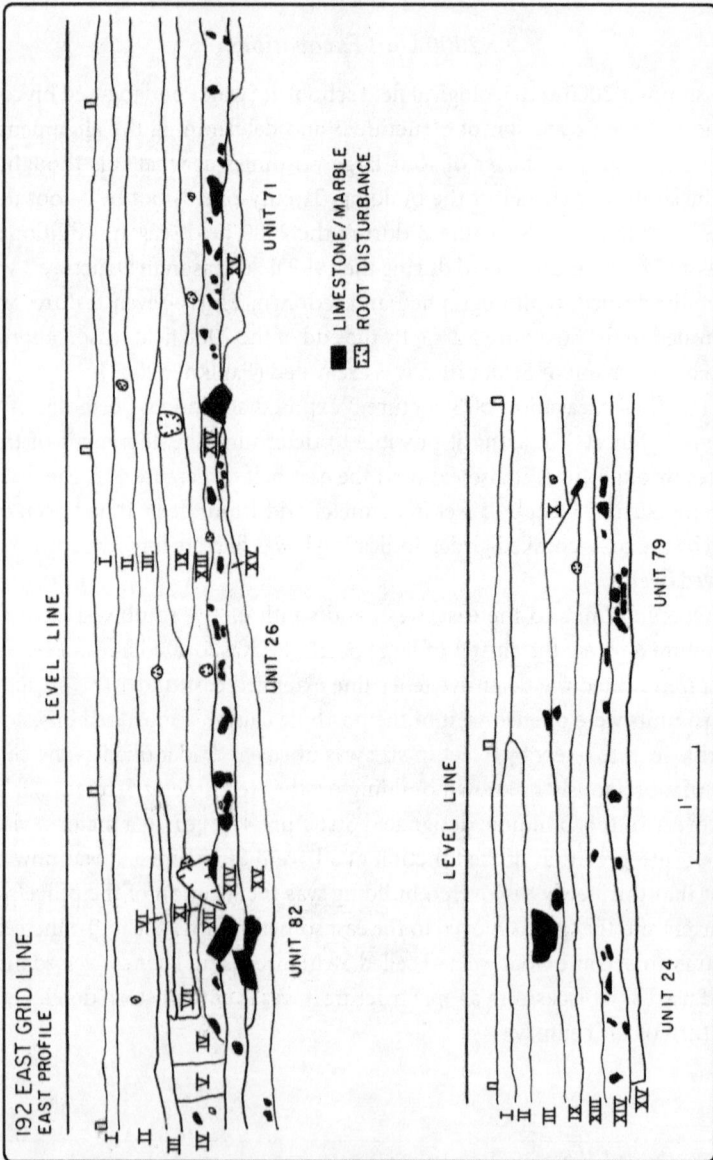

FIGURE 15. 192 east profile of Structure 3. I. Humus (10YR2/2). II. Loamy fill (10YR4/2). III. Cinder stratum (10YR3/1). IV. Clay/loam intrusion, lightly mottled (7.5YR4/6). V. Clay/loam intrusion (7.5YR3/4). VI. Clayey loam/silt (7.5YR4/3). VII. Clayey loam/silt, heavily mottled (7.5YR3/3, 7.5YR5/6). VIII. Clayey loam/silt, lightly mottled (7.5YR3/4, 7.5YR5/6). IX. Red clay stratum (5YR5/8). X. Silty loam/clay (10YR3/2). XI. Light ash stratum (7.5YR4/4). XII. Ash stratum (10YR3/6). XIII. Silty loam/clay (7.5YR3/4). XIV. Silty loam/clay with limestone/marble (7.5YR3/4). XV. Clay/silty loam (7.5YR4/6).

A profile baulk was maintained along the north-south (192 East grid line) axis through the Structures 3 and 4 area. The profile in this baulk confirmed that a depression/crawlspace had existed under Structure 3, the wall line of adjacent Structure 4, and served as a guide for the natural/structural stratigraphy these structure areas. The principal guide for the excavations from the 1999 through 2001 field seasons was the 15-foot-long profile maintained along the 192 East grid line (Figure 15).

Fifteen distinctive strata were evident in this profile, designated roman numerals I–XV and described by soil type and Munsell color. Temporally sensitive artifacts in the strata and features were used to date this sequence and its relationship to the former structures and changing activity patterns in the east side yard. The stratigraphic sequence below is from earliest to latest in time.

Clay/Silty-Loam Stratum (XV). This strong brown (7.5YR4/6)[4] clay/loam stratum grades into the yellowish brown (10YR4/6) clay subsoil that underlies most of the site . The lower level of this stratum contains prehistoric Native American artifacts. The upper level represents the earliest historic occupation of Swan Pond by the Ramsey family. This was determined by dating the historic ceramics and window glass in this upper portion of the stratum (Faulkner 2003a:5).

Silty-Loam/Clay Stratum (XIV). This stratum differs from underlying Stratum XV in that the soil appears to be more organically enriched (loamy), ranges from a dark brown (7.5YR3/4) to yellowish brown (10YR5/6) in color, and contains lenses and pockets of wood ash and fairly dense rubble from the foundation of Structure 4 (Faulkner 2003a:5).

Silty-Loam/Clay Stratum (XIII). Superimposed on Stratum XIV is another stratum of loam/clay that differs very little from the former stratum in color but contains far less wood ash and few foundation rocks. Ceramic dates from this stratum are in the mid-nineteenth century (Faulkner 2003a:5).

Ash Stratum (XII). Consisting primarily of wood ash and fragments of burned clay, this stratum is the lower peripheral deposit from the fireplace (Feature 159) of Structure 4. The Munsell color of this stratum is 10YR3/6, dark yellowish brown. This feature was observed in both the 1995 field season and 1999 field season (Faulkner 1996a:29, 2000a:13). Like Stratum XIV, it dates from 1793 to the mid-nineteenth century (Faulkner 2003a:6).

Ash Stratum (XI). This is the upper level of the ash stratum associated with the Structure 4 fireplace. It differs from the lower level of the ash stratum

4. From the standardized Munsell color chart, similar to a paint sample book with each color having its own code number.

in having less ash content, being very close in color to Stratum XIII (7.5YR4/4, brown clay loam), and having the same date range (Faulkner 2003a:6).

Silty Loam/Clay Stratum (X). Resting against the clay spoil deposit (Stratum IX), from the excavation of the cistern (Feature 20) in the center of the Structure 4 area, is a dark gray-brown silty loam stratum containing mottled clay (10YR3/2). This appears to be a colluvial fill that was deposited to level the side yard after the clay spoil (Stratum VIII) was spread around the cistern. It is closely related to Strata VII and VIII and probably dates from the same time period (ca. 1884–1900) (Faulkner 2003a:6).

Red Clay Stratum (IX). This is a yellow-red clay (5YR5/8) mottled with a dark brown clay/loam (7.5YR3/3) that was removed to install the cistern (Feature 20), the clay then being spread around this feature. This fill contained sherds from an undecorated whiteware plate dating between 1860 and 1890 with a mean date of 1875 and 10 window glass sherds with mean dates of 1871 and 1882 (Faulkner 2003a:6).[5]

Clayey Loam/Silt Strata (VIII, VII, and VI). Stratum VIII partially capped the red clay stratum and, like Stratum X, may have been laid down to level the area over and around the thick red clay spoil stratum, being especially thicker at the south end of the Structures 3 and 4 area. Besides being thicker at the south end of this area, there was also a change in the soil consistency and color between the north and south ends of this stratum. This difference in thickness, consistency, and color is probably due to the disturbance evident around the fireplace of Structure 4 and the fact that the ground surface began to slope to the south as well as the east in this area of the yard. These strata also cap the depression under Structure 3. Strata VIII, VII, and VI are believed to date from about 1884–1900 (Faulkner 2003a:7).

Clay/Loam Intrusion (Strata V and IV). This is a dark (7.5YR3/3) to strong (7.5YR4/6) clay/loam deposit or disturbance that intruded through Strata VI, VII, and XI, truncated Stratum XII, and extended slightly into Stratum XIV. The origin of this disturbance is not clear, and it is very localized. The point of origin of this disturbance was just beneath the base of Stratum III, indicating a pre-1900 date.

Cinder Stratum (III). A deposit of coal cinders across the east side yard has been one of the most visible temporal horizons in the landscape history of

---

5. The mean ceramic date is obtained by taking the median manufacturing date of each ceramic type, multiplying it by the number of sherds of that type, adding these products, and then dividing the sum by the total number of sherds in the collection (South 1977). The mean window glass date is based on glass thickness as window glass became thicker from the late eighteenth century through the early twentieth century.

this area of the house yard. This sometimes mixed cinder/loam/clay stratum ranges from as thick as ½ foot over portions of Structure 3 to a thin lens on the west side of Structure 4. Ceramics, coins, and window glass in this stratum indicate it began to accumulate in the 1890s and continued to accumulate in various areas of the east side yard until the late 1940s (Faulkner 2003a:7).

Loamy Fill Stratum (II). This is a dark grayish brown (10YR4/2) to dark yellowish brown sandy loam fill that was brought to the site to level a former slope on the east side of the front yard (Faulkner 2003a:7). Remnants of a gravel driveway are visible at the base of the fill, indicating it was laid down after the purchase of the property by the APTA in 1952 (Faulkner 2003a:7).

Humus Stratum (I). The present surface soil found over the entire excavated area of the east side yard is a very dark brown (10YR2/2) to black (10YR2/1) organic-rich humus resulting from the maintenance of a lawn here since the 1960s (Faulkner 2003a:8).

2001 Unit Excavation

The last summer field school at Ramsey House in 2001 finally placed the late-eighteenth- to early-nineteenth-century buildings found in the east side yard during the previous four field seasons in clearer perspective (Faulkner 2003a). The excavation of Structure 3 was completed by opening the last three units

FIGURE 16. Excavation of Structure 3 looking south. Note the girder running down the center.

over this building, a final mapping of all features within it, and the removal of the girder (Figure 16). A key posthole was revealed after the girder chinking rocks were removed. This posthole was the final link of the fence between the southeast corner of the smokehouse to the northeast corner of Structure 4.

Thirty units were opened over the Structure 4 area (Figure 17). Using the chimney/fireplace as a focal point, units were placed along all four wall lines of this building. It was immediately obvious that the chimney/fireplace was in the southeast corner of Structure 4, with the foundation lines outlining a 20-foot by 20-foot building. Virtually all of the large stones of the foundation had been removed, but remnants of rubble and a heavy concentration of domestic and architectural artifacts such as ceramics, nails, and window glass clearly marked the foundation lines. The corner fireplace, 6 feet by 4 feet in size, and the late-eighteenth-century date of the associated artifacts identified this building as the original Ramsey cabin described by J. G. M. Ramsey, Francis Alexander Ramsey's eldest son, who was born in this cabin in 1797 (Ramsey 1853).

It was now obvious that the cluster of postholes thought to be located at the southwest corner of Structure 3 were actually at the southeast corner of Structure 4, the original cabin. The posts of this fence extended a short distance east from the corner of the cabin, then turned north, passed under

FIGURE 17. Excavation of Structure 4 looking south.

Structure 3, and connected to the southeast corner of the smokehouse, Structure 1. This indicated that Structure 3 was later than Structure 4, and its close proximity to the latter building and similar size supported the assumption that Structure 3 was actually the original cabin, which had been moved east of its original location (Structure 4).

During our excavations at Swan Pond interested visitors often observed us carefully troweling and brushing soil away from buried artifacts and features from long-past human activities. It was difficult during those fleeting moments on hot July afternoons to explain how these fragments of the past were enriching the story of the people who lived at this site as told by the Ramsey House docents. What follows is a more complete and dynamic interpretation of the Swan Pond site and Ramsey House and their environs based on the archaeologically discovered vestiges of the past.

Chapter 2

A PREHISTORIC WILDERNESS

Like many early settlers who carved homesteads out of the North American wilderness, Francis Alexander Ramsey named his farm after an extraordinary natural feature, Swan Pond. He built his new home on a peninsula in a large pond, created by an ancient beaver dam built across Swan Pond and Sand Branch creeks. This ancient dam was located just north of the present-day intersection of John Sevier Highway and Strawberry Plains Pike. The shallow pond stretched for over two miles south to where the community of Marbledale is located today and was about ½ mile across at its widest point. In 1875, Francis Ramsey's son J. G. M. Ramsey described the former pond as follows:

> It had been for many years the favorite resort of trappers and hunters who came there to procure beaver pelts and feathers of swans and other aquatic birds. . . . This pond was a small but beautiful lake of placid water, extending from the beaver dam to the present residence of Alexander and Robert Armstrong, on one of the arms of the pond, and on the other arm of the pond nearly to the late Jas. Pickle's residence, these covering a large area of submerged land and enclosing between its two arms a considerable extent of upland in an insular position still known as the island field now owned by Dr. Vaun Anderson. It could be reached only by canoes. The depth of the lake varied from one to six feet: it was at first perfectly clear; over this the swans, wild geese and ducks, swam in joyful serenity, being in many places beyond the reach of the rifle ball. The flocks of this game were very large, almost beyond present belief, the noise made by them after

the report of a hunter's gun was frequently heard at Gilliam's and Gillespie's Stations. The pond was made by beavers that had constructed a dam across two or three spring branches, tributaries to the creek below, hence called Swan Pond. This dam was probably once higher than when I first saw it; it was then four feet high at the highest point, and lower as it approached the uplands which is connected. There was admissible ingenuity, skill and sagacity displayed, not only in its construction but in its boundary [Ramsey 1918:26–27].

When archaeological excavation began at Swan Pond in 1985, we were not surprised when over 1,000 prehistoric Native American artifacts were recovered during that first season. The bountiful environment around Swan Pond that had attracted the early historic hunters would certainly have been intensively utilized by native people, who relied on wild game for their subsistence for thousands of years. Archaeological excavations in nearby Tennessee Valley Authority (TVA) reservoirs by University of Tennessee archaeologists have revealed that Native Americans lived in East Tennessee at least 10,000–12,000 years ago (Chapman 1985:33–37). The history of Native American occupation of this area is usually divided into five major cultural periods.

Paleo-Indian Period (12,000 b.c.–8000 b.c.). The Paleo-Indians were the first native people to arrive in Tennessee, before the end of the last Ice Age. Hunters of big game, including such extinct Ice Age animals as the mastodon, an extinct forest-browsing elephant, these people moved seasonally between small hunting camps over a broad territory. Their distinctive lanceolate spear points have been found scattered throughout East Tennessee.

Archaic Period (8000 b.c.–1000 b.c.). At the end of the Ice Age, the appearance of modern environments caused changes in the lifeways of native peoples. Hunting of now-extinct Ice Age mammals was replaced by the taking of smaller game such as deer and turkeys, and fishing and shellfish collecting became important. Plant foods also became a mainstay in the diet, especially hickory nuts, acorns, walnuts, and chestnuts. Bands still moved seasonally, but a growing population now lived longer on campsites that were usually seasonally established on the floodplain terraces of larger rivers.

Woodland Period (1000 b.c.–a.d. 1000). By the end of the Archaic period, native peoples in East Tennessee were beginning to plant gardens, growing a small gourdlike squash and herbaceous annuals such as sunflowers. The most significant technological developments were the introduction of pottery and, later, the bow and arrow. Gardening now supported small, permanent villages with evidence of permanent housing. The dead were often buried in earthen mounds.

Mississippian Period (a.d. 1000–a.d. 1600). In addition to small villages, the Mississippian people also established town centers of political and religious life, with planned layouts of substantially built houses around a plaza and large flat-topped mounds on which religious structures were situated or that served as the residence of elite leaders. These towns were often encircled by a stout palisade with spaced bastions or defensive towers. The large population was supported by intensive farming of corn, beans, and squash.

Historic Period (A.D. 1600–A.D. 1783). When the Spanish explorer Hernando de Soto entered the eastern Tennessee River valley in the sixteenth century, he found Mississippian villages and towns occupied by the ancestors of the historic Cherokee tribe. Shortly thereafter, due to European-introduced disease and warfare, their population declined dramatically, and they moved into smaller villages in the Great Smoky Mountains, where they remained until they were removed by the United States government in the nineteenth century. A few intrepid survivors remained in their mountain fastness, where their descendants still live today.

NATIVE PEOPLE DISCOVER SWAN POND

There is no doubt that the beaver pond and its environs attracted numerous prehistoric hunters and gatherers. We do not know when the beavers began building their dam; J. G. M. Ramsey says it was "ancient." Thus far no distinctive projectile points of the Paleo-Indians have been found at Swan Pond. Perhaps the low peninsula was still being formed by deposition from the small adjacent streams that often overflowed their banks until the end of the Ice Age. The earliest artifacts that we have recovered in our excavations are from the early Archaic period: small chert (a type of flint) dart points thrown with a spear thrower and dated in the nearby Little Tennessee River Valley between 6000 and 7000 B.C. These dart points have a distinctive notched base and are called bifurcate points (Figure 18A). In fact, most of the projectile points found at Swan Pond date from the Archaic period, with larger numbers appearing between 4000 and 1000 B.C., during what we call the late Archaic, when the form of the projectile points changed to one with a wide-stemmed base. Other implements such as chert scrapers, drills, and knives were also used by these Archaic residents at Swan Pond (Figure 18D–G).

The preponderance of Archaic hunting and butchering artifacts recovered here and the virtual absence of features such as structures, formal cooking and storage facilities, and burials indicate these people used Swan Pond as a temporary hunting and gathering camp. Only two apparent Archaic features have been recorded here, in the form of concentrations of unfired and fire-fractured river cobbles of quartz and quartzite. Such fire-cracked rock is common on Archaic sites because these people did not make pottery and cooked their food by roasting it on hot stones or boiling it by dropping heated rocks into a skin bag full of water. Unfortunately, no animal bones or charred plant remains associated with the Archaic or later Native occupation were found, so we do not know what kind of animals or plants they were procuring from the pond and surrounding forest.

While the presence of their triangular-shaped arrow points (Figure 18B–C) indicates that later Woodland and Mississippian groups visited Swan Pond,

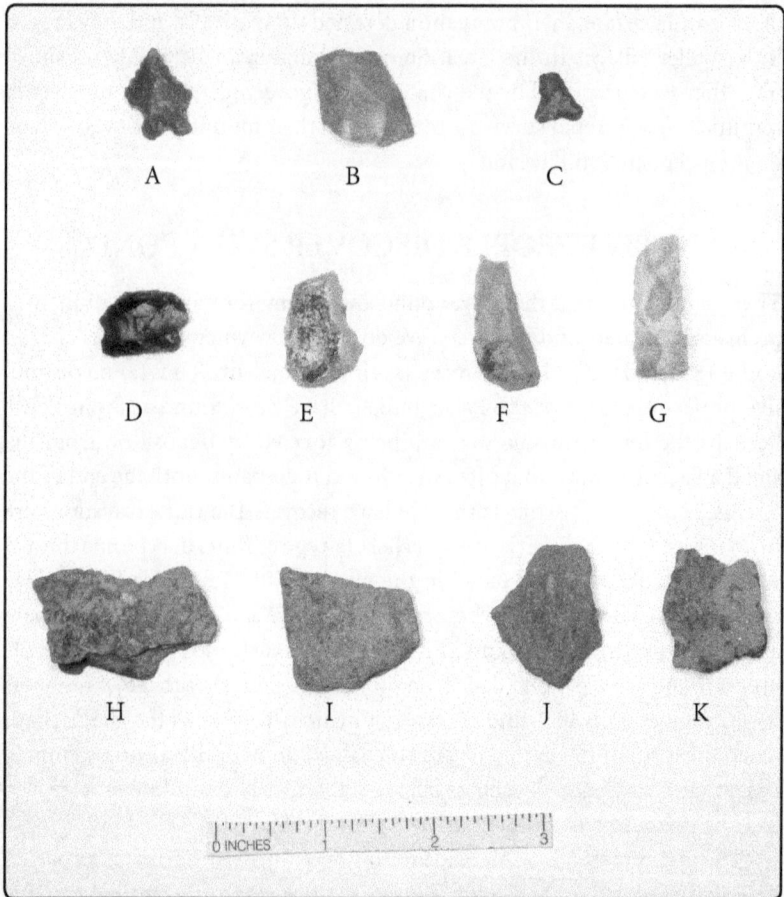

FIGURE 18. Prehistoric artifacts. A. Early Archaic bifurcate projectile point. B. Early to middle Woodland large triangular projectile point. C. Late Woodland small triangular projectile point. D. Notched scraper. E. Uniface end scraper. F. Perforator. G. Drill. H. Early Woodland quartz-tempered, cord-marked body sherd. I. Middle Woodland limestone-tempered, check-stamped body sherd. J. Early to middle Woodland quartz-tempered, cord-marked body sherd. K. Late Woodland limestone-tempered, cord-marked body sherd.

these artifacts are rare in comparison with the dart points of the Archaic hunt-ers at Swan Pond. The most distinctive artifact associated with the Woodland occupants is their distinctive pottery. The early Woodland pottery is rather thick and crude, tempered with crushed quartz,[1] and roughened on the outer surface with a fabric or cord-wrapped paddle (Figure 18H). Later, around 2,000 years ago, the Woodland potters began using crushed limestone as a temper and stamped the exterior with a wooden paddle that had a carved surface (Fig-ure 18I). No Mississippian-period pottery has been recovered at Swan Pond, and there is no evidence that the historic Cherokee hunted here, although by the seventeenth century native peoples were using metal arrow points, guns, and other European trade items. These artifacts are impossible to distinguish from those used by the Ramseys when they first settled on the site.

1. Tempering is material such as crushed rock or shell that is added to the clay to prevent the vessel from cracking during air-drying and firing.

Chapter 3

THE RAMSEYS REACH NORTH AMERICA: THE EARLY RAMSEY PERIOD, 1793–1820

There is disagreement among Francis Alexander Ramsey's descendants as to who his grandfather was. According to a genealogical chart of the Ramseys published by William Spencer Jarnigan in 1976, Francis Alexander's grandfather was one Alexander Ramsey who emigrated to America from Scotland in the 1720s. Frederic R. Ramsey in his 1982 book entitled *Ramsey of Swan Pond* states that a William Ramsey who came to America in 1730 was Francis Alexander's grandfather. Both authors, however, agree that Francis Alexander Ramsey's grandfather landed in what is now New Castle, Delaware, the heart of the Swedish settlement established in the Delaware River valley in 1638 (Weslager 1969). They also agree that Reynolds Ramsey, Francis Alexander Ramsey's father, was born in New Castle in 1736 and learned his trade as a miller there. The Ramsey family later moved to Marsh Creek, Pennsylvania, then on to York County, now Adams County, Pennsylvania, where Reynolds built a merchant mill and his son Francis Alexander was born in 1764 (Hesseltine 1954:1–2). J. G. M. Ramsey said his well-educated father left Pennsylvania when he was only 19 years of age and came to the Tennessee backwoods with only his horse and a surveyor's compass and chain (Hesseltine 1954:7). John Alexander, Francis Alexander Ramsey's maternal uncle, had invited his nephew to live with him on Big Limestone Creek in what was then Washington County, North Carolina (now Greene County, Tennessee) (Hesseltine 1954:6–7).

In August 1783, Francis Alexander Ramsey, in the company of James White, the founder of Knoxville, and Robert Love, explored the upper

Tennessee River valley as far south as the mouth of the Little Tennessee River for the purpose of locating land warrants (Ramsey 1853:278). Ramsey's expertise as a surveyor was a definite advantage to this expedition. It was on this trip that these hardy explorers chose the land they were later to home-stead. In 1786, Francis Alexander Ramsey obtained grants for the Swan Pond lands: "200 acres in Greene County upon a water of the Holston, including Swan Pond" (Bowman and Folmsbee 1965:207). Ramsey purchased additional property after he settled at Swan Pond, eventually raising his holdings to more than 2,000 acres (Hesseltine 1954).

THE EARLY RAMSEY PERIOD AT SWAN POND
(1793–1820)

While residing on Big Limestone Creek, Francis Alexander Ramsey became secretary of the Franklin Convention and a member of the Council of State. During negotiations with North Carolina on the separation of the ill-fated state of Franklin from her parent state, he met and married Margaret "Peggy" Alexander on April 7, 1789, in Mecklenburg, North Carolina, and brought his 23-year-old bride back to his East Tennessee home (Hesseltine 1954:4). J. G. M. Ramsey states that his father remained in Limestone "till 1792 or 1793, when he removed to Swan Pond and began the cultivation and improvement of that large and beautiful property" (Ramsey 1918:26). However, in his autobiography, written in 1868, he says his family moved to Swan Pond in 1790–1791 (Ramsey 1868).

It is puzzling that J. G. M. Ramsey, the eminent East Tennessee historian, who was so meticulous in recording the history of his family, is unclear about the exact date his parents arrived at Swan Pond. Historians have suggested several factors that delayed Francis Alexander Ramsey's settling at Swan Pond, including fear of hostile Indians and his preoccupation with the affairs of the state of Franklin and later the court proceedings of Washington County under the government of North Carolina. When Governor William Blount formed a new judicial district consisting of Knox and Jefferson counties in the Territory of the United States South of the River Ohio in the spring of 1793, he appointed Francis Alexander Ramsey clerk of the superior court of this district (Ramsey 1853:576). It has been suggested that Ramsey changed his residence to his Knox County lands as a result of this appointment (Bowman and Folmsbee 1965:208). Evidence points to the year 1793 that Ramsey and his family moved from Little Limestone Creek to Swan Pond. By that year he had two children, William B. (1791–1799) and John McKnitt (1793–1808). Five children were born to Francis and Peggy Ramsey after they settled at Swan Pond:

Samuel (1795–1800), James Gettys McGready (1797–1884), William Baines Alexander (1799–1874), Eliza (1801–1838), and an infant born in 1804.

Peggy Alexander Ramsey died in 1805. After her death, Francis Alexander journeyed to Gettysburg to visit his parents in 1806. While there he met and courted Ann Agnew, marrying her in August of that year. They had one son, John McKnitt Alexander Ramsey, born December 16, 1807. His father called him Jackie (Ramsey 1982).

According to J. G. M. Ramsey, when his family arrived at Swan Pond his father "erected a temporary residence twenty by twenty feet a little in the rear and east of the site he had selected for his family mansion." This was on the low peninsula extending into the pond, the site of present-day Ramsey House. Shortly after arriving, Francis Alexander, "wishing to drain the land, and use it for husbandry and safeguard for health, cut a wide ditch from north to south transversely to the beaver dam and the lake disappeared with all the game, and the land was converted into meadows, and the dam almost obliterated" (Ramsey 1918:27).

J. G. M. Ramsey, who was born in the early cabin, described it as being built "of hewn logs, one story high, a stone chimney in one corner, and covered with lap shingles" (Hesseltine 1954:9). With such a detailed description, one would think that the remains of this building would be easy to find. However, on closer examination, the meaning of some of J. G. M. Ramsey's words and phrases seem unusual or vague. For example, what did he mean by a chimney in the corner? Corner fireplaces are rarely if ever found in southern Appalachian log cabins, although they do occur in areas settled by the Swedes and Finns in eastern Pennsylvania and Delaware. Most importantly, what did J. G. M. Ramsey mean by the location being "a little in the rear and east of" the site of the stone house? Did he mean a little in both the rear and east of the stone house? If only the former, then how far east was the cabin situated?

While it was not until the 1995 archaeological field season that we began excavation at the possible site of this cabin, its precise location was already speculated upon shortly after we began excavation at the Ramsey site in 1985 (Faulkner 1986:8–10). At that time, two likely locations were discussed. One was the present location of the modern caretaker's house, which is a little to the rear and east of the stone house. The other location was to the east (Areas E, D, and K on Figure 3) across a former arm of Swan Pond on a hill above a spring (Faulkner 1986:8–10). Unfortunately, these two locations dominated our thinking about the site of the early cabin until the 2001 field season.

During the 1995 field season, two possible early buildings dating to the early Ramsey period were found in the east side yard, Structures 1 and 3 (Faulkner 1996a). At that time, Structure 1 was correctly identified as the early smokehouse. As we excavated along the west wall line of Structure 3, we did not realize the dense artifact concentration we encountered was actually from adjacent Structure 4, the early cabin. Our line of units was less than one foot east of the foundation remnants of the latter building. Discovery in archaeology can be a matter of inches.

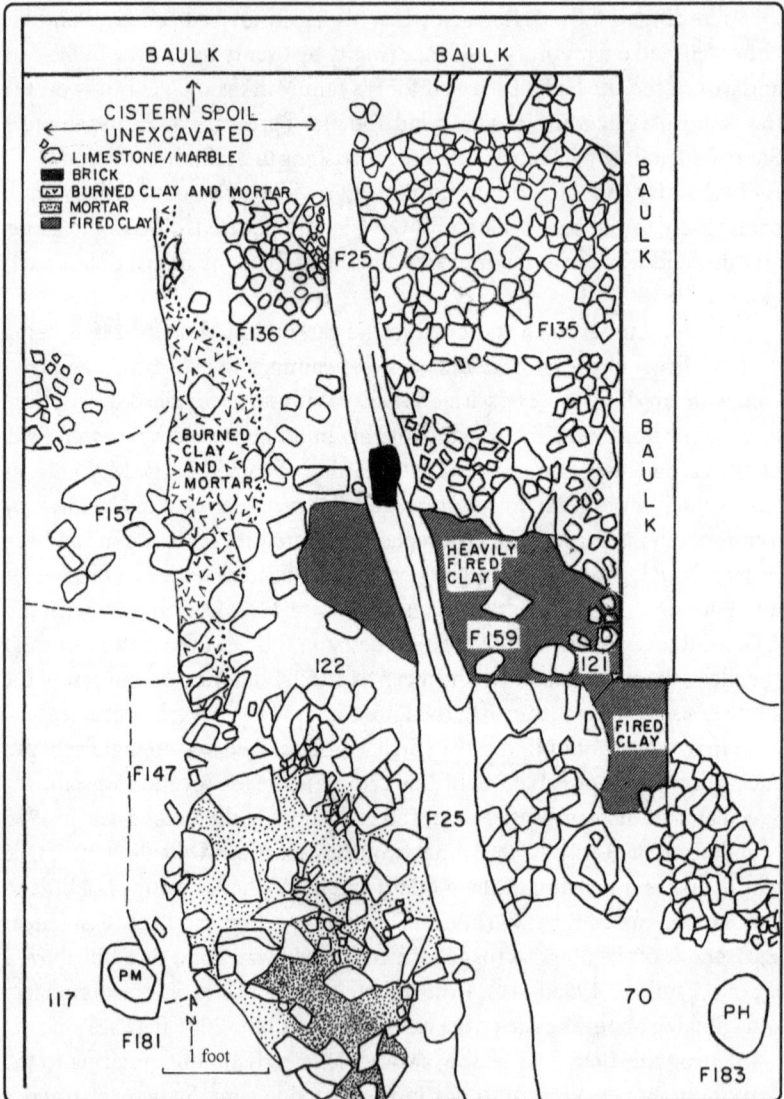

FIGURE 19. Structure 4 fireplace and chimney base.

When we returned to continue excavating Structure 3 in the 1999 field season, a rock and ash concentration (Feature 96) was found, but because it was badly disturbed by a modern PVC waterline (Feature 25), it was misidentified as part of the domestic debris that had accumulated around Structure 3 (Faulkner 2000a:14). However, when the excavation was extended to the west the following summer, the undisturbed portion of Feature 96 was found to be a chimney base of mortared limestone/marble. The report on that season's work (Faulkner 2001) concluded that this building was possibly Francis Alexander Ramsey's office that originally anchored the southeast corner of a fortified compound and was later moved to become Structure 3 (p. 34). Privately, however, we began to speculate that Structure 4 was the early Ramsey cabin.

Soon after our excavation on Structure 4 began in the 2001 field season it became clear that Feature 96 was the corner fireplace in the original Ramsey cabin. Three separate features were recognized in this fireplace (Figure 19). Feature 96 was a roughly rectangular base of mortared limestone/marble that measured about 6 feet east-west and 4 feet north-south. The absence of fired daub/clay in and around the chimney base indicated, as J. G. M. Ramsey related, that it had been built entirely of stone, the larger blocks having been removed, leaving the rubble base at or below grade. Postholes (Features 181 and 183) on either side of the chimney are believed to have supported a scaffold raised to build this stone structure.

The hearth of the fireplace was designated Feature 159. The hearth was basin-shaped and measured 2.6 feet by 1.8 feet. It had a fired clay base and was filled with fire-reddened soil, ash, and charcoal. No datable artifacts were found in the hearth fill.

Behind the hearth was a pavement of densely packed flakes and chunks of limestone/marble that merged into the rubble base of the east and south foundations. Such a structure might indicate that the cabin originally had an earthen floor, but it seems unlikely that such a floor would be used in this dwelling over the four years the Ramseys resided in it. Mean ceramic dates for Feature 135 ranged from 1796 to 1811.

Unlike the corner chimney, the foundation of the cabin was much more difficult to trace. This was due to the disturbance of the remaining features of this foundation by the moving of this building to the Structure 3 location, the intrusion of a late-nineteenth-century cistern, and a PVC waterline that was laid through the east side yard in 1993. The scattered nature of the small limestone/marble debris reflects this disturbance, as does the almost complete absence of larger foundation stones. The dispersed concentrations of these small rocks also led to an initial assignment of separate feature numbers to these deposits, which in retrospect is confusing because all of this material is from the same architectural feature, the cabin foundation. However, this fact was not clear when these rock concentrations were first discovered.

The removal of the foundation rubble did not reveal any builder's trenches; apparently a continuous foundation of larger stones was laid on a rubble base directly below the humus, which was simply scraped off in preparation for construction (Figure 20). Such a procedure would seem to be typical for what the

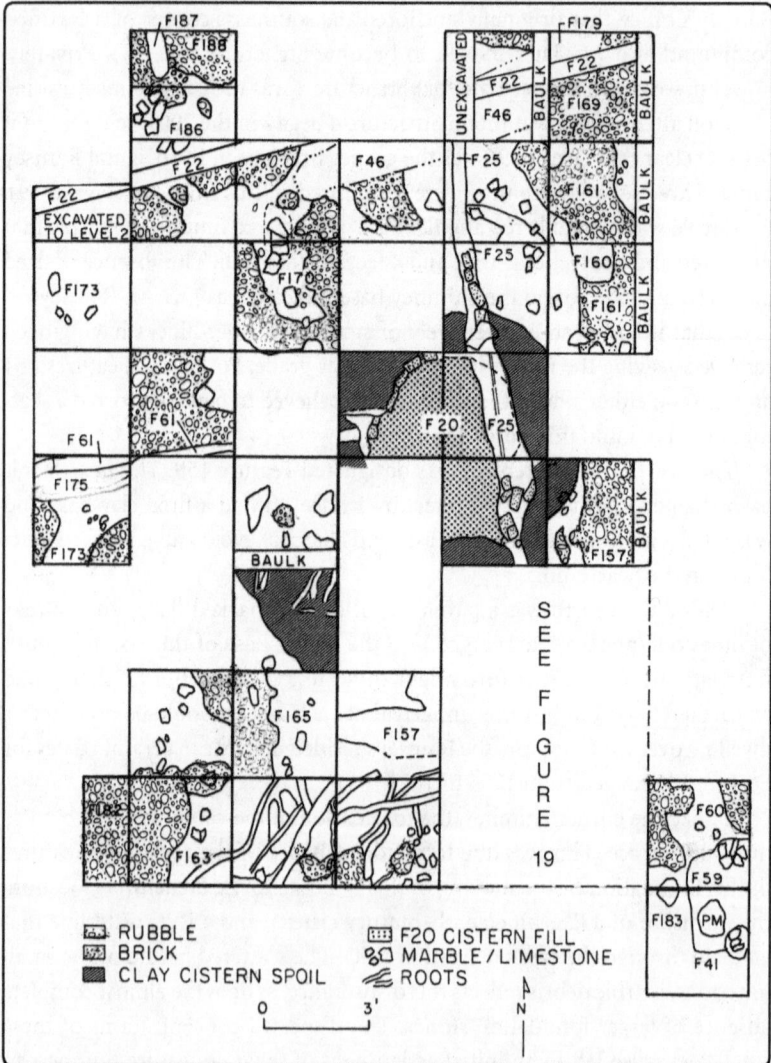

FIGURE 20. Structure 4 features.

Ramseys believed would be a temporary structure. Mean ceramic dates for the levels within and under the foundation rubble range from 1797–1811. If the location of the fireplace/chimney is considered the southeast corner of the cabin and the northwest wall is identified by footer remnant Features 186 and 187, the cabin appears to have been about 18–20 feet square, close to the dimension described by J. G. M. Ramsey. The orientation of the cabin was almost exactly to the cardinal points, the north-south axis aligned with magnetic north.

The disturbance from the cistern and waterlines within the cabin area made it impossible to establish activity areas that would be indicated by artifact scatter patterns within the cabin. Another problem was the apparent multiple uses of this building after it was used as a dwelling by the Ramsey family. The location of the fireplace indicates that the kitchen area or informal area (hall) was at the south end of the cabin. Presuming the cabin was divided by a framed dividing wall, the formal end (parlor/sleeping quarters) was at the north end.

Artifact distribution around the periphery of the building provides more details than are found in J. G. M. Ramsey's description of the cabin. For example, the dense concentration of domestic artifacts, especially late-eighteenth-century ceramics along the east foundation line indicates a doorway in this location. The large number of foodways artifacts here also suggests this doorway probably accessed the kitchen end of the cabin. A door was undoubtedly present facing west, but we did not excavate far enough along the west wall line to find the telltale doorway scatter around this entrance.

Nails are not very well preserved on the Ramsey site, many of them being unidentifiable blobs of rust. However, excavation of units in the early cabin area produced 43 identifiable wrought or handmade nails. Even taking preservation into account, this is a small number of nails from a dwelling site. While wrought nails, being hand-forged, were not manufactured in standard lengths or pennyweight like later cut and wire nails, these nails ranged from the equivalent of a 2-penny nail (ca. 20 mm long) to a 12-penny nail (ca. 70 mm long) with over half being between 5- and 8-pennyweight in size. The 5–8 pennyweight nails were probably all-purpose construction nails for interior framing and further suggest the interior was divided into at least two rooms.

The infrequency of very small nails used to fasten shingles or "shakes" and finishing nails (L or T hammered heads) also reveals details about the construction of the cabin. If shingles were not nailed to rafters or roof boards, it is likely the roof was covered with 2- to 3-foot-long rived boards (probably what J. G. M. Ramsey called "lap shingles"), laid in double overlapping fashion and fastened with poles laid on top, a roof sometimes called a "weight-pole" roof (Martin 1984:18–23).

While the Ramsey cabin could have had a simple dirt floor, the absence of a packed surface and the fact that the building continued to be used for many years suggest that a wood floor of some type was installed when it was built. The almost complete absence of flooring/finishing nails (only one wrought T-head nail was recovered) indicates the floor was probably constructed of puncheons, split logs 12 to 18 inches wide, smoothed on the top with an adze and pegged into the floor joists and/or sills (Martin 1984:21). This type of flooring does not require nails.

Window glass increased in thickness from the late eighteenth century to the early twentieth century and can be dated by measuring the thickness and using it in a formula with an accuracy of within 5 to 10 years (Moir 1987). Four hundred and twelve window glass sherds dating from 1793 to 1820 were concentrated at the northeast and southwest corners of the building, indicating small glazed windows in the east front and west rear walls.

The architectural features of the Ramsey cabin are unusual in two respects. First and foremost is the presence of a corner fireplace. A perusal of the literature on early log cabins and houses in the southern Appalachians did not yield any reference to such a placement of a fireplace (Glassie 1965; Morgan 1990). The closest examples of such fireplaces are found in the early Fenno-Scandinavian cabins in the Delaware River Valley of present-day Pennsylvania, New Jersey, and Delaware (Weslager 1969; Bealer and Ellis 1979; Jordan and Kaups 1989; Case ca. 1969). Weslager (1969:158) states: "The placement of the fireplace in a corner appears to have been a characteristic trait of the earliest Swedish log houses, as it was in the crude log ports, and in some, but not all, of the more sophisticated hewn log dwellings built by the Finns."

A mid-eighteenth-century Swedish log house with corner fireplaces still stands on Upper Darby Creek in Delaware County, eastern Pennsylvania (Weslager 1969:167–168; Bealer and Ellis 1979:147–150; Case ca. 1969). The fireplaces and chimneys of this double-pen (room) log house (30 by 15 feet) are built of stone, the chimney placed inside the walls of the cabin (Bealer and Ellis 1979:149; Case ca. 1969:2).

How close, then, is the style of the Ramsey cabin to a Fenno-Scandinavian log house, and more important, why did Francis Alexander Ramsey build it this way? Addressing the first part of this question, there does not seem to have been a single style of Finnish or Swedish log houses. They ranged from square to rectangular one- or two-room structures with gable end or side doorways, some with central, side, gable, or corner fireplaces (Kaups 1986; Palmqvist 1986). The most unusual characteristic of the Ramsey log house in comparison with other log houses in southern Appalachia appears to be the corner fireplace. An almost square cabin is also not common in this area, but it does not appear that this characteristic can be attributed to the Finns or Swedes any more than to the English or Germans.

Where did Francis Alexander Ramsey learn about building in the Fenno-Scandinavian style? The Ramseys were of relatively "pure" Scotch-Irish and English ancestry; therefore, this was certainly not a family architectural tradition. There is also no record of early Swedish or Finnish settlements in the Adams County area of Pennsylvania where Francis Alexander Ramsey was born (Elwood Christ, personal communication 2002); thus he may not have personally observed this architectural style as a young man. However, when Francis Alexander's grandfather emigrated from Scotland, he landed in the heart of the Delaware valley Swedish settlement established in 1638 (Weslager 1969). Francis Alexander's father, Reynolds, was born in this Swedish community, and it is likely that Reynolds Ramsey passed on his knowledge of Fenno-Scandinavian architecture to his son Francis Alexander.

Finally, despite his knowledge of this building style, why did Francis Alexander Ramsey build in the Fenno-Swedish style, particularly since corner fireplace construction was uncommon in the southern Appalachian "back-woods"? It would have been more difficult to construct, and his cabin was apparently raised as a "temporary" residence until a permanent home could be built. A quote from two Dutchmen who were traveling through the Swedish area of New Jersey perhaps best explains Francis Alexander's choice of frontier housing:

> The house, although not much larger than where we were last night [they had spent the previous night in an English clapboarded cottage which was cold and uncomfortable] was somewhat better and tighter, being made according to the Swedish mode, and as they usually build their houses here, which are block houses, being nothing else than entire trees, split through the middle, or squared out of the rough, and placed in the form of a square.... These houses are quite tight and warm; but the chimney is placed in a corner [Weslager 1969:157–158].

Thus the Ramsey log cabin, though temporary, was built like a little "blockhouse" or defensive fort, with logs tightly fitted. The fireplace, radiating outward from a corner, would have heated the room(s) more completely. Although erecting a temporary cabin until he could build his more permanent home (of stone, in the Pennsylvania style), he expended extra labor and materials to make the most secure and comfortable dwelling for his family, even for a short period of time.

A contemporary building with the Ramsey cabin was Structure 1, the smokehouse, discovered during the 1995 field season. Two additional units were

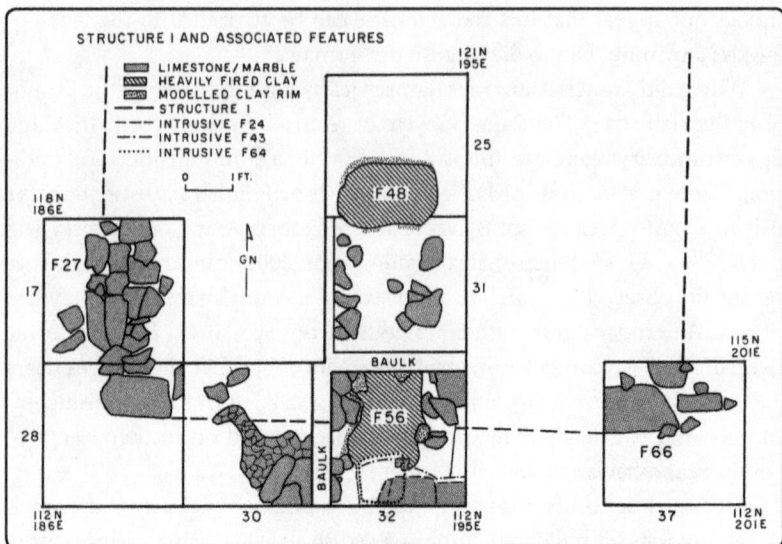

FIGURE 21. Structure 1 and associated features.

excavated during the 2001 season to verify the location of the southeast corner of Structure 1. The east-west dimension of this building was 12 feet, and while the north end of Structure 1 is covered by the modern caretaker's house, its position at the northeast corner of a fenced residential compound (see below) indicates a north-south dimension of approximately 18 feet (Figure 21).

Two features were associated with Structure 1. Feature 48 was an interior oval basin with a heavily fired clay base and rim, the basin filled with wood ash and charcoal. Numerous fires apparently burned down in the basin, and the remaining ash was removed and spread around the hearth on the packed earthen floor. Feature 56 was a heavily fired clay hearth centrally located along the 12-foot east-west wall line of Structure 1. Its location at the gable end of this building and heavily fired base suggest it was the remains of a simple exterior stick and clay chimney (Faulkner 1996a:27). A concentration of faunal remains, especially pig bones, was found in the ash deposit on the floor of this building (Patterson 1998).

The interior fire pit with a heavy concentration of wood ash containing numerous animal bones clearly identifies Structure 1 as a smokehouse. The mean ceramic date of 1803 for sherds in this ash stratum indicates this building was in use during the lifetime of Francis Alexander Ramsey (Faulkner 1996a:34). The exterior chimney corresponds to similar features on early German smokehouses in Pennsylvania (Long 1972:180). Like the plan for his cabin, Francis Alexander probably brought this idea with him when he moved to Tennessee from Pennsylvania. It appears, however, that the gable end chimney was replaced with the central interior hearth at a later time, more in keeping with practices in the southern Appalachian area.

The 1985 testing of the northwest corner of Area H in the rear inner yard also produced evidence of an additional early building in the domestic compound. A concentration of creamware, an early English refined earthenware dating from ca. 1762–1820, was indicated by an artifact density map generated by the SURFER computer program (Faberson 2003:Figure 14). A concentration of early wrought nails was also found in this area (Roberts 1986). This indicates that a structure also anchored the northwest corner of the compound. A tight scatter cluster of wrought and early cut nails suggests that a fourth early corner building was located in the southwest corner of the west side yard (Faulkner 1995:91–93). The small number of early ceramics recovered in the 1994 testing of this area indicates this early building was not a domestic structure. Since it is certain that the Ramseys had horses and milk cows, it is possible that this was the location of the stable or barn at the southwest corner of the compound.

A question often asked by visitors to Swan Pond is where the Ramsey's privy or outdoor toilet was located. If found, privies are usually easily identified due to a deep pit beneath the structure containing a distinctive dark, organic waste fill and/or a sealed deposit of household trash placed there after the facility was abandoned. A likely location for the Ramsey privy is near or behind the smokehouse. Privies were often situated near smokehouses since the smoky smell would mask the offensive odor of the privy. It may also be significant that twentieth-century privies at Swan Pond were located in this area, which is now under the caretaker's house.

Another feature associated with the early Ramsey farmstead is a well. The well was described by an early-twentieth-century resident of the area as having a square, dressed stone casing. It was said to be 35–40 feet deep, the water being dipped out with a bucket. The well was later lined with a cast concrete pipe and a cement block pump house built on top of it in the twentieth century (Faulkner 1986:61–63). Since there is no evidence that a natural spring existed on the peninsula in Swan Pond near the cabin, it is likely that the Ramseys would have dug a well because the water table was much higher at that time. It was located at or near the location of the modern water spigot near the west kitchen door.

Besides providing his family with a substantially built and comfortable cabin when they settled at Swan Pond, Francis Alexander Ramsey also constructed a stout defensive fence around the farmstead, placing the blockhouse-like cabin at the southeast corner and buildings at the other three corners of this fortified compound (Figure 22). One must remember that on September 25, 1793, the same year the Ramseys established their home at Swan Pond, 1,000 Creek and Cherokee Indians approached Knoxville with the intent of attacking this small frontier post, ultimately wiping out Cavett's Station and killing 13 people (Ramsey 1853:580–581). Excavation at William Blount's mansion in Knoxville also revealed that the governor of the Southwest Territory lived within a defensive compound at this time (Faulkner 1993), indicating that the fortification of pioneer homesteads on the East Tennessee frontier in the 1790s was not an uncommon practice.

This defensive fence was built of stout vertical logs, from ½ to 1 foot in diameter, placed in deep square or rectangular shovel-dug postholes and wedged with large limestone/marble rocks (Figure 23). Either horizontal boards were nailed to these upright posts or horizontal stringers were attached to the posts and planking or "pickets" were nailed in vertical fashion to the stringers (Faulkner 2003:37).

Completely excavated postholes of the defensive fence include five in the east side yard and six in the rear house yard (Area H) (Figure 12). A cluster of three postholes was found at the southeast corner of the cabin, indicating at least three post replacements there. These were connected to large posts 10–12

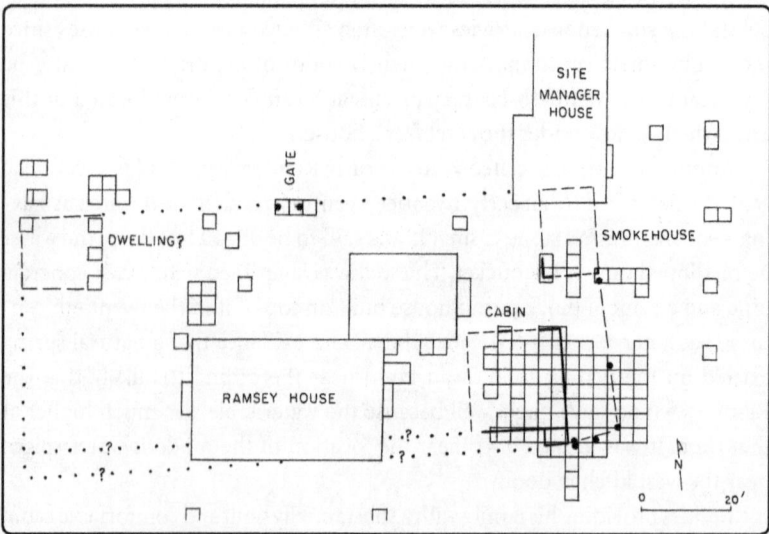

FIGURE 22. Locations of buildings and postholes of the defensive fence in the early Ramsey compound.

feet apart paralleling the east cabin wall at a distance of 10 feet forming a narrow forecourt in front of the east doorway (Figure 25). This space between the cabin and the fence also served as a convenient dumping area out the kitchen end door. There is no evidence of a gate along this east fence line. These posts aligned with another cluster of postholes (Feature 58) at the southeast corner of the smokehouse. This cluster was exposed at the edge of the unit and the number of posts represented there could not be determined. These postholes contained a number of large wedge rocks.

The six postholes found in the rear yard were in two clusters of two and four posts in separate installations. One post in the cluster of two superimposed posts contained the remnants of a red cedar post about a half foot in diameter. The post was heavily wedged with limestone/marble fragments, the only post in the rear fence line having such heavy chinking (Figure 24).

Four feet east of these paired postholes was a cluster of four superimposed postholes (Figure 12). The location of these clusters opposite the rear door of the Ramsey House suggest this was the north gate of the defensive fence. Gate posts would have been replaced more frequently because of the stress of opening and closing the gate. Until the pond was drained and present-day

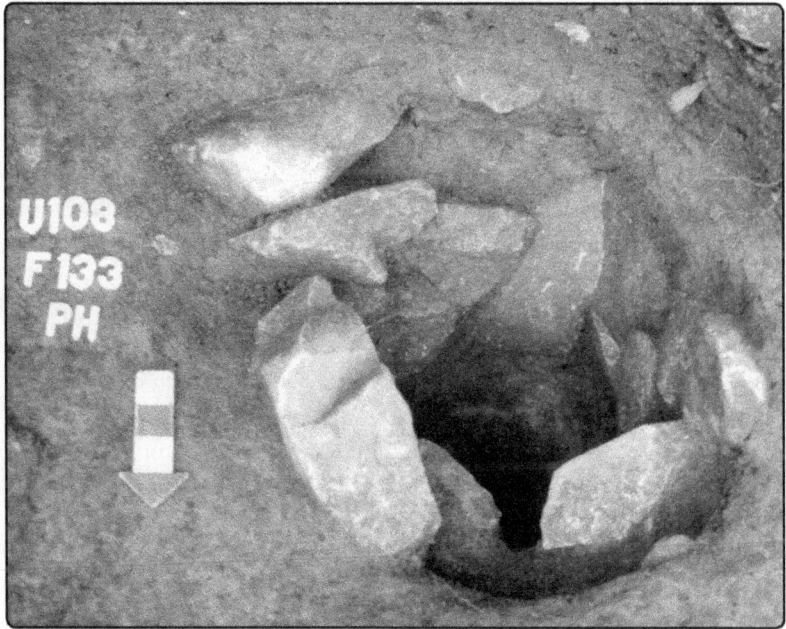

FIGURE 23. Feature 133 posthole and post mold with limestone/marble chinking.

FIGURE 24. Feature 74 posthole and post mold with limestone/marble chinking. Modern water pipe to right.

Thorngrove Pike built, access to the farmstead could only have been from the high ground to the north. However, these closer-spaced postholes on 4-foot centers might also mark a stouter section of the fence, since this would have been the main avenue of attack by hostile forces.

The disposal of trash or domestic debris around a dwelling not only produces large numbers of artifacts used in daily household activities but can also reflect a family's level of sanitation, identify doorways in the dwelling, reveal the location of surrounding outbuildings, and expose shifting activity areas in the house yard. Accumulations of trash on archaeological sites are called "middens." Middens can be concentrated in a small area or within an open feature such as an abandoned cellar hole or privy. These are often referred to as sealed middens. They are usually the result of short-term dumping and restrictions on the dispersal of debris through cultural or natural agencies. A "sheet midden" is a thin, widespread scatter of trash that accumulates over a longer period of time and is dispersed through human activity such as yard cleaning and natural agencies such as erosion.

Testing and unit excavation in the inner house yard indicated the heaviest dumping during the early Ramsey period was in the east inner house yard between the east wall of the early cabin and the defensive fence along the east side of the peninsula and around or within the smokehouse, Structure 1.

The midden between the cabin and the fence was dense, suggesting that household trash was simply thrown or swept out the east door of the cabin. Such refuse disposal behavior appears to be common on late-eighteenth to early-nineteenth-century sites in eastern North America. On seventeenth- to eighteenth-century coastal Carolina domestic sites this method of refuse disposal is called the Brunswick pattern (South 1977).

In 1796, construction began on the "stone mansion," now known as the historic Ramsey House, which was completed the following year (Ramsey 1918). The house was designed by the English architect Thomas Hope, who moved to Knoxville from Charleston, South Carolina, in 1794 and designed and built other houses in Knox County including the Strong House (ca. 1814) in Knoxville and Charles McClung's "Statesview" (1805) eight miles west of town (Tate 1972). Ramsey House, however, was Hope's crowning architectural achievement, J. G. M. Ramsey proudly remarking, "At the census of 1800 it was the most costly and most admired building in Tennessee" (Hesseltine 1954:9).

Recent descriptions of the Ramsey House architecture include an article by Elizabeth Scaggs Bowman and Stanley J. Folmsbee in the *Tennessee Historical Quarterly* (1965), a short description by architectural historian James Patrick (1981:82–83), and a section in a master's thesis on Thomas Hope written by Susan Douglas Tate (1972). The house is a three-bay structure with a Federal I-house floor plan (two over two rooms with central hall) built of local pink limestone/marble. There is a full cellar with an outside stone-lined bulkhead entranceway at the east gable end and an attic, the latter being reached by a steep, narrow staircase. The styling of Ramsey House is late neoclassic Georgian, with quoins, a string course, and flat-arched openings with voussoirs and keystones of distinctive blue limestone (Patrick 1981:83).

The pink limestone/marble was cut from a nearby stone quarry that was still in operation in the 1990s. Ike Rader, a retired superintendent of the local quarry, told me that the Ramsey quarry could still be seen in the 1920s in a draw east of the house. This early quarry was buried by rock and debris from recent quarrying activities (Ike Rader, personal communication 1985).

An interesting story concerning the building of the Ramsey House appeared in a column in the *Knoxville Journal* (7 June 1931). Dr. J. M. Kennedy wrote:

> Dr. Aaron Armstrong now living at the age of 75 in comfortable circumstances in a pleasant home on the east side of Knoxville, told me that his father, when a young man, was riding down the Virginia Trail in search of fame and fortune. On his journey he came upon a six-horse team and wagon, the wagon loaded with large building stone. The outfit was mired in a ditch from which several men were vainly

trying to extract it. On request, young Armstrong was given permission to assist. Having adjusted the harness and soothed the irritated horses with gentle hand and voice of the born horseman, he took the reins into practiced hands, got the common strength of the team to pull as one, and brought the wagon to firm ground. Col. F. A. Ramsey was the man in charge, and he continued Armstrong on the job as teamster for hauling stone from a nearby quarry, until the famous "Rock House" was finished.

While Thomas Hope planned the house and directed the overall construction, the fine workmanship of the masonry indicates it was laid by an expert stonemason. Unfortunately, there is no firsthand documentation as to the identity of this stonemason. Robert Van Deventer, who conducted extensive research and directed some of the restoration of Ramsey House, believed the master mason was a man named Seth Smith, who was said to have built other stone houses in East Tennessee (Coughlin 1996:14). James Patrick also remarks, "The house was a three-bay stone house of the type Ramsey probably remembered from Limestone, where he had spent his youth, and where the Gillespie house had stood since the 1780s . . ." (1981:83). Seth Smith has been identified as one of several Quaker stonemasons who lived around Jonesborough, Tennessee, and built the Gillespie house in 1792 (Fink 1989:173). It is also possible that, as when he built his log cabin, Francis Alexander was influenced by the building techniques used in the houses that dotted his native Pennsylvania countryside when he built his permanent stone house.

It is interesting that although immediately adjacent to the log house, which was oriented to the cardinal points (north-south) like most early houses I have studied in Knox County and probably faced west (toward the interior of the compound), in Figure 22 the stone house has an orientation of 7 degrees east of magnetic north and faces south. While Hope may simply not have been precise in laying out the foundation, the fact that Francis Alexander Ramsey was a surveyor makes this difference even more intriguing.

The fact that the stone house faces south indicates that when it was built, either Francis Alexander envisioned present-day Thorngrove Pike being built across the south end of the peninsula, or this road had already been constructed. Since the road could not have been there when the Ramseys arrived in 1793 because it crosses the bed of the former Swan Pond, the original access to the Ramsey farmstead was undoubtedly from the ridge to the north, where there is a gradual dry descent onto the peninsula. The apparently rebuilt gate on the north side of the defensive fence also indicates an access route from the north. A line of ancient osage orange trees once snaked across the field north of the house. Robert Van Deventer believed these may have been part of a natural

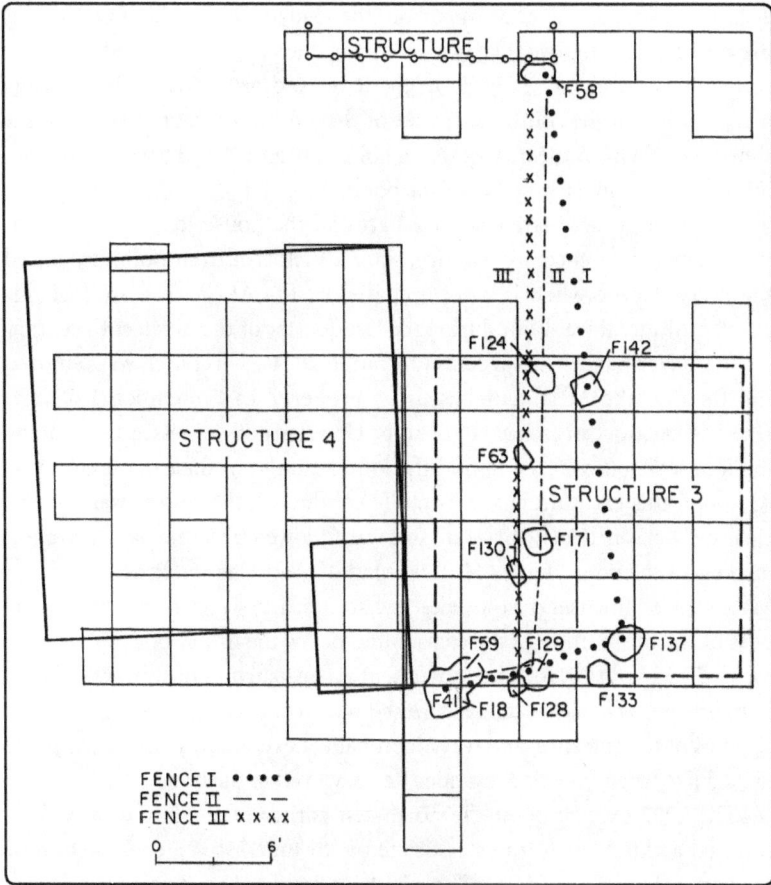

FIGURE 25. Early fences in the east side yard. Note the different orientation of the early cabin (Structure 4) and later fence lines.

fence that bordered the old entrance lane from the north. These trees were bulldozed during the early landscaping of the rear yard (Van Deventer 1985).

The building of what later became Thorngrove Pike in front of the stone house depended on how long it took for the pond bed to dry sufficiently for a road to be built over it. What J. G. M. Ramsey calls "the road to Dandridge" (Hesseltine 1954:10) is shown on an early map that indicates this road was already in place by 1815 when the pond bed was being farmed (letter from F. A. Ramsey to J. G. M. Ramsey, 24 July 1815, Ramsey Papers, University of Tennessee Special Collections Library, Knoxville). That it may already have been built by 1796 is hinted in the narrative of Aaron Armstrong's father, who encountered the stone-laden wagon on "the road to Dandridge." That this was present-day Thorngrove Pike is suggested by the fact that this road led to the early ferry crossing at the Forks of the River and on to Knoxville. Crossing the pond bed at the southeast corner of the peninsula would have been the shortest route from the quarry to the house site and would have passed over one of the narrowest stretches of the pond.

Two excavations were conducted around the house to determine what the original front entrance was like, since a Victorian front porch enhanced the house facade when it was purchased by the APTA. The style of this porch indicates it was built during the last quarter of the nineteenth century (Bernard Herman, personal communication 2004). This porch was removed shortly after the APTA purchased the property. In September, 1973, Dr. D. Bruce Dickson, an archaeologist at the University of Tennessee, tested along the Ramsey House facade to find the foundation(s) of the earliest entrance. Although this excavation was carefully conducted, the results were inconclusive (Dickson 1974). Dickson's test was followed by a one day excavation in front of the door by Alex H. Townsend of West Chester, Pennsylvania, in March 1976. Townsend exposed a few stones that were interpreted as the possible reconstruction of the steps found below the front door of the house today (Townsend 1976). The subsequent reconstruction of this arc of stone steps is believed to have destroyed most if not all of the original archaeological remains of the entrance, and we will probably never know what the entrance looked like when Francis Alexander Ramsey lived in the house.

The 1997 excavation at the northwest corner of the house in Area H revealed a cluster of features associated with the 1796–97 construction of the house (Figures 7 and 26). These include Feature 70, a dressed limestone/marble pad or footer; Feature 76, the builder's trench along the north wall of the house; and Features 90 and 92, large construction postholes chinked with large limestone/marble rocks (Faulkner 1999:25–26). The context and configuration of these features indicate they are the archaeological remains of a substantial scaffold used to build the walls of the stone house.

Feature 70 was approximately 5 feet long, built of large flat limestone/marble slabs laid perpendicular to the northwest corner of the stone house (Figure 26). This was first thought to be part of a foundation of a small building adjacent to the house, but excavation of six units and posthole tests around it revealed no connecting foundation remains. Units placed in the same grid position at the southwest and southeast corners of the house revealed similar features. Feature 75, a flat limestone/marble slab or footer was laid 12 feet from the southwest corner of the house. A large slab or footer was not found at a comparable distance from the southeast corner, but a heavy concentration of

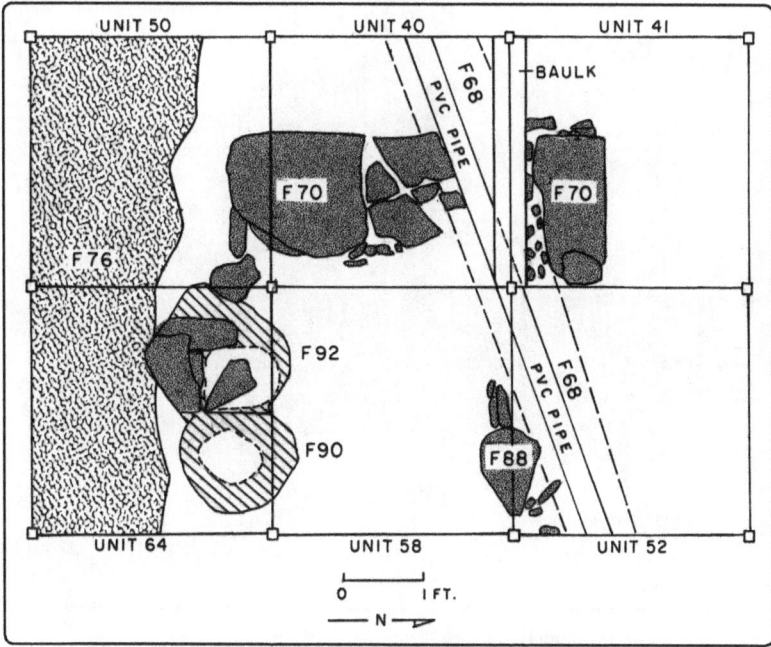

FIGURE 26. Feature 70 and associated postholes (Features 90 and 92).

limestone/marble chunks and flakes occurred at this location. The location and composition of this feature suggest it had a similar function to Feature 70.

Excavation of units between Feature 70 and the wall of the house revealed the top of a clay-filled builder's trench for the house foundation (Feature 76). This sloping trench was completely excavated to the south profile of the unit. This revealed that the overall width of the trench was approximately 5 feet from the house wall. This width from the house wall is unusual, since the house has a full cellar and the house wall could have been expediently built against the trench wall, making a wide exterior builder's trench unnecessary. However, the large postholes Features 90 and 92 on the edge of the builder's trench are believed to explain the exterior width of this feature. The 5-foot width allowed the placement of large vertical posts on the outside edge of the builder's trench so that individual postholes of a scaffold would not have to be dug along the wall. Large rocks were piled around the posts for support, and the trench was then refilled with the removed subsoil clay after the house wall reached above ground level. This secured the substantial scaffold needed to hold the heavy stone blocks used to build the wall. This scaffold may have resembled the example illustrated in Diderot 1959:Plate 284 except there is no evidence of vertical

Figure 27. Scaffold construction for building the walls of Ramsey House.

support posts abutting the walls of the house. Since this is a two-story house, the horizontal ledger boards supporting the decking were probably placed into pockets in the stone wall later filled with matching stone (Figure 27).

The proximity of the Feature 70 stone footer to the builder's trench and postholes indicates it was an integral part of the scaffold. However, until more excavation is conducted on the builder's trenches along other sections of the house wall, the function of this footer and what appears to be remnant footers at the southwest and southeast corners of the house will remain unclear. They may have been bases of ramps or lifting devices for moving stone to the upper levels of the scaffold.

The cellar is also interesting from an archaeological standpoint because there is no evidence of what happened to the subsoil spoil clay when it was dug. Normally, such spoil would be conveniently spread around the house. Posthole testing and the opening of units around the house and along the edge of the peninsula did not reveal a stratum of clay that might have been dumped around the house, nor was there such a deposit evident on the eastern slope of the peninsula above the pond bed. While the cellar could have been dug by hand with slave labor, the magnitude of this undertaking suggests the soil might have been removed by a horse-drawn slip scraper. If this was the case, the clay spoil could then have been easily dumped into the pond bed in front of the house to build the road. This is additional evidence that the present-day Thorngrove Pike was built early in the history of the house.

In 1994, heavy rains caused major flooding of the Ramsey House cellar. The digging of drainage trenches in the cellar floor exposed a large number of artifacts at the bottom of the steps in the bulkhead entrance. In February 1994, I collected artifacts from the trench backdirt, recorded the stratigraphy exposed in the trenches, and cored the cellar floor to determine the nature of the deposition occurring there (Faulkner 1994b). In 1996, a 1-foot by 2-foot unit was excavated by natural/cultural strata at the base of the cellar steps where deposits reached a depth of 1 foot (Coughlin 1996). This excavation indicated that except for the colluvial deposit at the base of the steps, artifacts in the remainder of the cellar are of recent origin and lay on a thin band of silty soil atop the yellow clay subsoil packed hard by years of foot traffic.

The excavations conducted in the cellar in 1994 and 1996 revealed an early drain along the cellar walls. The Ramsey House drain is an open system that diverts floodwater out of the cellar (Fay 1986:22). Mortared gutters extend along the north and west walls of the cellar and converge at an opening in the wall in the northwest corner. When the cellar was first dug, the floor probably sloped from east to west, directing any water on the floor toward this drain. Outside the house, the drain appears to lead to the creek bank on the west side of the peninsula (Faulkner 1994b:4). We attempted to find the buried drain on the outside of the wall during the 1997 field season by digging a unit opposite the interior opening in the cellar, but encountered two modern drain pipes near the surface. preventing further excavation (Faulkner 1999:21).

Recent study of the cellar has also revealed some early features. Aligned with the space under the stairway to the second floor are modifications to the original ceiling/floor joists that suggest an interior stairway to the cellar once descended there. Such an interior access to the cellar would not be unusual for a house of this period and elegance. Features include cut mortises for what may have been newel posts at the base of the stairs and a remnant of a stringer or stringer board. At what would have been the base of the stairs is a large dressed limestone block that may have served as a landing on the dirt floor. Unfortunately, the area of the possible cellar stairs is largely covered by the heating and air conditioning unit attached to the ceiling, making a study of these features difficult. It is very surprising that they were not noted when the house was restored after 1952. If a stairway did exist here, it is not known when or why it was removed, although it may have been because of continued flooding or dampness in the cellar.

Despite possible moisture problems, the cellar may have been initially used for more than simple storage of foodstuffs. The cellar walls were plastered, and evidence of whitewashing on the main floor beam suggests some other domestic activities may have taken place in this area. It was also recently discovered that the original cabinet in the relieving arch beneath the west end fireplace once had a door. Robert Van Deventer (1985) suggested that this cabinet was used to store jellies or other canned goods. James Hooper, who identified the late-eighteenth-century woodwork on this cabinet, believes that because it was set into the wall it might have served as a cooler for perishable foodstuffs (personal communication, 2006).

Food preparation activities may also be indicated by the ceramics and container glass recovered in the unit excavated in 1996 at the base of the outside stairway, although the presence of numerous window glass sherds indicates that most of this material is domestic debris that reached the cellar via the bulkhead entrance. There has also been a persistent rumor that Ramsey slaves may have lived in the cellar. This seems unlikely, as the cellar lacks a heat source and it was obviously very damp, at least initially.

One of the most distinctive features of the Ramsey House is the attached stone kitchen. In her M.A. thesis on Thomas Hope, architect of Ramsey House, Susan Tate was the first to note the unusual construction of the attached kitchen, observing that the attachment of this structure to the corner of the house was "an unusual procedure in the area at the time" (1972:75). Most kitchens of late-eighteenth-and early-nineteenth-century houses in East Tennessee were either detached for fire safety or connected to the rear of the main house by an ell addition attached at the gable end (short axis) opposite the chimney. The Ramsey kitchen is attached on the side (long axis) of the structure, which is not only unusual but, according to modern house builders, a poor method of construction because it has caused drainage and leakage problems between the two buildings to the present day.

There is no question that the kitchen is a later addition to Ramsey House because it covers the detailing (quoins) on the northeast corner, and the stonework of the kitchen is definitely inferior to that of the main house. The quality of the stone is poorer, there is no detailing with special stone at the corners and over the doors and windows, and the doors and windows are asymmetrically placed; in other words, it completely lacks the neo-Georgian styling of the stone house.

One of the outstanding features of the kitchen is the huge fireplace with a massive poplar lintel. The most curious and controversial feature of this fireplace is the so-called welcome window, a small opening on one side the structure. According to the story told in tours of the house, a candle was placed in this small window to alert weary travelers on the nearby road that they were welcome to come into the kitchen to eat and spend the night.

There are certainly other, more practical reasons for placing such an opening in the fireplace. One is that it was an opening into an exterior beehive oven. Beehive ovens were not uncommon on German-American farms in Pennsylvania, although most were free-standing (Long 1972). This theory was briefly tested by Townsend (1976), who found no evidence of the buried foundation for such an oven. I examined the outer wall of the chimney in this location but failed to find any evidence of the attachment of such a structure. There is also no evidence the rocks within or around this opening were subject to the intense heat of an oven.

The most likely function of this feature is that it produced additional light for persons working at this large fireplace (there are no regular windows on this end of the kitchen), or else it was a means of transporting wood from the outside rather than carrying it through the door. A similar feature is found in the early-eighteenth-century Buck House in Newcastle County, Delaware, believed to be a light source for a seat in the jamb or end of a large fireplace (Bernard Herman, personal communication 1985).

Edith Watson, whose father, Sam Pitner Watson, lived in the Ramsey House at the turn of the twentieth century, told me that her father said it was an opening for transferring firewood into the kitchen fireplace. An examination of the stones in this opening revealed that one of the original interior sill stones shows considerable wear/polish as though something, possibly wood, was passed through this opening regularly.

Although the unusual construction of the kitchen is curious, determining the construction date of the kitchen has been just as problematic. Unlike the house, which is well documented as being constructed in 1796–97, there is no known written record about the construction of the kitchen. Until my research, only one date had been suggested in a study of Ramsey House conducted by the UTK School of Architecture in 1980, which concluded that the kitchen was built in 1799 (Cashion et al. 1980). However, these researchers present no documentary or architectural evidence supporting this construction date.

The most opportune time to have dated the kitchen would have been during restoration after the property was purchased by the APTA. The APTA conducted two restorations on this structure. The first was shortly after 1952, when a wood floor was constructed over what was then apparently a dirt floor. No primary documents have yet been found indicating who built this wood floor, but it is certain that the exposed earth was not an original floor but the result of an earlier removal of a wood floor. The very poor condition of the building in 1952 may have been due to its having been used to store corn prior to its purchase by the APTA (Van Deventer 1985).

The major restoration of the kitchen was conducted by Robert Van Deventer in 1960. Although Van Deventer kept notes on this restoration, took photographs, and retained artifacts found under the wood floor when it was torn out due to termite damage, replacing it with the present stone floor, he did not try to date the kitchen by hardware or other artifacts that might have been in plain view beneath the floor (Van Deventer 1960).

A report by the UTK School of Architecture in 1980 describes the restoration of the kitchen floor:

> The floor of the kitchen at the time of purchase [1952] was wood planks nailed to log joists laid on the ground. This was found to be badly damaged by termites. After removal of the wooden floor by Mr. Van Deventer, what seemed to be an infill of rubbish and dirt was noticed. Digging then revealed a rock ledge, which was determined to be the perimeter of a stone floor [Cashion et al. 1980].

Van Deventer related that when the house was purchased in 1952, the kitchen had been used as a crib with an earth floor covered with hay and domestic trash dating from the late eighteenth to the mid-twentieth century. He wrote that a wood floor was installed shortly thereafter, the floor joists resting on stones and other recent trash that had been left in place on the earthen surface. Because of termite damage and moisture caused by the debris under the floor, this modern floor was removed in 1960 and replaced with the stone floor; it had been determined that there had been a stone floor because of the presence of a rock "ledge" around the perimeter of the walls (Van Deventer 1960). Such paved floors are found in eighteenth-century German houses in Pennsylvania, usually associated with kitchens (Bernard Herman, personal communication 2005).

It is unfortunate that the "rock ledge" was not studied in more detail at the time, as it could have been used to support the ends of wood floor joists rather than being the remnants of a stone floor. A common Pennsylvania-German building practice was to construct a ledge around the perimeter of the foundation and lay the joists on top of the ledge but unattached to the wall (Bernard Herman, personal communication 2005). Evidence that this was the case at the Ramsey House kitchen includes the presence of a large quantity of eighteenth-century artifacts under the modern termite-infested floor, which seems unlikely to have accumulated under a stone floor. One must also ask why a substantial stone floor would have been removed, considering the labor involved in such a renovation.

Finally, Van Deventer described a "baffling problem" discovered in front of the fireplace: a pavement of brick about 18 inches below the rock ledge that he thought dated from the construction of the kitchen. The origin and function of these bricks were not explored at the time they were exposed, though they were described as being "of varying ages but . . . as old as the house or kitchen" (Van Deventer 1960).

Van Deventer kept a scrapbook of color prints showing progress on the restoration of the house and grounds from January 1960 to October 1975. These photographs included several taken in July 1960, when the wood floor was replaced by the stone floor (Van Deventer 1975). The line of bricks is visible in two photographs, and their location substantiates Van Deventer's description that they were laid only in the fireplace opening. What is interesting about these bricks is that they appear to be covered with rubble fill on which the rear wall of the fireplace rests. If this was a brick hearth, which was not unusual in early American fireplaces, then the presence of the rubble fill above it suggests that the hearth was rebuilt sometime during the later history of the kitchen.

In 1996, Sean Coughlin conducted an intensive study to date the construction of the kitchen, examining previous architectural studies, archaeological data that had accumulated by that time, and Van Deventer's notes and the artifacts he found while renovating this structure (Coughlin 1996). While Van Deventer's notes lacked solid contextual evidence and he reported boards and other debris that dated from the late eighteenth century to the early 1950s, the artifacts in his collection included 20 handwrought rose-head nails and seven spike-sized wrought nails probably pulled from boards in or under the floor. If these nails were indeed used in the construction of the original floor of the kitchen, it would mean it was built not much later than 1800. However, it is also possible that the various boards found under the 1952 modern floor could have come from anywhere in the house during earlier repairs and discarded in the later abandoned kitchen (Coughlin 1996:17–18).

Some nails pulled from timbers in the kitchen during more recent renovation and repair have also been studied. When the flooring in the second floor was repaired in 1998, some of the cut nails removed from the floor were dated both before and after ca. 1836 (Dr. Amos Loveday, personal communication 1998). The professional historic house restorer who repaired the floor believed that this flooring had been replaced perhaps two or three times since the kitchen was built (James Hooper, personal communication, 1998).

The second-floor room of the kitchen also warrants mention because it retains much of the original construction of the kitchen. Reached by a narrow staircase along the west wall of the kitchen, the windows and fireplace indicate that the room was originally a domestic living quarters. Original plaster covers the stone walls, including the decorative limestone quoins on the northeast corner of the house. While we have no direct evidence of who lived in this room, it is likely that it was the residence of the cook and other enslaved house servants of the Ramseys.

In the 1997 field season we attempted to date the builder's trench of the south wall of the kitchen from artifacts in the fill by placing a unit in the corner where the south kitchen wall meets the east wall of the house. Unfortunately, excavation revealed that this corner was badly disturbed by recent repair to the adjacent bulkhead wall of the cellar entrance, and no clear evidence of a builder's trench along the kitchen wall could be seen (Faulkner 1999).

During the 1999 field season another excavation was conducted adjacent to the kitchen wall to determine the date of its construction. Two units were opened below the window in the south kitchen wall to collect a sample of flat glass from this window and conduct a further search for an undisturbed portion of the builder's trench (Figures 13 and 14). Eighteen window glass sherds were recovered in the level just above the top of the builder's trench. Twelve of 17 sherds clustered between 1796 and 1813, with a mean date of 1803. These sherds are believed to be from the original pane(s) in the south window of the kitchen.

The point of origin of the builder's trench (Feature 109) was found at the base of Level 3 in these units. The lower levels of the trench contained a concentration of hammer-dressed limestone/marble flakes and mortar discarded into the open trench while the kitchen was being constructed. Besides these construction materials, no other artifacts were found in the trench (Faulkner 2000a:26–28).

The absence of domestic artifacts in this section of the builder's trench suggests an early date for the construction of the kitchen. An early date is also indicated by the mean date of 1803 on glass from the south wall window. The age range of the window glass (1796–1815) also correlates with the wrought nails recovered by Robert Van Deventer during the 1960 kitchen restoration (Faulkner 2000a:28).

A construction date of ca. 1803 implies Thomas Hope might have been involved with the construction of the kitchen. Four of Hope's children were born at Ramsey House, the last, Ralph Izzard Hope, being born there on December 30, 1803. The next child, John Hope, was born at Charles McClung's plantation in 1805, where Hope was building McClung's brick home called "Statesview." The unusual method of attaching the kitchen block to the house and the lack of the masonry detail matching that on the house are difficult to explain, however, if Hope was still the architect. While it is also possible, of course, that a master stonemason could not be found at this later date, the rather coarse construction of the kitchen does not seem to be characteristic of the meticulous Hope. On the other hand, why would Hope remain at Swan Pond until 1803, after the stone house was completed, if not to direct the construction of the kitchen?

Perhaps it is significant that the year 1805 also saw a major change in the Ramsey family with the death of Francis Alexander's first wife, Margaret "Peggy" Alexander. The next year he married Ann (Agnew) Fleming, a widow he met on a trip to visit his parents in Gettysburg (Rothrock 1946:468; Hesseltine 1954:12). If Francis Alexander did not build the kitchen for his first wife, perhaps he presented his second wife with this convenience when they returned to Swan Pond, although the absence of domestic artifacts in the excavated section of the builder's trench seems to argue against a date this late in the nineteenth century.

The location of Francis Alexander's office has also been the focus of testing and excavation in the inner house yard. Because he was a respected and lifelong public servant as clerk of the first state senate of Tennessee and clerk of the circuit court, it is likely he needed a place to conduct business in private. J. G. M. Ramsey says that his father:

> was a steady patron of schools and learning in his neighborhood. Common school teachers on the frontier were not always at hand and were often incompetent. To supply this great deficit he often employed educated young men as clerks in his office ... and as instructors of his children [Hesseltine 1954:13].

Three of these young clerks, John Naylor Gamble from Pennsylvania, New England native William Smith, and Lyle Humphreys from Limestone, Tennessee, kept a journal together, the remaining portion containing entries from November 29, 1802, to February 4, 1803 (Francis Alexander Ramsey's Clerks' Diary, University of Tennessee [UT] Special Collections Library, Knoxville).

Since the clerks' journal never specifically mentions an office building, I originally speculated that perhaps the office was in a room of the Ramsey House (Faulkner 1986:14). However, there are enough inferences in their daily accounts to indicate the existence of an office building. For example, on January 18, 1803, a clerk spends the forenoon *in* the office and attends an arbitration *at* Colonel Ramsey's in the afternoon. It appears that two different locations are spoken of here. On January 22, 1803, a court session was held at the office. It seems unlikely that a court session would have been held in the Ramsey's house.

If the office was in a separate building, where was it located? There is now substantial archaeological evidence that the Ramsey log cabin continued to stand in its original location until after 1865, when it was moved a few feet to the east to become what we call Structure 3 (Faulkner 2002:28). While the question of why a log house would continue to stand next to the beautiful stone residence throughout Francis Alexander Ramsey's life and after he died is somewhat perplexing, the most logical reason is that it continued to be useful in daily operation of the farm. Despite the architectural beauty of the house, parsimony seems often to have been the bottom line for Francis Alexander Ramsey.

It is also possible that the original cabin, Structure 4, functioned as a detached kitchen before the stone kitchen was constructed, and once the kitchen was built the cabin's convenient location adjacent to the residence made it ideal as Ramsey's office. If Francis Alexander's office that the clerks referred to was indeed in the cabin, it means the kitchen was built before 1802. This is a good example of the proxemic and functional relationship between outbuildings and the house and why such should never be studied in isolation.

In my study of the locations of offices at other early-nineteenth-century farms and plantations in Tennessee, I discovered that of 14 offices studied, five were at the side of the main house and parallel with it, five were in front of the house, two were behind it, and two were at the side or attached to the main house (Faulkner 1986:15–18). This suggests that offices were attached to or very near the main house so that daily business matters could easily be attended to in a private yet convenient setting. This certainly fits the location of the Ramsey cabin.

Other evidence that an office stood at this location are a slip-glazed ceramic inkwell, a British brown stoneware inkwell and ink bottle sherds, and slate writing pencils found around Structures 3 and 4 (Figure 28). Four writing desks and two inkstands are listed in Francis Alexander Ramsey's estate inventory (Knox County Administrator's Settlements 1821).

Francis Alexander Ramsey's estate inventory contains the names of six slaves: Jude, Vinnie, Cate, Dorcas, and Saphrona (Knox County Administrator's Settlements 1821). There is also a note in the inventory that the court ordered that all Negroes belonging to the estate of Francis Alexander Ramsey be sold at public sale by the administrators to satisfy claims against the estate. The Knox County bills of sale one year later record the disposition of some of these enslaved persons. Dorcas (no age given) and her infant daughter Mary Hannah were sold to Eliza Ramsey. W. B. A. Ramsey bought a man (name unintelligible), 30 years of age, and a woman, Sophie (probably Saphrona), about age 14. J. G. M. Ramsey bought Venus (Vinnie?) 47 years old, and an unnamed mulatto man, age 22 (Knox County Deed Records 1822). Thus six enslaved persons were duly sold, but except for two they do not correspond

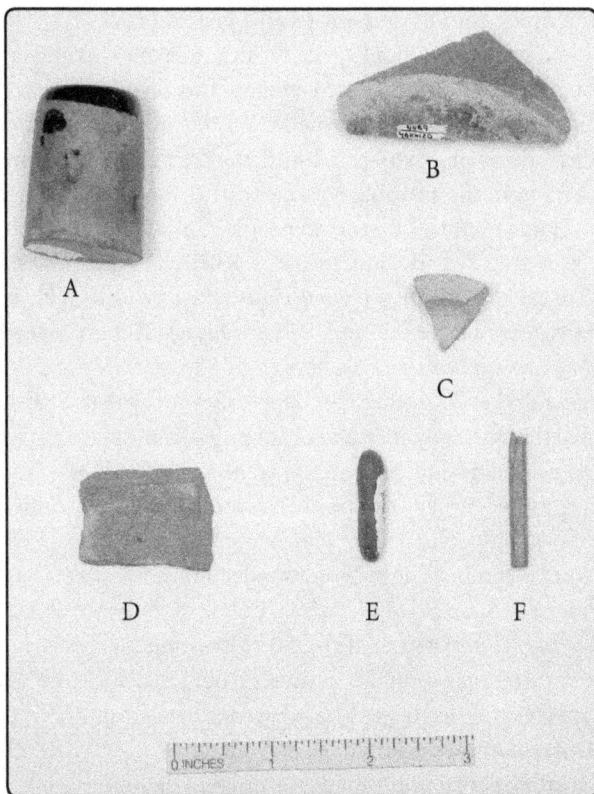

FIGURE 28. Office ceramics. A. Ceramic inkwell. B. Base of British brown ink bottle. C. Base of British brown inkwell. D. Writing slate. E and F. Slate pencils.

to the names on the inventory. Part of this discrepancy is probably due to the poor handwriting or carelessness of the recorders, a not uncommon occurrence at that time.

Evidence of the earlier presence of slaves at Swan Pond is found in the Knox County Deed Records. In July 1804, Francis Alexander sold a woman, Hannah, age 16, to Charles McClung (Knox County Deed Records 1804). During the years 1810 and 1811 Francis Alexander Ramsey was involved in a flurry of slave trading. In 1810 he bought six slaves from Deverous Gilliam: four females (Hannah, 42; Anny, 14; Tanny, 10; and Mandy Moriah, 2) and two young males (James, 6, and Billy, 8). It is possible that some or all of the children were Hannah's. In the following year, Francis Alexander bought a woman named Debe, age 29, and her son Charles, not quite 2 years of age, from

William Davenport for $400 (Knox County Deed Records 1811a). However, he sold Debe and her son to John Crozier for the same amount during that year (Knox County Deed Records 1811b). Perhaps this suggests he was not in the slave trading business for profit. In the 1812 listing of Knox County taxpayers Francis Alexander is shown to own four slaves (Tennessee Ancestors 1986).

It appears from the available documents that Francis Alexander Ramsey never had a large number of enslaved people at Swan Pond. This is interesting because by 1812 he had acquired almost 2,000 acres (Tennessee Ancestors 1986) and one could infer that it would have taken a considerable number of laborers to clear and farm the land. Perhaps his acquisition of several slaves around that time indicates he was expanding his farming activities as the pond became dry; on the other hand, it is noteworthy that almost all of his documented slaves were women and children. We know that enslaved women often worked as field hands, but the apparent rarity of adult males for heavy labor is surprising. Perhaps most of his slaves had domestic duties, and the farming was largely conducted by white tenants.

The exact location of Francis Alexander Ramsey's slave quarters during his lifetime at Swan Pond is unclear. The most likely possibility is that it anchored the northwest corner of the defensive compound where a scatter of late-eighteenth-century ceramics indicates a domestic structure once stood. Another possibility is that is was located in Area I, where posthole testing and five excavation units produced late-eighteenth- and early-nineteenth-century ceramics. In any case, the apparent domestic focus of his slaves suggests it was close to the house.

Other dwellings also existed on the Ramsey farm in the early nineteenth century, but the number of these houses and location is unclear. We know that Francis Alexander's aged mother and father moved from their Gettysburg, Pennsylvania, home to Tennessee in about 1807 and lived out their last years at Swan Pond (Hesseltine 1954). However, the reference to this move suggests they lived in the main house with their son. Another elderly relative also moved to Swan Pond about the same time. John Alexander, Francis Alexander's maternal uncle, who had invited his nephew from Pennsylvania to live with him on Big Limestone Creek and thus start his successful Tennessee career, was settled on the Ramsey farm "near to the old mansion in a neat frame cottage where he ended his days at an advanced age" (Hesseltine 1954:13).

In 1812, James Rogers, the son-in-law of Ramsey's uncle John Alexander came to Swan Pond to care for his aged father-in-law, who was blind and feeble and lived on a 200-acre tract east of the Ramsey House and south of Swan Pond Creek. For a decade thereafter, Rogers and the Ramsey heirs fought a legal battle over this property. The details are extremely complex, but basically the Ramseys claimed that Rogers did not make the necessary payments for the property and Rogers claimed that he did. This 200-acre tract was not included in the Ramsey estate after Francis Alexander's death, and Rogers was still living on the property in 1832 (Knox County Court Records, Knox County Archives, Knoxville, Tennessee).

A cabin was said to have stood south of the Ramsey house on the west side of Thorngrove Pike until the turn of the twentieth century when it was torn down (Van Deventer 1985). In describing the collection of rocks used to build the kitchen floor, Van Deventer mentions that some were obtained from an early foundation in a field west of the house. This area near the northeast corner of John Sevier Highway and Thorngrove Pike has not been tested for evidence of this foundation.

In addition to Francis Alexander Ramsey's parents and uncle, other relatives and employees also lived at Swan Pond during the early nineteenth century. J. G. M. Ramsey relates that "my father brought around him other distant relatives, old destitute and infirm: Hanna Moreton, Mrs. Patton, and Mrs. Hawthorn and others" (Hesseltine 1954:13). In addition, the clerks who authored the aforementioned journal were boarded at the farm, and Thomas Hope and his family lived there until 1805. Counting the Ramsey's slaves, there was a veritable community of Ramsey relatives and workers living at Swan Pond.

The location of other outbuildings is also not known at this time, although there is considerable indirect evidence of additional farm buildings. Francis Alexander Ramsey's estate inventory (Knox County Administrator's Settlements 1821) records that 4 horses, 3 mares, 2 colts, 13 cows and calves, 9 cattle, 6 steers, 2 oxen, 1 bull, 16 sheep, and 40 hogs were sold in October 1821. Only two poultry are listed. While the cattle, steers, bull, sheep, and hogs were probably not provided with substantial shelter, the horses must have been kept in a stable and milk cows and the oxen in a barn. While the stable would presumably have been located near the house, buildings housing other stock may have been elsewhere on the large farm. Early log outbuildings such as barns often do not produce a significant scatter of artifacts, and their simple rock footer foundations are easily removed from areas later cultivated or built upon.

Three of the most interesting contrivances listed on the estate inventory that might have been housed in separate buildings include a cider mill, a "gethsemane," and a 75-gallon still with tubs. The "gethsemane" was apparently an oil or juice press. It is possible that this apparatus and the cider mill could have been housed in separate building(s). However, on the estate inventory, the cider mill was sold for 50 cents and the gethsemane for 25 cents.

Either they were badly in need of repair or they were small machines that would not have required a separate building for their operation.

The size of the still apparatus suggests it was used in a building called a still house. Assuming there was a still house on the Ramsey farm, it is interesting to note that while this might be considered strong evidence that Francis Alexander was producing liquor, his probate inventory does not contain any specific serving vessels such as decanters, wine glasses, or goblets for the consumption of alcoholic beverages. Although the Ramseys frequently entertained because of their social position in the community, they apparently did not serve their guests spirituous beverages. This is confirmed in the account of Bishop Francis Asbury, who, while visiting Knoxville in November 1800, was a guest at Swan Pond (Williams 1928:312). After delivering a sermon in the Knoxville statehouse, Bishop Asbury met Francis Alexander Ramsey, who

> pursued us to the ferry, franked us over, and took us to his excellent mansion—a stone house: it may not be amiss to mention, that our host has built his house, and takes his harvest without the aid of whiskey. We were kindly and comfortably entertained.

Considering the apparent abstinence of Francis Alexander Ramsey, how does one reconcile the presence of a still in his possession. Perhaps this can be explained by a statement in an nineteenth-century journal that "Before markets became convenient, almost all large plantations had stills to use up the surplus grains, which could not be sold to a profit near home" (Continental Monthly 1862). Another possibility is that a still came into the possession of Francis Alexander during the property dispute with James Rogers, who is known to have had a still house (Faulkner 1986:26–27).

Also listed on the estate inventory are three wool and flax wheels, one reel, two pairs of wool cards, three flax hackles, and a flax break, suggesting to the compiler that the Ramseys had a weaving and spinning room (Van Deventer 1985) or perhaps a loom house (Carnes and Chapman 1984:7). A loom is not included in Francis Alexander's inventory, and the spinning and flax wheels could have been used in the main house, perhaps in the small room at the head of the stairs where such devices are displayed today. Flax breaking and hackling might have been done in the barn. In any case, there is no direct documentary evidence of a separate loom house.

An agricultural census does not exist for the early Ramsey period at Swan Pond, so we do not have an inventory of the crops grown on the farm. J. G. M. Ramsey relates that the peninsula on which the stone house stood was "sufficiently large for the yard and grounds around the site of the buildings and also for a large garden and orchard" (Hesseltine 1954:8). The cider mill indicates apples were grown in the orchard. Posthole-testing in Area B, directly north of the caretaker's house (now being appropriately used as the heritage garden), produced virtually no artifacts but showed that the area had deep, homogeneous soil, suggesting that it was the original and long-standing kitchen garden area. Archaeological testing of the known turn-of-the-century garden area at Governor John Sevier's home at Marble Springs produced the same kind of virtually artifact-free, homogeneous soil (Faulkner 2003b:22).

Information in the probate inventory relates to the growing of corn and wheat and the cutting of hay. The inventory items include a shelling machine, a corn basket, two mowing scythes, and a cradle. Fodder for the animals is also listed in the inventory. In a letter to his sons J. G. M. Ramsey and W. B. A. Ramsey in 1815 while they were attending Washington College, Francis Alexander writes about the difficulty of getting in the wheat. In the same letter he also states, "I have this morning begun to cut the meadow but am still afraid we shall have wet weather" (Ramsey Papers, UT Special Collections Library, Knoxville) He was probably talking about making hay in what had been the bed of Swan Pond.

The faunal remains excavated at Ramsey House through the 1995 field season have been studied in stratigraphic context in a master's thesis by Judith Patterson (1998). In addition, preliminary analyses have been conducted on faunal remains from the 1999 field season (Jacobson 2000) and 2000 field season (Windham 2002). However, the latter two studies in general do not separate the material by time period.

Based on the deep stratigraphic deposits, mean ceramic dates, and window glass thickness in the east side yard, Patterson distinguished four occupation periods. The earliest, Period I, corresponds to the early Ramsey period. Strata representing this period yielded 67 bones of six vertebrate species, including (in order of frequency) 49 (73.14 percent) pig (*Sus scrofa*), 14 (20.90 percent) cattle (*Bos taurus*), 2 (2.99 percent) freshwater drum fish (*Aplodinotus grunniens*), 1 (1.49 percent) white-tailed deer (*Odocoileus virginianus*), and 1 (1.49 percent) cotton rat (*Sigmodon hispidus*) (Patterson 1998:Table 4.2). In addition, there were 163 unidentified mammal bones from medium- to large-sized animals (Patterson 1998:65–67).

This inventory suggests that pork was by far the prime meat source in the early Ramsey diet, with beef constituting an important secondary meat source. That cattle played a significant role in their diet may also be implied by the analysis of faunal material from Feature 96, the fireplace/chimney base of the early cabin. Six of the 33 bones from this feature were identified as cow (n = 3) and pig (n = 3) (Jacobson 2000:4). Studies of southern foodways have indicated that while pork was the most common meat served because it could easily be preserved, beef was still the preferred meat of wealthy farmers and planters in this region (Hilliard 1972).

Two other observations are noteworthy in this faunal assemblage. The almost complete absence of wild game is unexpected for an early frontier homestead and could indicate that from the time the Ramseys arrived at Swan Pond they were already very proficient in raising domestic stock. They were also wealthy enough to purchase meat from local sources. In any case, the Ramseys apparently did not have to supplement their diet with wild game. The other observation is the absence of chicken bones in the early Ramsey period. While this could be attributed to poor preservation of the thinner and more fragile bird bones, it may correlate with the rarity of fowl on the estate inventory. The occurrence of eggshell in the early Ramsey period kitchen ash deposits may also mean chickens were primarily raised for their eggs rather than their meat in this period.

Examination of the specific elements and their condition also reveals something about food preparation and meat consumption in the early Ramsey household. The amount of nonmeat butchering waste such as teeth and cranial fragments and the practice of chopping to dismember the animals indicate home butchery was practiced (Patterson 1998:86). Identifiable pig elements indicate that 32 percent came from high-yield cuts of meat and 68 percent were from medium-yield cuts; all of the cattle bones are from high-yield cuts (Patterson 1998:87–97).

MATERIAL CULTURE
OF THE EARLY RAMSEY PERIOD

A description of the artifacts possessed and used by the Francis Alexander Ramsey family has been made much more complete by the existence of Francis Alexander's estate inventory. Thus we not only know what artifacts were present during the early Ramsey period on the site but we also have excellent data about the ones that survived in archaeological context.

A number of classification schemes have been proposed to inventory and describe artifacts found on historic sites in North America. One of the best known is the classification scheme of Stanley South (1977), in which artifacts are placed into functional groups, classes, and types. Groups are distinguished by functional activities reflected in the archaeological context. Classes within groups are based on form and/or function. Artifact types in classes are distinguished from other types by form and/or such attributes as decoration, etc. Artifact groups in this study include kitchen, furniture, clothing, firearms,

personal/grooming/health, leisure/entertainment, hunting/military, and edu-
cation/office. The architecture group (nails, window glass) has been discussed
in the descriptions of construction and buildings on the site.

The artifacts listed in the Ramsey estate inventory and those recovered
in the archaeological excavation are described below. It is important to note
that in no way can it be expected that those artifacts in the systemic context
(inventory) will be expected to match those in archaeological context due to
the vast amount of perishable items in the former (wood, cloth, paper, etc.)
and the vagaries of sampling, differential preservation, and disposal patterns
in the archaeological record. Therefore, only the frequently described non-
perishable artifacts in the inventory are discussed here.

KITCHEN GROUP

Ceramic artifacts are often the most frequently noted in the kitchen group
class. Forty-six plates, 4 dishes, 3 Delph dishes, 2 pitchers, 1 Delph pitcher, 1
Delph coffeepot, 5 punch bowls, 7 teapots, 8 cups and saucers, 12 China cups
and saucers, 12 Liverpool cups and saucers, 1 sugar bowl, 2 cream pots, 7
crocks, 4 earthen jugs, 2 jars, and 3 earthen pans are listed in the inventory.

Other items in the kitchen group that could have been lost or broken and
were found in archaeological context are glass container and tableware artifacts, including 4 quart bottles, 4 glass bottles, 6 tumblers, 2 salt holders, and 2
glass pitchers. Other small kitchen items that might have been lost around the
house are 6 metal spoons, 18 silver tablespoons, 12 silver teaspoons, 10 other
teaspoons, 1 pair of sugar tongs, 31 knives and forks, 1 nutmeg grater, and 4
pot hooks. Other kitchen ware such as metal tin cups, pails, racks, sieves, pans,
etc. would normally be represented in the archaeological context as badly
rusted fragmentary pieces.

Several thousand artifacts were found associated with the original cabin,
Structure 4. While architectural artifacts such as wrought nails and window
glass made up a large percentage of this assemblage, a large number of kitchen
artifacts were recovered as well. Most prominent was refined earthenware used
to set the Ramsey table, virtually all imported from England and available by the
1790s in the mercantile stores in Knoxville. These wares included creamware
(ca. 1762–1820) and pearlware (ca. 1785–1830), the latter replacing creamware
in the 1790s and becoming the predominant ware on East Tennessee historic
sites in the first two decades of the nineteenth century (Figure 29).

The most frequent creamware vessels are plates, platters, cups and saucers.
Many dinner plates are embossed on the rim in what is called the Royal pattern (Figure 29A) (Noel-Hume 1969:116). Other decorated creamware vessels

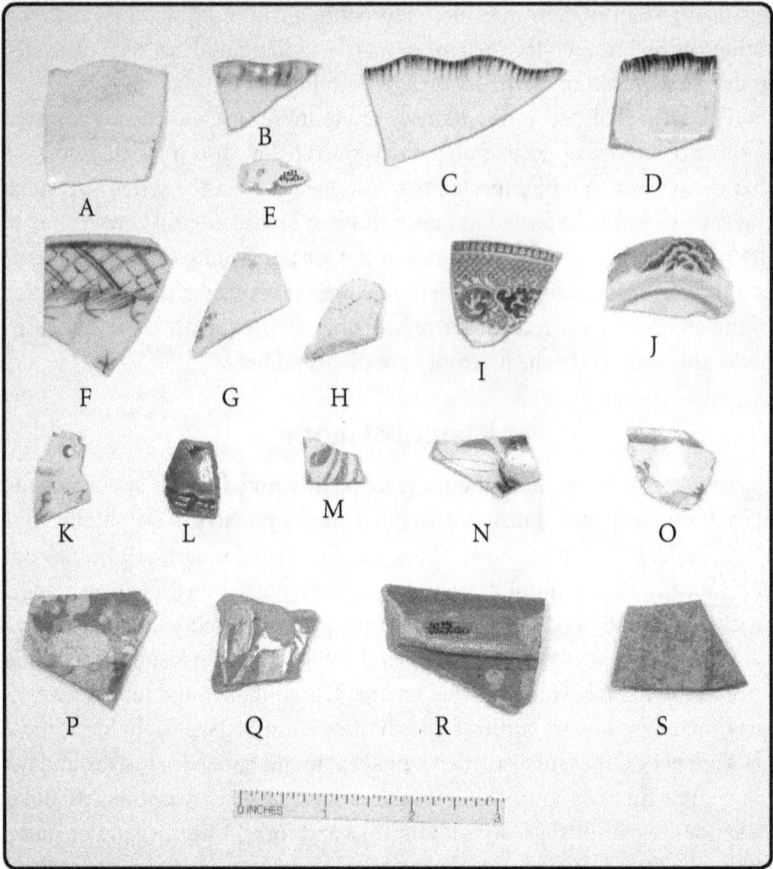

FIGURE 29. Early Ramsey ceramics. A. Creamware dinner plate with a Royal pattern. B. Pearlware dinner plate with a green shell edge. C and D. Pearlware dinner plates with a blue shell edge. E. Creamware pepper pot. F. Chinese export porcelain dinner plate, hand-painted blue and underglazed, Canton pattern. G. Chinese export porcelain tea cup/bowl, hand painted, enameled, and overglazed. H. Chinese export porcelain saucer, hand painted, enameled, and overglazed. I. Pearlware dinner plate, transfer printed with a blue willow pattern. J. Pearlware tea cup/bowl, blue transfer printed. K. Pearlware teapot, hand-painted blue, fine-lined, and underglazed. L. Refined redware teapot with an embossed basket design. M. Delph saucer, hand-painted blue, tin-glazed and underglazed. N. Pearlware saucer, hand-painted polychrome, underglazed, and broad lined. O. Pearlware teacup/bowl, hand-painted polychrome, underglazed and broad lined. P. Creamware mocha cat's eye hollow ware. Q. Earthenware slip-decorated, lead-glazed hollow ware. R. Earthenware bowl, lead glazed. S. Stoneware, British brown hollow ware.

include mocha bowls and pitchers that accompanied the dinnerware during daily meals and overglazed enameled creamware cups and saucers used in afternoon tea. These cups and saucers might be the "Liverpool" tea ware listed in the estate inventory. The perforated top of a creamware pepper pot was also recovered (Figure 29E).

Pearlware was usually decorated, types including blue and green shell-edge dinner plates, soup plates, and platters used for casual dining (Figure 29B–D), and fancier transfer-print dinner sets for more formal meals. The Ramseys had a blue transfer-printed dinner set in the "blue willow" pattern, a pattern still in use today (Figure 29I). Underglaze pearlware blue and polychrome painted tea sets eventually replaced the creamware sets as the Ramseys kept abreast with the latest entertaining fashions in the early 1800s. Four teapots are represented in the archaeological ceramic assemblage, an underglaze blue hand-painted pearlware vessel (Figure 29K), a refined redware teapot molded in the shape of a basket (Figure 29L), and two porcelain vessels, one a possible Castleford teapot of molded unglazed porcelain, and the other a Chinese export teapot.

Two sherds from a tea set of tin-glazed refined earthenware were also recovered around the cabin (Figure 29M). Decorated with underglaze blue hand-painting, this ware could have come from England, Holland, or France. Tin-glazed ware was a popular table setting before the advent of creamware, with a median date ca. 1750 in England (South 1977:211). It is believed that this might have been from an heirloom tea set brought from North Carolina by Peggy Alexander Ramsey.

For entertaining special dinner guests, even in their humble log cabin, the Ramseys used a set of Chinese export porcelain. Two types of export porcelain were present in the ceramic assemblage. Several sherds from a table setting of underglaze blue hand-painted plates and serving pieces in the Canton pattern were found (Figure 29F). Such sets have only occurred archaeologically at the eighteenth-century house sites of Knoxville's elite families such as the William Blounts and the James Whites (Faulkner 2000b). The other type of Chinese export that occurred more frequently at Swan Pond was overglaze enameled tea ware (Figure 29G–H). Several hand-painted decorative patterns were found on cups, saucers, and a teapot, these sets undoubtedly being the china cups and saucers listed in the estate inventory.

The ubiquitous kitchen utilitarian ceramic ware used in the early Ramsey period was a lead-glazed earthenware often called redware. No American-made stoneware could definitely be identified dating from this time period although sherds of British brown stoneware, imported from England with a median date of 1733 (South 1977:210), were recovered (Figure 29S). The

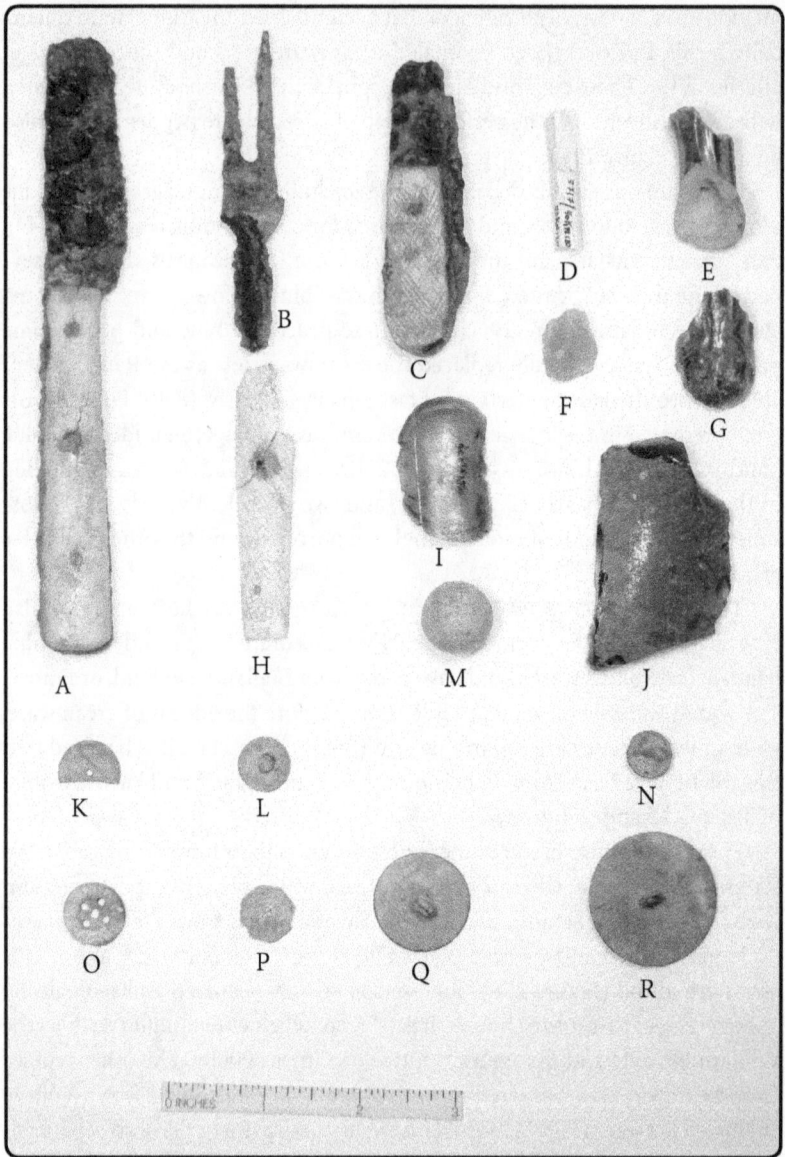

FIGURE 30. Early Ramsey artifacts. A. Bone-handled table knife. B. Two-tined iron fork.
C. Bone-handled clasp knife. D. Kaolin clay pipe stem. E–G. Lead-glazed, stub-stemmed pipes.
F. French gun flint. H. Incised bone handle. I. Cobalt glass medicine bottle. J. Olive glass wine
bottle. K. Single-hole bone button. L. Yellow metal sleeve button. M. Stone marble. N. Brass
tack. O. Five-hole bone button. P. Pewter button. Q–R. Yellow metal jacket/vest buttons.

majority of sherds from the redware vessels were from utilitarian bowls, pans, crocks, and jugs. The "earthen pans" in the estate inventory were undoubtedly shallow redware bowls used to prepare and store food (Figure 29R). A few sherds from slip-decorated, lead-glazed plates (Figure 29Q) and a pitcher were also found, vessels possibly made in Pennsylvania or North Carolina, where such pottery was popular among the early German settlers. It is likely, however, that most of the utilitarian kitchen vessels were locally manufactured in East Tennessee (Smith and Rogers 1979).

Identifiable glass artifacts such as containers and glass tableware (glassware) occurred much more infrequently, suggesting these expensive items were more carefully curated by the Ramseys. These include glass containers such as case bottles and glassware such as tumblers. A few olive-green bottle glass sherds were present in the early Ramsey strata. In the late eighteenth and early nineteenth centuries olive-green bottles often contained wine (McKearin and McKearin 1941:423–425). Of the 70 sherds of olive-green glass found in the east inner side yard, only seven, or 9.9 percent, occurred in the early Ramsey levels (Figure 30J). Comparing this frequency of wine bottle glass to that recovered on the homesites of other elite Knoxville families, it was found that in one of the test excavations at Blount Mansion, 100 percent of the olive-green glass occurred in the early Governor Blount levels (Faulkner 1985:Table 4). In the excavation of the James White Second House site, 80 percent of this glass was found in the early horizon (stratum), dated to the occupation of the James White family (Faulkner 1984:Table 10). The infrequency of wine and other alcoholic beverage bottles in the early Ramsey levels supports the observation of Bishop Asbury that Francis Alexander Ramsey did not drink or serve alcohol.

Other foodways-related artifacts recovered in the early historic archaeological context include fragments of cast-iron cookware (probably from kettles), a pewter spoon handle, table knives with riveted bone plates with incised decoration, and iron two-tined forks (Figure 30A–B, H).

FURNITURE GROUP

Because of the size and wooden construction of most furniture, only a few metal furniture artifacts were found. Most frequent are round-headed brass tacks, either from upholstered chairs or leather-bound trunks (Figure 30N). A brass escutcheon plate from a Hepplewhite (ca. 1785–1800) piece of furniture was also found. A few mercury/silver-backed mirror sherds also occurred, this mirror type dating to the early nineteenth century (Roenke 1978).

Clothing Group

Clothing artifacts can be placed into three functional categories: manufacture/sales, wearing apparel, and repair. The most frequently recovered items of clothing on archaeological sites are fasteners from wearing apparel. Common early Ramsey buttons are disc buttons made of "yellow metal," a generalized descriptive label for eighteenth-and nineteenth-century buttons manufactured from brass, copper, bronze, or a combination of these metals (Figure 30L, Q–R). After about 1800 many of these buttons were back-stamped with the manufacturer/trade name, which can be used to date their period of manufacture. The majority of the copper alloy disc buttons from Swan Pond are not back-stamped, indicating an early Ramsey date for these artifacts. Some of these disc buttons were originally covered with cloth and many were gold-plated. A two-piece embossed button from the early Ramsey strata still had the surface gilting preserved and was probably from a woman's dress.

Two other early metal button types were found in the Structure 4 area. One type is a disc button made from "white brass." Most of the yellow and white metal disc buttons are probably from men's coats, jackets, vests, and breeches. Another common late-eighteenth-century metal button found there is the cast pewter button (Figure 30P). Bone buttons with one to five holes (Figure 30O) are also common in this early clothing assemblage, the most distinctive late-eighteenth-century bone type having a single hole (Figure 30K). These latter buttons are believed to have been covered with cloth. Another early fastener type occurring around Structure 4 is the brass hook-and-eye, usually found on women's garments.

Clothing repair artifacts include a pair of iron scissors and a brass thimble. The most common manufacturing/repair artifacts, however, are wire-wrapped headed straight pins that date before 1824 (Noel-Hume 1969:254). These were largely retrieved through flotation of soil samples around Structure 4.

One artifact representing manufacturing/commerce is a stamped (illegible) lead cloth-bale seal. Two lead bale seals were also found at the James White house site (Faulkner 1984:160). These seals were used to seal or identify bales of cloth, and their occurrence at the White and Ramsey house sites indicates these families were buying cloth in bulk and manufacturing some of their clothing.

Personal/Grooming/Health Group

Personal artifacts are those carried on oneself or are ones' personal property. These often include grooming aids such as combs or personal implements such as a clasp ("pocket") knife. Coins may also be personal artifacts although, like a comb or knife, they can be shared by family members. Health care artifacts are also personal; for example, medicine often came in virtually indestructible glass containers that can be found on archaeological sites.

Only one personal artifact from the early Ramsey period was recovered, this being a clasp knife with an incised bone handle (Figure 30C). Similar clasp knives with incised bone handles were found at the Tellico Blockhouse, occupied from 1794 to 1807 (Polhemus 1977:248).

Surprisingly, no grooming aids could be definitely identified from the early Ramsey strata. The health artifact class is represented by the hand-formed finish or rim from a clear glass medicine phial and a body sherd from a small cobalt bottle (Figure 30I). Cobalt glass was often used for medicinal containers in the late eighteenth and early nineteenth centuries (Jones and Sullivan 1985:14). Other glass fragments from free-blown bottles occurring in early context could have also been from medicine bottles, but the absence of content embossing precluded determining the function of these containers.

LEISURE/ENTERTAINMENT GROUP

At Ramsey House this group includes the toys and smoking pipe classes. Stone marbles represent the only toys (Figure 30M). These are made of limestone and are considered an early marble type on American sites since their impor-tation reached a peak in the mid-eighteenth to mid-nineteenth centuries, declining in popularity after 1870 (Baumann 1970:19; Randall 1971:102).

Two types of tobacco pipes were found in the early strata at Ramsey House. Most frequent are the earthenware stub-stemmed pipes that were made in the United States. These were made from the late eighteenth century through the late nineteenth century. One type of stub-stemmed pipe found at Swan Pond is a green-glazed redware type, believed to have been made by Moravian potters in North Carolina (Figure 30E–G) (Bivins 1972).

The other pipe type found here is the long-stemmed white kaolin clay pipe (Figure 30D), sometimes called the "church warden pipe" (Noel-Hume 1969:296). Most kaolin pipes were probably made in England or on the Con-tinent. They have only been found in late-eighteenth-and early-nineteenth-century context on domestic sites in Knox County.

HUNTING/MILITARY GROUP

Surprisingly, only five firearm artifacts were found in and around Structure 4. These include a round lead shot, lead sprue, two gun flints, and a possible trigger part.

While the sprue and residual melted lead could have been from the home manufacture of other artifacts (pewter buttons, for example), it is believed that such amorphous blobs of lead on frontier sites are usually from the molding of spherical shot. The gunflints include a rectangular gray flint artifact, accidentally burned in a fire, and probably of English origin, and a honey-colored French gunflint (Figure 30F). The possible trigger part is broken and cannot be positively identified as being from a firearm.

The rarity of firearm artifacts in the early Ramsey period is difficult to explain. Although the scarcity of wild faunal remains from this period indicates the Ramseys did not rely on hunting wild animals for food, we know that all settlers also kept firearms for militia duty and for protection from hostile Indians. A likely possibility is that during this time, firearms were largely used/discharged away from the homesite; flints and shot may have been too expensive to waste and would therefore not be found in abundance around the house.

EDUCATION/OFFICE GROUP

Education and office activities are combined in this study because many classes and types of artifacts were used in both of these categories of activity. Such artifacts found at the Ramsey site include a ceramic inkwell, ink bottles, and slate pencils. The inkwell was found in the deepest level near Structure 4 and is cylindrical in shape, covered with a dark brown slip glaze (Figure 28A). A similar inkwell was found at the Tellico Blockhouse (Polhemus 1977:Plate XXXI). It appears to be a type that would fit on a writing desk. A sherd from a British brown stoneware inkwell was also in the early Ramsey strata (Figure 28C). Several sherds of British brown stoneware from cylindrical ink bottles were also recovered around Structure 4 (Figure 28B). The British brown inkwell and bottles were probably imported from England (Noel-Hume 1969:78–79). The slate pencils are round, thick rods of slate, sharpened at one end (Figure 28E–F). Several pieces of dark gray/black writing slate were found in Structure 4 (Figure 28D), suggesting that Alexander Ramsey's children were instructed in this building.

Chapter 4

THE LATE RAMSEY PERIOD, 1820–1866

WILLIAM B. A. RAMSEY

Francis Alexander Ramsey died on November 20, 1820. His estate was divided between his four surviving children in 1822, the house and the Swan Pond tract being inherited by his second-oldest son, William Baines Alexander Ramsey (Hesseltine 1954:10; Knox County Court Records 1825). After W. B. A. Ramsey (called "Billy" by his father) graduated from Washington College, he returned to live at Swan Pond with his parents, and when his father died, he took over management of the farm (*In Memoriam: Col. Wm. B. A. Ramsey*, 1874, Ramsey Papers, UT Special Collections Library, Knoxville).

In April 1820 Francis Alexander Ramsey married Mrs. Margaret (Russell) Cowan Humes, who gave birth to a son, Francis Alexander Ramsey, five months after his father's death in November. Margaret Ramsey moved to Knoxville shortly after her husband's death. In 1850 Margaret Ramsey was living with her son Francis "Frank" A. Ramsey, a respected physician in town (United States Census 1850).

A map in the University of Tennessee Special Collections Library shows the tracts of Francis Alexander's estate that were inherited by the four Ramsey children (Figure 31). W. B. A. Ramsey inherited 558 acres including the home place. Francis Alexander's oldest surviving son, James G. M. Ramsey, inherited the 353¼-acre farm in the fork of the Holston and French Broad rivers, an estate he called "Mecklenburg" after Mecklenburg, North Carolina, the home of his mother, Margaret "Peggy" Alexander Ramsey

(Hesseltine 1954:17). Their younger brother, John M. A. Ramsey was given a tract of 874 acres north of Swan Pond Creek. Eliza Ramsey received 343 acres south of the family home, including acreage on the French Broad River. While this map is not dated, it was certainly drawn between the recording of Francis Alexander's will in 1816 and the building of J. G. M. Ramsey's Mecklenburg house at the Forks of the River in about 1823.

The map also shows houses on three of the properties and a saw mill at the confluence of Swan Pond and Cruze creeks. It is assumed that these buildings represent all or most of the dwellings found on the Ramsey property at that time. Support for this assumption is based on map details such as cleared land. Noteworthy cleared or cultivated land includes a large area at the Forks of the River, an area just west of the stone house, and a meadow south of this

FIGURE 31. Map showing those portions of Francis Alexander Ramsey's estate inherited by his four children. A: W. B. A. Ramsey. B: J. G. M. Ramsey. C: John M. A. Ramsey. D: Eliza Ramsey. The arrow denotes the Ramsey House. Courtesy University of Tennessee Special Collections Library.

dwelling. If these represent the only cleared and/or cultivated ground on the Ramsey farms, the growing of crops appears to have been diversified among the four farms. The Sutton and Plumblee families were also tenants on the Ramsey land. It is also possible that some of Francis Alexander's relatives who were mentioned as residing on the farm lived in these houses (Faulkner 1986:30).

Unfortunately, the history of and the activities at Swan Pond are not well documented between 1820 and the year 1857 when J. G. M. Ramsey's son, Francis Alexander Frost Horlbeck Ramsey ("Alex" or "Elick"), inherited the property. There is some evidence that W. B. A. Ramsey may not have lived at Swan Pond for several years of his ownership. This is indicated by the fact that he is not listed in the 1830 Knox County census (U.S. Census 1830). While this might simply have been an oversight, it is difficult to believe that such a large landowner would have been overlooked by the census taker. The explanation probably lies in the following account from J. G. M. Ramsey's *Autobiography:*

> A scheme was also projected to give East Tennessee the advantage of steamboat navigation as far at least up the river as Knoxville. This enterprise was inaugurated by my brother, W. B. A. Ramsey, Doctor James King, William Swan, James Kennedy, Dr. C. W. Crozier, and others—all of Knox County. I took one share—my brother two—he was the largest stockholder and was commissioned by a unanimous vote of the shareholders to repair to Cincinnati Ohio, to purchase or build a boat of such form and tonnage as would best suit the navigation of our shoal rivers. Under his direction the steamboat *Knoxville* was built and brought around to the town for which it was named [Hesseltine 1954:33].

Articles in the *Knoxville Register* indicate W. B. A. Ramsey was in Cincinnati in 1831. He was back in Knoxville in 1832, when he served as clerk and master of the chancery court from that year through 1848 (Goodspeed Publishing 1974:814). From 1835 to 1836 W. B. A. Ramsey was a member of the Knoxville Board of Aldermen, and in 1838 he was elected mayor of Knoxville, serving a one-year term from 1838 to 1839 (Deaderick 1976:627, 636). This indicates that he either lived in town or was spending a great deal of time there.

William B. A. Ramsey is found in the 1840 Knox County census, apparently living at Swan Pond. Perhaps he moved back to the property in 1839, the year his wife Eliza died (Ramsey 1982:174). The census lists a 40- to 50-year-old male (presumably W. B. A. Ramsey), three males between 20 and 30 years of age, an elderly female between 50 and 60 years old, and two young girls under five years old living in W. B. A. Ramsey's household (United States Census 1840).

According to a memorial written for W. B. A. Ramsey when he died in 1874, he married his first wife, Mrs. Eliza C. White, widowed daughter of John Craighead, in 1834. Since a woman of her approximate age is not listed on the census, his wife must have already been deceased when it was taken in 1839. The two young girls were probably daughters born of Eliza. A Ramsey genealogist states that W. B. A. Ramsey had two daughters born in 1835 and 1837 (Bivins 1987), but primary documentation of their birth and life at Swan Pond is unavailable. The names of these two girls appear later in letters from J. G. M. Ramsey to his brother in Nashville in which he mentions "Maggie and Liddy, my two nieces" (McIver Collection, Tennessee State Library and Archives, Nashville).

The elderly female in the household was probably W. B. A. Ramsey's deceased wife's mother. Eliza Craighead White was the daughter of John and Temperance Nelson Craighead, who also had two sons, James Patterson Nelson Craighead (b. 1812) and Robert Craighead (b. 1814). Temperance Craighead was born in 1787 (Howell 1986). This would make her 52 years old when the census was taken in 1839 and her sons 27 and 25. W. B. A. Ramsey's involvement with the Craighead family is also seen in the fact that he and Robert Craighead published the *Knoxville Register* from 1837 to 1839 (Adamson 1976:295).

Seven enslaved African Americans also lived at Swan Pond at this time. The 1840 slave census lists three children (two males and a female) under ten, an adult male, and three adult females (United States Census, Slave Schedule 1840). We do not know the Christian names or surnames of these enslaved individuals.

The same types of artifacts found on late-eighteenth- and nineteenth-century African American sites in Knox County and elsewhere in the South were also found around and under Structure 4. This suggests that slaves were living in this structure, the former Ramsey cabin/office, sometime after Francis Alexander's death in 1820. These distinctive artifacts include glass beads, a quartz crystal, and fragments of homemade clay pipes (Figure 32). Unfortunately, ceramics and other domestic artifacts used by these enslaved people could not be differentiated from those used by the Ramsey family. Slave ceramics were often hand-me-downs or were obtained by the enslaved by barter or purchase, and sometimes even included expensive porcelain pieces, such as the ones found under the slave quarters at Blount Mansion (Hamby 1999).

Although only a few artifacts can be associated with the African American presence at Swan Pond, they do tell us something about the lifeways of people in bondage there. Beads, especially those made of blue glass, are common on African American sites, and it is thought not only that they were used for personal adornment but that the color blue may also have been believed to protect individuals from evil spirits and bad luck (Stein et al. 1996).

Sixteen beads have been analyzed from the Swan Pond excavations. Ten of these artifacts were found in mid-nineteenth-century strata in the area of Structures 3 and 4. Four of these (40 percent) are of blue glass, three of them typical later-nineteenth-century faceted types (Figure 32G). Four remaining glass beads include one green faceted, two white, and one trapezoid shaped, color indeterminate. A brass or copper bead and a wooden bead are also included in this assemblage.

Various types of crystals have been found on African American sites throughout the eastern United States (Wilkie 1997). According to African

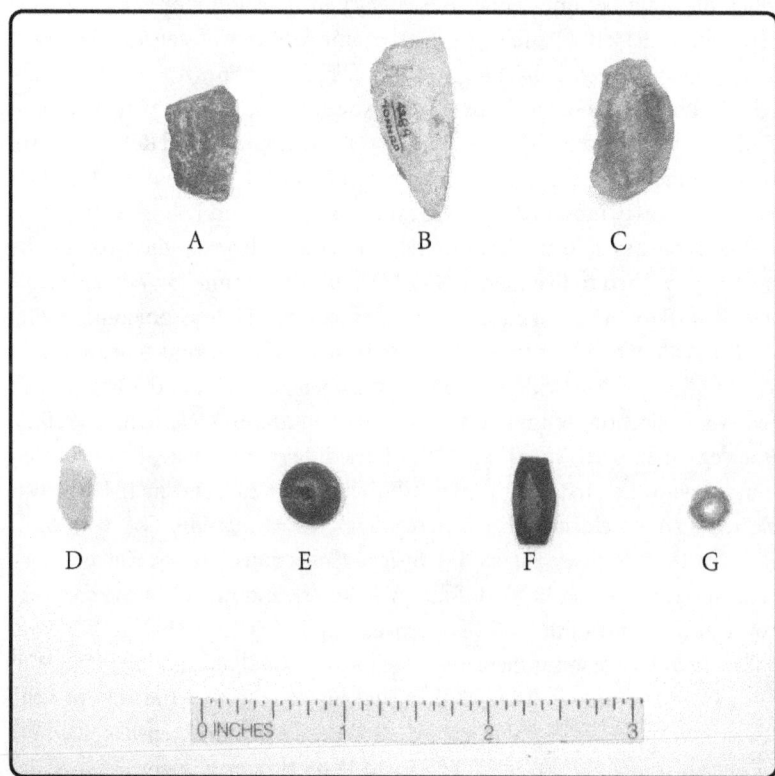

FIGURE 32. African American artifacts. A–C. Handmade clay pipes. D. Quartz crystal. E. Black glass spheroid bead. F. Black glass faceted bead. G. Blue glass faceted bead.

and African American traditions, these objects may have been used as amulets or charms. A small quartz crystal was found under the chinking stones of the Structure 3 girder, indicating a pre-1866 date for this artifact (Figure 32D).

The handmade clay pipes (Figure 32A–C) are also interesting in that factory-made pipes were readily available in the United States during this time, yet someone at Swan Pond chose to make his or her own. A home-made clay pipe was found in the slave quarters at the Mabry site in west Knox County (McKelway 2000), and it appears this craft was also practiced at Swan Pond. The entire African American assemblage at Swan Pond suggests some African traditions were still alive and well in mid-nineteenth-century enslaved communities at this time in East Tennessee.

JAMES G. M. RAMSEY

J. G. M. Ramsey states that his brother William sold the old home place to him when the latter became Tennessee secretary of state and moved to Nashville (Hesseltine 1954:10). W. B. A. Ramsey became secretary of state for Tennessee in 1847 (Goodspeed Publishing 1974:823). This date does not, however, correlate with a deed filed in Knoxville on November 6, 1840, in which W. B. A. Ramsey sold 465 acres to J. G. M. Ramsey (Knox County Deed Records 1840). It is assumed that this was the majority of the 558-acre home place that W. B. A. Ramsey inherited from his father. Bowman and Folmsbee state that William Ramsey sold the farm to his brother after his wife died because he no longer wished to live there (1965:14). This time frame for William's selling Swan Pond and leaving Knoxville is incorrect. He was obviously living in Knoxville when he wrote 21 letters to his future second wife, Susan P. Washington, in Nashville between November 20, 1841, and May 1, 1842 (McIver Collection, Tennessee State Library and Archives, Nashville). W. B. A. Ramsey's memorial, states that "While residing in Knoxville, he connected himself with the First Presbyterian Church of that city, and in 1841, he was elected a ruling elder of that congregation" (*In Memoriam: Col. Wm. B. A. Ramsey,* 1874, Ramsey Papers, UT Special Collections Library, Knoxville, 4). Goodspeed states that W. B. A. Ramsey was clerk and master of the chancery court in Knoxville until 1848 (Goodspeed Publishing 1974:814), and William still owned acreage somewhere in the vicinity of Swan Pond after the Civil War.

J. G. M. Ramsey is listed as living on his 353 acres at the Forks of the River in both the United States census and the agricultural census (Schedule 4) for Knox County for 1850. The Swan Pond property is not listed under J. G. M. Ramsey's name, and thus far only one family has been identified that occupied the old home place in the 1840s. Two other Ramseys are found in the Schedule 4 census for 1850. John McKnitt Alexander Ramsey, the son of Francis Alexander Ramsey and Ann Agnew, lived on a 263-acre farm, probably the remainder of the 874 acres of the family estate that John McKnitt inherited from his father (Knox County Court Records 1825; Ramsey 1982:179). A William Ramsey was living on a 200-acre farm in Knox County, and while the location of this property is not precisely known, the 1850 census listing suggests it was not in the area of the original family estate. This is apparently William S. Ramsey, a minister age 42 (United States Census 1850). The relationship of this man to the Francis Alexander Ramsey family is not known.

Apparently Swan Pond was occupied by renters during this time, since neither W. B. A. Ramsey nor J. G. M. Ramsey seems to have lived there after 1840. The John Christopher Kinzel family were tenants here from about 1841 to 1844. John Kinzel, with his wife, Sophia Anna, and four young children sailed from the port of Bremen, Germany, for Baltimore, where they worked to pay passage to Charleston, South Carolina. In Charleston they were met and cared for by wealthy kinsman John Adam Horlbeck Sr., a master mason in Germany and later in Charleston. In 1788 it is recorded that Horlbeck and Thomas Hope participated in the federal procession to celebrate South Carolina's ratification of the United States Constitution (John Christopher Kinzel—Father of the Seven Brothers, Kinzel Family Papers, private collection). No doubt Horlbeck and Hope knew each other, and it is possible that Hope learned masonry skills from the senior Horlbeck. Obviously Francis Alexander Ramsey knew the elder Horlbeck and his son John Adam Horlbeck Jr., also a master mason, as did J. G. M. Ramsey, whose son Francis bore the middle name of Horlbeck.

It is certainly through this connection to the John Horlbeck family that Francis Alexander Ramsey was acquainted with the building skills of Thomas Hope and invited him to build his stone house. It is also through the Horlbeck family that J. G. M. Ramsey invited John Kinzel to Tennessee to take care of the Swan Pond property. The Kinzel family narrative recounts that J. G. M. Ramsey greeted them when they arrived at Swan Pond. Two sons were born to John and Sophia Kinzel when they lived at Swan Pond: Jacob John Kinzel born June 8, 1841, and Edward John Kinzel born August 9, 1843 (Kinzel Family Papers ca. 1997). On August 5, 1844, John Kinzel acquired 120 acres of his own land in east Knox County (Knox County Deed Records 1844).

We are unsure who lived at Swan Pond from 1844 to the time J. G. M. Ramsey's third eldest son, Francis Alexander Frost Horlbeck Ramsey began to oversee the property. From a letter from J. G. M. Ramsey to W. B. A. Ramsey dated October 7, 1852, we know that a family named Burnett were tenants on four tracts still owned by the two Ramsey brothers. The reference is probably to Joseph Burnett and Jesse Burnett (brothers?) who on the 1850 agricultural census are shown as renting two tracts of 185 and 50 acres, respectively (United States Census, Schedule 4 1850). J. G. M. states that "Burnett is a good tenant" and seems to imply that he lives on or close to the "home place" (McIver Collection, Tennessee State Library and Archives, Nashville). It might be significant that the combined acreage farmed by the Burnetts (235 acres) is close to the 225-acre Swan Pond farm acquired by Francis A. F. H. Ramsey from his father in 1857.

There is no evidence in the Swan Pond archaeological record that any new buildings were added to those in the inner house yard or that the alignments of any fences were shifted during this time. It is possible that whatever structure had existed in Area I in the peripheral outer yard was destroyed before, or immediately after the death of Francis Alexander Ramsey, since most of the thinly scattered ceramics found in this area date before about 1820. It is also difficult to accurately separate most of the artifacts used between about 1820 and 1850 because the majority could overlap with the earlier and later Ramsey occupations. Clues to foodways through faunal remains can also only be placed within the late Ramsey time frame (1820–1866).

FRANCIS A. F. H. RAMSEY

On December 9, 1852, J. G. M. Ramsey wrote to his wife, Peggy, from Charleston, South Carolina, that his third-eldest son, Francis Alexander Frost Horlbeck Ramsey ("Alex" or "Elick"), was looking after the old home place. The exact date of Alex's birth seems somewhat controversial in the family history. One family historian estimates he was born about 1828 (Ramsey 1982:204). Eubanks (1965:53) states he was born January 2, 1829, probably the correct date. In any case, by 1852 Alex was a responsible adult, fully capable of taking care of his father's interests. Further evidence of this young man's maturity is the fact that he had accompanied his older brother Wilberforce to the California gold fields in 1849, returning to his father's home after his brother's untimely death in 1850 (Hesseltine 1954:136–137). According to J. G. M Ramsey, Alex was seriously ill when he arrived home from California (Hesseltine 1954:137). In a letter to his brother W. B. A. Ramsey dated October 7, 1852, J. G. M. states that "Alexander reached us more than a week ago" but does not mention that he was ill (McIver Collection, Tennessee State Library and Archives, Nashville). Apparently he was fully recovered and taking care of Swan Pond two months later when his father wrote:

> Alexander you had better employ some one say Harvey Plumblee to
> make 2 or 3,000 rails around the Stone House fields—especially those

above the house—Down near home rails ought to be made of chestnut [in and against?] spring they will be light and dry. But I know you are looking into all of these things (Ramsey Papers, University of Tennessee Special Collections Library, Knoxville).

Sometime after returning from California Alex went to work for his brother-in-law Daniel Breck Jr. in Richmond, Kentucky. J. G. M. wrote that

> ... my son-in-law, Col. Breck, had become interested in a large landed property high on the Kentucky River, and wishing to improve it and develop it by erection of machinery invited my son, Alexander, to become an active partner. This he did. Under his direction a mountain was tunneled and one of the forks of the Kentucky River diverted through it. The mills proved to be valuable, furnishing to Frankfort vast quantities of plank and lumber transported in rafts down the river [Hesseltine 1954:137].

There is no record as to how long Alex remained with his brother-in-law. On March 19, 1856, J. G. M. wrote to W. B. A. that "At last account from Richmond Col. Breck was falling into consumption. . . . Alec was well" (McIver Collection, Tennessee State Library and Archives, Nashville). Daniel Breck actually died on March 13, 1856 (The Family of Mary Lincoln, http://members.aol.com/beaufait/biography/geneology.htm). It is not known how long Alex remained in Richmond after Breck's death, but in his autobiography J. G. M. states that upon Alex's return to Tennessee, "becoming acquainted with Miss Presley of South Carolina [he] went there and married her. I gave him the property sometimes known as Swan Pond, more recently as the Stone-house" (Hesseltine 1954:137). On October 15, 1857, J. G. M. closes a letter to his brother by mentioning "Alexander left via the cars for South Carolina this morning" (McIver Collection, Tennessee State Library and Archives, Nashville). According to the South Carolina marriage records, on October 27, 1857, Col. Alexander Ramsey married Nannie R. Pressley in York County, South Carolina.

J. G. M. Ramsey kept the deed for Swan Pond for several years, until he passed it on to his son in 1857. Deed records for the property indicate that on December 4, 1857, J. G. M. Ramsey sold 225 acres of the "Swan Pond Place" to Francis A. Ramsey. The warranty deed says in part "that the said James G. M. Ramsey for and in consideration of love and affection and Four thousand five hundred dollars, to him in hand paid, the receipt of which is hereby acknowledged, had bargained and sold" the property to Francis (Knox County Deed Records 1857).

Why would J. G. M. Ramsey say he gave his son the Swan Pond Place when the deed states he sold the property to him for $4,500? The answer lies in the phrase "for and in consideration of love and affection." This is standard legal jargon used when property is given as a gift.

It is interesting that J. G. M. Ramsey gave Swan Pond to his second-oldest surviving son rather than the eldest, John Crozier (b. 1824). Was Alex a favorite of his father, or was he the only son who was truly interested in being a farmer and maintaining the old home place?

According to Bowman and Folmsbee (1965:14–15), J. G. M. Ramsey bequeathed Swan Pond to Alex in 1856, transferring the title to his son in 1857. They further suggest that since J. G. M. Ramsey was being sued at that time by Parson William G. Brownlow, a perpetual antagonist of the Ramsey family, a consideration of $3,000 was included in the deed and Alex's note for that amount was later torn up. The consideration was actually $4,500, and the note was never torn up. This promissory note from Alex to his father was found in the UT Special Collections Library and reads:

> $4500 on or before the twenty-eighth day of February 1867 I promise
> to pay J. G. M. Ramsey for value received forty five hundred dollars.
> Witness my hand December 4, 1857.

On the back of the note is written: "To be cancelled. J. G. M. Ramsey."

J. G. M. Ramsey and Margaret Crozier Ramsey had 11 children, and in 1860 nine lived in his household or nearby. The three youngest children, Charlotte Barton Ramsey (b. 1838), Arthur Crozier Ramsey (b. 1846), and Susan Alexander Ramsey (b. 1846) apparently lived in J. G. M.'s household in that year. William Wilberforce Ramsey had died in California in 1850, and the oldest surviving son, John Crozier Ramsey (b. 1824), an attorney, lived in a hotel in Knoxville. Crozier, as his family called him, apparently never married. Besides the Swan Pond acreage that Francis Alexander Ramsey now owned, before 1860 J. G. M. had acquired an additional 874 acres of nearby property that were farmed by three other children. These were his oldest child, Elizabeth Alexander "Hannah" Breck (b. 1823), who married Col. Daniel Breck in 1845, her husband dying in 1856; Robert McGready Ramsey (b. 1832), who married Margaret Atwell in 1866; and James G. McKnitt Ramsey (b. 1835), who never married. While the U.S. agricultural census for 1860 lists these three Ramsey children as owning their own farms, widowed Elizabeth and unmarried Robert and James lived in J. G. M.'s household. The agricultural census lists different crops and animals raised on these three farms, suggesting a cooperative arrangement of production among the Ramseys. I speculate that J. G. M. acquired these three farms and then willed or sold them to his three children to keep them out of the clutches of William Brownlow in case he lost his lawsuit.

The 1860 U.S. census lists 30-year-old[1] Col. F. Ramsey, his 19-year-old wife Naomi (Nancy), and a one-year-old female child. The child was Elizabeth "Lizzie" Ramsey, born in 1858. Alex and Naomi Ramsey had 10 additional children. Archaeological evidence indicates that Alex Ramsey became the first family member to make major changes in the built environment of the farm. This is also substantiated in J. G. M. Ramsey's autobiography, in which he states that "[Alex] occupied and improved it for a few years" (Hesseltine 1954:137).

One of the major improvements was the final removal of the imposing defensive fence. This fence had been moved at least one time before it was finally removed and was one of five fences built across the east side yard between 1793 and the early twentieth century.

Figure 33 illustrates the location of these east side yard fences. Fence line A is the original defensive fence, this identification being based on an early date for some of the postholes in the east side yard and north rear yard, the size and spacing of these posts, and the orientation of this fence with the orientation of the early cabin. The terminus post quem (TPQ)[2] established by the artifacts in the posthole/mold fill for the first shift of this fence is unclear because the superposition of the three postholes (Features 18, 41, and 59) caused a mixing of the fill, but the relatively undisturbed posthole Feature 137 had a TPQ of 1837 for window glass and 1840 for ceramics (Faulkner 2003a:38), suggesting it might have been replaced at least once when the property was owned by W. B. A. or J. G. M. Ramsey.

It is significant that when the fence was moved to fence line B, the postholes remained large (Features 124, 129, and 171), as they were for the earlier fence, but the new fence now ran parallel to the east wall of the stone house. The spacing of the posts was somewhat irregular, being an average of 8 feet from center to center, with the remnants of cedar posts being found in Features 124 and 129. The TPQ for ceramics in Features 124 and 171 was as late as 1850 (Faulkner 2003a:40).

Another possible indicator that the defensive fence was removed in the 1850s is the fact that the posts at the southeast corner of the cabin had been replaced three times. Fence posts made of rot-resistant wood such as cedar

---

1. While Alex Ramsey was convalescing from his illness contracted in California, he was picked to fill a position of colonel in the local militia regiment. Thereafter, his father usually referred to him as Colonel Ramsey (Ramsey 1982:238).
2. The "date after which" for a feature established by the latest artifact(s) within it. The date can be any time after but not before the artifact was manufactured.

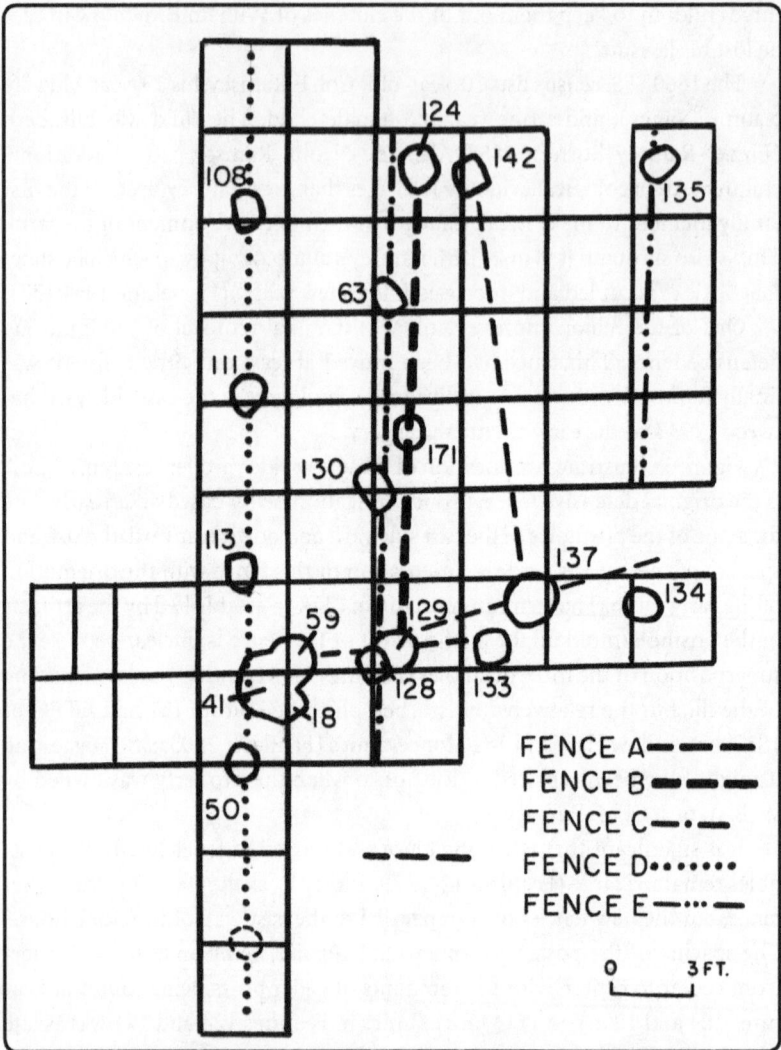

FIGURE 33. Fence lines in Structure 3 area.

may last 20 years (Stilgoe 1982:191). If the red cedar posts of the defensive fence lasted 20 years or more, and it was rebuilt at least three times, the fence may have stood from 1793 to at least 1853.

When Alex Ramsey removed defensive fence B, he replaced it with either a smaller board fence or palen fence C also aligned parallel with the stone house. Although fence C has a TPQ of 1830, it is believed to have been built by Alex because the three excavated postholes (Features 63, 128, and 130) have the usual later precise 6-foot spacing, Feature 128 was intrusive into Feature 129 of fence B, and two of the postholes were filled with wood ash when they were pulled, presumably from the continued occupation of the early cabin, immediately adjacent to the west (Faulkner 2003a:41). The fence also continued to connect the southeast corner of the cabin to the southeast corner of the smokehouse, indicating both structures were still standing at that time.

That a smokehouse still existed on the site when Alex lived at Swan Pond is also suggested from an interview in 1985 with Claudialea Ledger Watts, granddaughter of Alex Ramsey. Ms. Watts said her grandparents had a smokehouse, and it was fairly large because they put up their own meat (Faulkner 1986:44). This is also indicated by the 32 hogs that were raised on the site in 1860 (United States Census, Schedule 4 1860). As part of the "improvements" to the property, it might have been Alex Ramsey who tore down the gable end chimney of the smokehouse and installed a central interior basin hearth, more in keeping with the smoking of meat in East Tennessee.

Two slaves are listed in the 1860 United States Slave Schedule for the Ramsey farm: an 18-year-old female and a 15-year-old male. Since it is believed that slaves lived in the early cabin after Francis Alexander Ramsey died in 1820 and during the occupation of the farm by W. B. A. Ramsey, it is assumed that enslaved people continued to reside in the cabin in 1860. If this building continued to be the slave quarters during Alex Ramsey's tenure on the farm and he tore down the defensive fence, Alex may also have removed what may have been the first slave quarters at the northwest corner of the compound.

A feature that might date from either the W. B. A. Ramsey or Alex Ramsey occupations is the large pit, Feature 115. Its stratigraphic and spatial location within the east side yard indicates that it dates earlier than the moving of Structure 3, suggesting it was probably associated with this building when it stood in its original location (Structure 4) and may have had a functional relationship to Structure 4. More precise dating is provided by mean ceramic dates of 1808 and 1837. Only three window glass sherds were recovered, these having an average date of 1833 (Faulkner 2000a, 2001). Since one of the window glass sherds has a Moir date of 1867, it is possible that this pit could have been finally filled during the Alex Ramsey occupation because the silty clay fill apparently resulted from slowly accumulating colluvial wash, although the profile of this pit shows that it was capped before Structure 4 was moved over it.

The function of this pit is problematical. If it is associated with Structure 4, the time frame suggests it was used by the enslaved African Americans who probably lived in this building at that time. There are three possibilities. One is that it functioned as a refuse pit; however, it did not contain the large amount of refuse that would be expected in such a feature. Another possibility is that it was some type of outside storage facility, although such features do not appear to have been common on enslaved African American sites. The dimensions of the feature suggest that it may have functioned as a slave privy pit, but the fill does not contain the usual dark organic strata that are characteristic of this type of feature.

Refuse disposal during the late Ramsey period continued in the east side yard along the defensive fence and the buildings at the southeast and northeast corners of the compound. This suggests that the earlier activities in this part of the house yard continued through Alex Ramsey's occupation of the farm. The concentration of African-American artifacts in this midden is also evidence that these enslaved persons lived in the early cabin during this time.

The Schedule 4 agricultural census for 1860 also indirectly attests to the presence of other farm outbuildings on Alex Ramsey's farm. The seven horses, four milk cows, and two oxen indicate a stable and barn were present. The corn and oats were probably stored in some kind of crib. White and sweet potatoes were undoubtedly stored in the house cellar.

Other animals raised on the farm in 1860 were 32 swine, 12 "other cattle" and two sheep. The sheep produced 10 pounds of wool. Peas and beans were also grown. The production of 30 pounds of tobacco, 80 tons of hay, and 400 pounds of butter indicates a surplus sold or traded at market. It is likely that the 80 tons of hay were grown on the open meadows as it was when Francis Alexander Ramsey farmed at Swan Pond. The making of 7 gallons of wine listed on the 1860 census is interesting because there is good documentary and archaeological evidence that Alex's grandfather was an abstainer. It is worth noting in this regard that Alex's father, J. G. M. Ramsey, also made wine at Mecklenburg (United States Census, Schedule 4 1860).

The frequency of olive-colored glass, at this time largely associated with wine or other alcoholic beverage bottles also indicates an increased consumption of alcohol at Swan Pond in the mid- nineteenth century. Olive glass increased to 26 percent of the total of these glass sherds in the late Ramsey strata.

Unfortunately, no estate inventory exists for the Alex Ramsey family, their possessions largely being lost during or immediately after the Civil War. However, a deed of trust from John Lones to F. A. Ramsey dated July 1861 provides a glimpse into the material culture of this family. The transfer of farm products, food production equipment, and furnishings from Lones to Ramsey for a consideration of $5 was made on the condition that if a note for $225 owed Francis Alexander was paid off within 15 months, the sale was void; otherwise Ramsey could sell the items and apply the proceeds to the debt. The items included 35 hogs, one steer, one heifer, 300 "doz" (?) oats in the field (to be put into bags?), three stacks of hay, two stills and tubs, one corn sheller, one apple mill, two beds, bedsteads, a "lounge," and other illegible items. Apparently Alex Ramsey was still expanding his farming activities after the start of the Civil War.

A study of the faunal remains from the period 1820–1866 indicated domestic stock and fowl made up 96 percent of the faunal remains, with pig (83 percent), cattle (11 percent), sheep or goats (0.74 percent), and chicken (1.48 percent) represented (Patterson 1998:Table 4.3). This is the first time chicken bones appear in the faunal record, suggesting an increase in the consumption of this bird, since only chicken eggshell was found in the early Ramsey strata. The occurrence of sheep or goat bones also suggests these animals must have been occasionally eaten in addition to providing wool for clothing. Interestingly, wild species (eastern cottontail and freshwater drum) remain at about 4 percent indicating hunting and fishing by the Ramseys were still minor subsistence pursuits (Patterson 1998:Table 4.3). Another possibility is that enslaved Africans on the farm primarily ate this wild game, a practice often seen in other parts of the South to supplement their rations.

The major difference noted in the faunal assemblage between the early Ramsey period and the late Ramsey period is the quality of the meat cuts represented in the two periods. In the former period pork is represented by 65 percent medium- and 35 percent high-yield cuts, whereas in the latter period pork is represented by 50 percent low-yield cuts and 50 percent high-yield cuts (Patterson 1998:Figure 4.4). This could be due to the fact that the unknown persons (renters?) living there or perhaps even the young Alex Ramsey family were not in the same higher socioeconomic class as the Francis Alexander Ramsey family was. Low-yield cuts of meat may also represent food remains of the enslaved Africans who were living next to the stone house in Structure 4. The fact that all of the beef cuts were high yield (Patterson 1998:Figure 4.7) is good evidence that cattle were not butchered on the site, the 12 "other cattle" being sold on the hoof. As in the early Ramsey period, most of the beef was probably purchased or traded for from a butcher in town.

MATERIAL CULTURE
OF THE LATE RAMSEY PERIOD

Many artifacts at the beginning and end of the 46-year late Ramsey occupation at Swan Pond are difficult to distinguish from those made and used in the earlier and later periods. Also, there are no discrete strata or large artifact-bearing features that specifically date to the late Ramsey time period.

KITCHEN GROUP

Four new ceramic wares became predominant at Swan Pond during this period; bone china (English porcelain), stoneware, ironstone, and whiteware, all of these wares found throughout the east and rear inner active yards (Figure 34). Bone china porcelain, a "soft-paste" porcelain imported from England, replaced the earlier hard-paste Chinese porcelain. Unlike the earlier Chinese hard-paste ware that was acquired by the Ramseys in full table settings and was somewhat expensive, the bone china found at Ramsey House appears to be largely cups and saucers from a tea service (Figure 34H). That guests were still entertained, however, is indicated by sherds from an embossed porcelain chocolate cup and a porcelain dessert plate. Nevertheless, as time went on, bone china became less expensive yet seemingly more infrequent at Swan Pond, suggesting formal teas and other social events were less common at Swan Pond during this time than in the early Ramsey period.

During the period from 1820 to 1866 there was a major change in utilitarian ware at Swan Pond. By the mid-nineteenth century lead-glazed redware was replaced by salt-glazed stoneware crocks, churns, and jugs. This might have been largely due to the establishment of a stoneware pottery manufactory in Knoxville by a potter named Samuel Smith in about 1820 (Faulkner 2002). While no marked Smith sherds have been recovered at Ramsey House, sherds from several slip- and salt-glazed sherds from finely made stoneware vessels are very similar to Smith's wares. Sherds from a salt-glazed jug may be a vessel manufactured by the Graves pottery in nearby Corryton, dating to the mid-nineteenth century (Figure 34N) (Smith and Rogers 1979). Occasionally, this highly fired utilitarian pottery came from outside Tennessee; the most interesting stoneware sherds found at Swan Pond and dating from this period are from an alkaline-glazed, slip-decorated bowl made by Thomas Chandler (1845–1855) in the Edgefield district of South Carolina (Figure 34O)(Steve Ferrell, personal communication 2003). The presence of this bowl is particularly interesting because Alex's wife, Nancy Pressley, was from South Carolina, and the Ramseys visited that state on several occasions. Could this bowl have been a souvenir from one of their trips to that state or part of Nancy Pressley Ramsey's dowry?

Although it was invented in the early nineteenth century, a refined stoneware called white ironstone found at Swan Pond only became popular during the 1840s (Wetherbee 1996). Sherds of saucers in what is called the Ceres shape with the embossed "wheat and hops" pattern could date from the late 1840s to the 1880s (Wetherbee 1996:90–91). Portions of a slop jar and a cup sherd (Figure 34I) are embossed with what appears to be the "wheat and clover" pattern (Wetherbee 1996:100–101). Sherds from an ironstone pitcher and teapot or coffeepot were also found. Since ironstone was a more expensive tableware during its earlier years of manufacture, these vessels were probably used to set Alex Ramsey's table.

A major change also occurred in refined earthenware during the late Ramsey period. During the 1820s and early 1830s pearlware was replaced with whiteware, the latter becoming the most popular refined tableware in the United States. The appeal of whiteware was found in the widespread production of transfer-printed ceramics in a greater variety of bright colors including light blue, scarlet red, mulberry purple, and bright green. These colors were also applied to tea wares, usually decorated in hand-painted fine-line floral designs. Sets with transfer-printed designs including pastoral, exotic, and American views as well as floral patterns were probably used by the W. B. A. Ramsey family when they lived at Swan Pond (Figure 34D–G). Bold floral designs were also used on polychrome-decorated tea wares at this time (Figure 34J–K).

By the time Alex Ramsey lived at Swan Pond, transfer-printed flatware had become thicker like the contemporary ironstone, with shallow fluting on the brim and decorated in new colors like flow purple and flow black, often found in table sets. Transfer-printed flatware also included transfer designs decorated with underglaze enameling. New decorated sets appeared, such as spatter- (Figure 34C) and sponge-decorated tea wares (Figure 34L). Spatter colors included the always popular blue but also red, green, black, and yellow. Throughout the late Ramsey period, blue shell-edge decorated plates and serving pieces continued to be ubiquitous at informal meals (Figure 34A–B).

During the late Ramsey period, the finishes (rims) of bottles were made with a finishing tool, producing a more symmetrical shape. Several mid-nineteenth-century tool-finished bottle tops were found on the site, but the contents of most of these bottles is not known. Two functionally identifiable bottle sherds were from contact-molded historical whiskey flasks. Such historical flasks were popular between 1820 and 1870 (McKearin and McKearin 1941:456–613). One is from a green glass vessel in the scroll or violin design (Figure 35C); the design on an aqua-colored bottle sherd could not be identified.

Glassware became more common in the kitchen assemblage during this period due to the invention in about 1825 of pressed glass tableware, which was cheaper than hand-decorated cut glass. Pressed glass pieces that can be attributed to the late Ramsey period include tumblers, bowls, and a lidded bowl or dish. One sherd is from a small leaded clear glass tumbler or cordial in the Bellflower pattern, probably made between about 1840 and 1870 (Figure 35A) (Lee 1946:92–99).

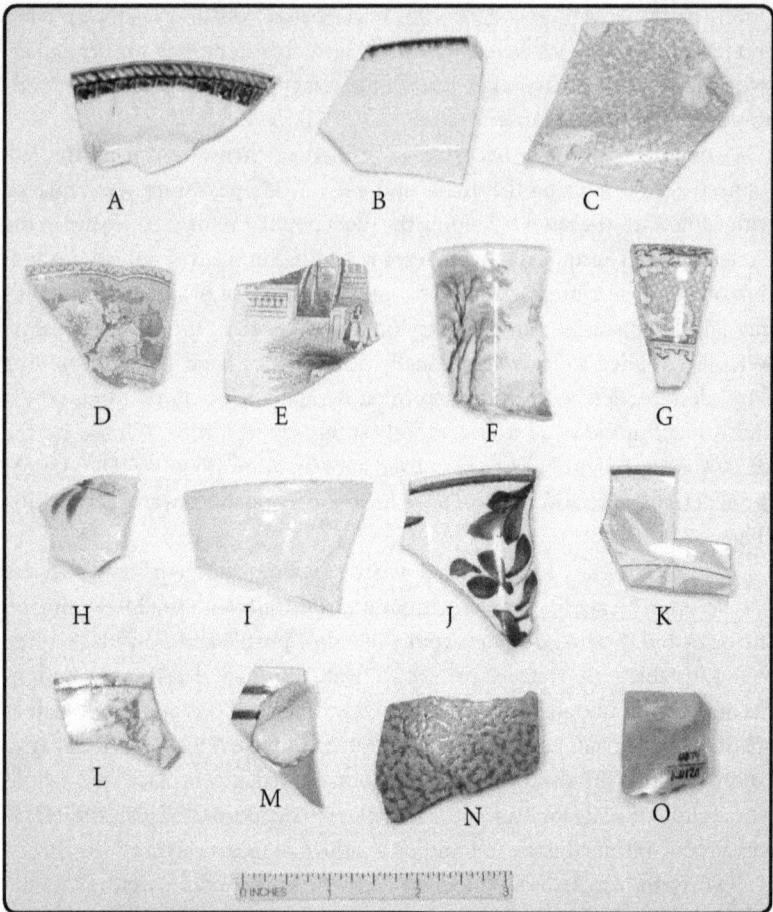

FIGURE 34. Late Ramsey ceramics. A. Pearlware dinner plate blue edge decorated.
B. Whiteware dinner plate with a blue shell edge. C. Whiteware dinner plate with green spatter.
D. Whiteware dinner plate with mulberry transfer print. E. Whiteware dinner plate with brown
transfer print. F. Whiteware teacup with light blue transfer print. G. Whiteware saucer with
light blue transfer print. H. English porcelain teacup, hand painted, overglaze. I. Ironstone
teacup embossed with a wheat and clover pattern. J. Whiteware teacup, hand painted, broad
lined, and underglaze. K. Whiteware saucer, broad lined polychrome underglazed.
L. Whiteware saucer with red and green sponging. M. Whiteware pitcher, annular ware.
N. Stoneware salt-glazed jug. O. Stoneware bowl, slip decorated and alkaline glazed.

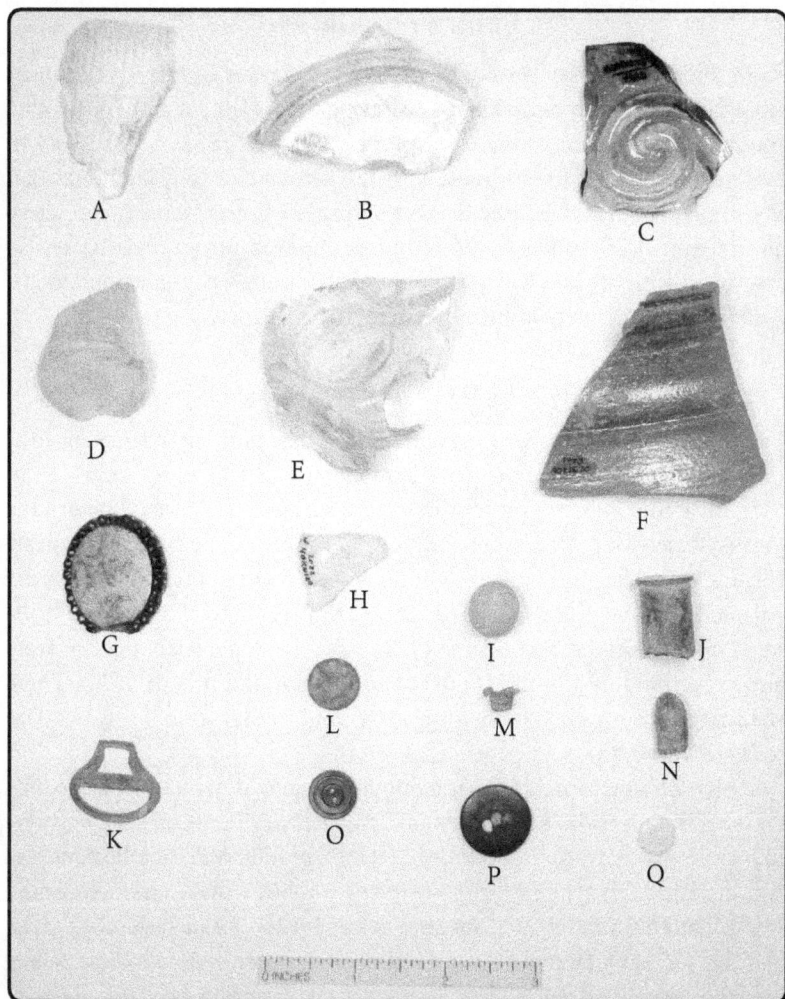

FIGURE 35. Late Ramsey artifacts. A. Clear pressed glass tumbler/cordial with a bellflower pattern. B. Clear pressed glass bowl. C. Green glass figural bottle with a scroll/violin design. D. Aqua glass medicine bottle, Curtis and Perkins Cramp and Pain Killer. E. Clear glass perfume bottle. F. Stoneware chamber pot, slip and salt-glazed. G. Black glass brooch setting. H. Porcelain doll head. I. Clay marble. J. .56-caliber cartridge from a Spencer carbine. K. Brass suspender buckle. L. Brass U.S. Army general service button. M. Brass percussion cap. N. .36 caliber lead bullet. O and P. Hard rubber buttons marked Goodyear. Q. Porcelain or "china" button.

Furniture Group

As in the early Ramsey period, there is a small variety of furniture artifacts from the late Ramsey period, but one type, the glass lamp chimney, becomes much more common in the latter period. This is due to the discovery of kerosene in 1854 and the invention of the kerosene or "oil" lamp. Another invention that greatly reduced the cost of furnishings is silvered mirror glass, also recovered in the late Ramsey context. An iron furniture caster is also associated with the late Ramsey period and is probably from a Sheraton or American Empire piece of furniture dating after 1820.

Clothing Group

Based on the number of wearing apparel artifacts, clothing styles changed at the Ramsey House during the late Ramsey period. This is not only seen in the increased number of buttons found dating from this period but also the greater variety of button types and the appearance of the suspender buckle (Figure 35K). The most numerous buttons are the white porcelain or "chinas," patented by an Englishman named Richard Prosser (also called "Prosser" buttons) in 1840 (Albert and Adams 1970). After 1850, porcelain buttons were also being produced in the United States (Albert and Adams 1970). These were largely worn on button-front shirts and undergarments, as they are today (Figure 35Q).

Other buttons found in lesser numbers include the brass two-piece Sanders type, iron (four-hole, sew-through), green glass with metal backing, bone four-hole, and hard rubber buttons. Like the prolific porcelain buttons, the two-piece Sanders type with cloth covering was being mass-produced by the mid-nineteenth century (Hughes and Lester 1981). The metal-backed green glass button has a faceted face and is probably from a woman's dress. While bone buttons appeared in Early Ramsey strata, the four-hole sew-through seems to be associated with the later Ramsey occupation of Swan Pond. Synthetic buttons also appear in the mid-nineteenth century, the earliest found on the site being two hard rubber buttons marked "Goodyear" with a patent date of 1851 (Figure 35O–P). These buttons were manufactured by the N.R. Company from 1851 to 1870 (Poole 1982:286). The only archaeological evidence of clothing manufacture is the flat-headed pin, which replaced the spun-head pin after 1824 (Noel-Hume 1969:254).

In the early nineteenth century, elements of clothing had taken their modern forms (Boucher 1967:419). From 1830 to 1850 the bourgeoisie in Europe set the fashion with trousers, jacket, and frockcoat for men, and trimmed gowns and bright colors for women. The sewing machine was also invented during this period. The larger number and variety of buttons found in the late Ramsey artifact assemblage correspond to these clothing changes. By the 1820s, men's breeches were being replaced by trousers (Braclawski 1995:214), and by the 1840s trouser buttons were common in the fly and also held suspenders (Braclawski 1995:212–214). Small buttons such as the porcelain chinas were now used on pleated-front shirts worn by the upper classes and the smock-frock with a buttoned opening worn by the working class (Braclawski 1995:178–180, 193). The formal gowns and dresses of women at this time did not seem to use many buttons (hooks and eyes were common), thus explaining the infrequency of typical women's buttons.

Personal/Grooming Group

At least one medicine bottle dates from the late Ramsey period. This is an embossed round container identified as "Curtis & Perkins, Cramp and Pain Killer," the Bangor, Maine, company dating from 1850 to 1865 (Figure 35D). Several other bottle fragments made with a finishing tool (ca. 1820–1870) probably contained medicine but could not be specifically identified as such because they were not embossed.

A hard rubber comb found at Swan Pond dates to about the same time as the rubber buttons described above. Other grooming aids include a clear glass contact-molded perfume bottle made in a two-piece hinge mold (Figure 35E). This type of mold was generally uncommon after 1870 (Jones and Sullivan 1985:27).

A molded set of opaque black glass from a woman's brooch was also found (Figure 35G). Black glass jewelry was very popular in the mid-nineteenth century.

Another personal artifact found on eighteenth- and nineteenth-century domestic sites is the chamber pot. Chamber pots in the late Ramsey context include utilitarian salt-glazed vessels and at least one more formal ironstone vessel. At least one of the salt-glazed chamber pots was probably manufactured by potter Samuel Smith in Knoxville (Figure 35F).

Leisure/Entertainment Group

The stub-stemmed pipe, which appeared during the early Ramsey period, became the sole smoking devise in the late Ramsey period, the kaolin pipe having largely disappeared. Drinking alcoholic beverages, probably wine, is indicated not only by the fact that Alex Ramsey is recorded as making this beverage but also by the fact that the number of olive glass bottle sherds increases from 9.9 percent in the early Ramsey period to 25.7 percent of the total in the late Ramsey period.

Other entertainment is evidenced by a musical instrument and several toys. Though invented earlier, an iron mouth harp was found in the Late Ramsey strata. A fragment of a white parian (unglazed porcelain) doll's head was found (Figure 35H), this type of doll produced in the 1850s (Hillier 1968:144). Stone marbles are now replaced with clay marbles (Figure 35I), several of the latter being found in the late Ramsey strata.

HUNTING/MILITARY GROUP

One of the most significant changes in firearms during this time was the replacement of the flintlock firing mechanism with the brass percussion cap. The percussion cap was adopted by sportsmen about 1840 and the military about 1842 in the United States (Chapel 1960:69). Several of these small fired caps were recovered at Swan Pond (Figure 35M). At least one brass cartridge found here might be from a sporting/hunting weapon manufactured before the Civil War. This is a back-stamped Union Metallic .22-caliber short cartridge dating between 1857 and 1911 that may have been used by sportsmen.

Given the involvement of the Ramseys in the Civil War and the fact that thousands of Union and Confederate soldiers occupied East Tennessee throughout the conflict, it is surprising that few definitive artifacts from either the Union or Confederate forces have been found at Swan Pond. Among the only six probable Civil War artifacts are two Spencer variant .56-caliber cartridges (Figure 35J), a Sharps .54-caliber conical shot, and two .36-caliber conical bullets (Figure 35N) (McKee and Mason 1995). Neither Spencer cartridge had been fired, one being both cartridge and bullet, with the latter being grooved as though someone may have been trying to remove it from the cartridge. The other cartridge had the powder removed and the edge of the casing crimped. Both Colt and Remington manufactured .36-caliber cap-and-ball revolvers for the Union army although other U.S. firms as well as Confederate arsenals produced revolvers and ammunition in this caliber (Donald Ball, personal communication 2005). The only other Civil War artifact is a badly corroded three-piece brass Union army general service button with a symmetrically spread eagle on a recessed shield (Figure 35L), a type of button manufactured between 1851 and 1880 (Wyckoff 1984:27–28). Since the Spencer and Sharps carbines were usually carried by the Union cavalry and the button is from the sleeve of a Union army enlisted man's jacket, Federal forces must have occupied Swan Pond for at least a short period of time.

During the battle of Knoxville, the Union cavalry corps in the area was under the command of Brig. Gen. James M. Shackleford (Seymour 1982:217).

EDUCATION/OFFICE GROUP

Slate pencils and slate writing boards continued to be used during this period, but the presence of the wooden lead pencil in the late Ramsey period is indicated by the recovery of metal ferules (eraser holders). The wood-encased pencil was first introduced in 1854 (Petroski 1989). With the refinements of the bottle-making industry by the mid-nineteenth century, the mold-blown "umbrella" ink bottle also appears (Munsey 1970:120).

How long Alexander Ramsey's family lived at Swan Pond after 1860 is unknown. J. G. M. Ramsey writes about his son's leaving the old home place during the Civil War:

> He occupied and improved it for a few years, and the war coming on, he took his wife and children to South Carolina, returned to Tennessee and entered upon the active duties of a soldier's life. He joined Captain Kain's Artillery, went to Chattanooga, bore a gallant part in the affair at Bridgeport, followed his captain in the campaign he carried across the Sequatchie and Walden and Cumberland Mountains [Hesseltine 1954:137].

This seems to indicate that Alex moved his family to South Carolina before or shortly after the beginning of the conflict. On May 24, 1862, Alex enlisted as a sergeant in Capt. W. C. Kain's Light Artillery of the Army of Tennessee in Chattanooga. Alex was captured in June 1864, at the battle of Piedmont, Virginia, and was held at Camp Morton in Indianapolis, Indiana, until the end of the war, when he returned to his family in Yorkville, South Carolina (Ramsey 1982).

It is not known who lived at Ramsey House during the last years of the war or if the house was even continuously occupied. That Alex occasionally returned to the home place is suggested by a statement by his father just prior to his leaving his home at Mecklenburg in September 1863, when the Federal army was about to occupy Knoxville: "My son, Francis Alexander Ramsey, was that night at home" (Hesseltine 1954:115). In light of the fate of Mecklenburg, which was burned by a Union soldier during the Federal occupation of the area, it is fortunate for us today that the Ramsey House was not destroyed, considering the antagonism against the Ramseys by the local Unionists in power at the close of the war. This is speculative, but it might mean Swan Pond was occupied and protected by person(s) sympathetic to the Union cause.

Like his father, who had been an official for the Confederate government, Alex was afraid to return to Tennessee when the war ended for fear of retribution. After the war, J. G. M. Ramsey and some of his children lived in exile at several locations in North Carolina. On December 7, 1865, Margaret Ramsey wrote in her diary that Alex had left North Carolina with his family for Georgia (Ramsey 1865–1876). He purchased a steam flowering mill near Rome, Georgia, but finding this operation unprofitable, he moved back to Rowan County, North Carolina, where he rented a large farm that also became the home of his parents (Ramsey 1982). The elder Ramseys returned to Knoxville in 1871, where they lived until J. G. M. died in 1884. In 1872 Alex Ramsey and his family moved to Texas.

Alex Ramsey sold the Swan Pond property while he was living in Georgia. In the warranty deed for the sale of the property, Alex's home is given as Chatooga County, Georgia. Alex's brother John Crozier, J. G. M.'s oldest son and an attorney, returned to Knoxville shortly after the war to try to settle the family's affairs and sell their property. In a letter to his father in North Carolina dated October 4, 1866, Crozier wrote:

> I have been trying to sell Lizzie's and Alexander's places. They are both anxious to sell. I have been offered thirty-five hundred dollars for Elicks place—but have had no offer for Lizzies. I ask thirty-five hundred dollars for her place and four thousand for Elicks. I think both places are low—but I fear that I can't even get that for them— money is scarce (Ramsey Papers, University of Tennessee Special Collections Library, Knoxville).

On December 12, 1866, Crozier, acting as an agent for his brother, sold the Swan Pond property "to a stranger" for $3,600 (Knox County Deed Records 1866). J. G. M. Ramsey later summed up the loss of their ancestral home when he lamented:

> It was a house of prayer, and of praise. A home for the minister of religion, the stranger, the widow, the orphan, the exile and the homeless! That old Mansion! With its pointed gables, quaint cornices and antique windows! Dear old home with its gay dreams and sunny hours, and cloudless skies, and visions of bliss and glorious happiness gone! All gone! gone! (Hesseltine 1954:10)

Chapter 5

THE VICTORIAN PERIOD, 1866–1914

The "stranger" that purchased the Swan Pond property from Alex Ramsey in 1866 was William C. Spurgin (or Spurgeon) from Washington County, Tennessee (Knox County Deed Records 1866). The 1867 Knox County tax list gives a value of $4,000 for the 225-acre farm. The 1870 census property value for the farm was $3,000, and the personal possessions of the Spurgin family were valued at $700. The family consisted of W. C. Spurgeon, age 37; his wife Narcissa, age 25; and three children: John R., 7; Mary T., 4; and Dorcas (?), 5 months (United States Census 1870).

It is not known what condition the farm was in when the Spurgins bought the property, since it is not known if anyone had cared for it after the Ramsey family left in 1863. Comparing the $8,000 cash value of the farm in 1860 to its value of $4,000 in 1867 suggests Swan Pond was run-down, although this depreciation was probably also due to the economic depression that followed the Civil War (United States Census, Schedule 4 1860, 1870). It should be noted, however, that although the improved acreage had increased slightly by 1870, the value of the farm had decreased by $1,000 (Knox County Tax List 1867).

That Swan Pond was still a working, productive farm in 1870 is indicated on the agricultural census for that year, although its total value of $525 for livestock was substantially lower than that of previous owner Alexander Ramsey ($1,800). The Spurgins' livestock included 4 horses, two mules, one milk cow, one "other cattle," 12 sheep, and 29 swine. Crops were corn, wheat, oats, and Irish potatoes. Some meat and butter were apparently sold or bartered based on value of slaughtered animals and pounds of butter produced.

Based on the stock and crops raised by the Spurgins at Swan Pond, it is likely that the barns and other food production and storage-related outbuildings did not change substantially from what existed there ten years before. One obvious change, however, was the end of slave labor at Swan Pond. Tenants might have continued to live on the farm, since $60 was paid for farm labor wages in 1870 (United States Census, Schedule 4 1870).

The Spurgins lived at Swan Pond for only five years. On October 24, 1871, they sold the 225-acre Swan Pond place to Joseph L. Keener and his brother Leroy S. Keener for $4,000 (Knox County Deed Records 1871). On January 22, 1878, Joseph L. Keener, his wife, Esther, and Leroy S. Keener and his wife, Mary, sold Swan Pond to Leroy's son William A. Keener and his wife, Margaret A. Keener, for $3,000. According to the warranty deed, the tract had been reduced to 100 acres (Knox County Deed Records 1878), but in the Schedule 4 agricultural census for 1880 the farm of William Keener is described as having 150 acres.

The 1880 Schedule 4 data indicate that mixed farming continued to be practiced by the William Keener family, although the stock had been further reduced; two horses, one milk cow, 12 sheep and eight swine were recorded. More wheat and corn were grown in 1880 but slightly less Irish potatoes and no oats. The absence of oats was probably because there were fewer horses and no mules on the farm at that time. The only products sold were 25 cords of wood valued at $50. The Keeners continued to pay someone farm wages of $200 for that year.

The date range of the faunal remains in Patterson's study is from 1866 to 1912 and includes the tenure of the Spurgin and Keener families, as well as the later Watsons who owned the property from 1884 to 1924. Domestic stock and fowl still made up a little over 90 percent of the faunal remains found, with pig occurring slightly less, at 77 percent of the total. This could mean that some pork was purchased from a market during this period, but the presence of cranial parts and most of the axial skeleton indicates pigs were still slaughtered and butchered on the farm. Cattle remained the same at 10 percent and the presence of selective prime cuts continues to indicate beef was largely purchased at market, since the Spurgins had one "cattle" and the Keeners raised no cattle in 1880. Chicken bones constituted 3 percent of the total, and caprines (sheep and goats) less than 1 percent. That hunting and fishing continued to provide a minor amount of meat but perhaps remained important in their subsistence is indicated by wild mammals and fish constituting about 9 percent of the faunal remains, with cottontail (6 percent), white-tailed deer (1 percent), and freshwater drum (2 percent) represented (Patterson 1998:Table 4.4).

There is no archaeological or architectural evidence that the later Ramsey family members remodeled the house. However, there is architectural evidence that either the Keener or Watson families removed the original porch and built the Victorian porch that was present on the house by the late 1890s. The Victorian porch was removed shortly after the APTA purchased the property in 1952 and a portico entrance porch constructed in its place. This latter porch was removed shortly before Dickson's 1973 excavation when the Ramsey House Association turned to archaeology to discover what the original entrance looked like. Unfortunately, the two archaeological excavations conducted in 1973 (Dickson 1974) and 1976 (Townsend 1976) failed to find conclusive evidence of an early porch; nevertheless, questionable data from the later Townsend excavation was used to construct the stone steps that are now found at the front of the house.

There is little doubt that a covered entrance or porch graced the front doorway when the house was built (Bernard Herman, personal communication 2004). Certainly the most compelling evidence is the central exterior doorway in the small room at the head of the stairs. Such a doorway is not uncommon above the front door in Federal period I-houses in East Tennessee. Questions about the function of this door are commonly asked by visitors to Ramsey House. At least three reasons for such a door have been suggested. One is that it would have provided a convenient fire escape from the second floor. Another likely function is that it would have provided excellent ventilation for the second floor of the house. Thirdly, it has been suggested that such an entrance could have been used to move furniture too cumbersome to negotiate the narrow staircase to the upstairs rooms. Like many features in houses, it undoubtedly had several functions. Nevertheless, it seems likely that it opened onto a flat roof of some sort.

It is indeed ironic that the portico entrance built after the Victorian porch was removed may have been close to what was constructed by Francis Alexander Ramsey in 1797. The Historic American Building Survey and recording of the house in 1936 states that "From indications on the south wall the original porch was two storeys high and ran three-quarters the length of the front elevation. The present porch is a later addition" (Historic American Building Survey 1936). What is even more disturbing is that the construction of the present steps probably destroyed significant archaeological evidence of the original porch.

The 1973 excavation exposed portions of the brick foundation of the Victorian porch. The foundation on the west end was largely intact, consisting of a single line of bricks laid side by side providing a foundation of the Victorian porch approximately 30 feet long and 6 feet wide. Except for being described as "solid, uniform, apparently kiln-hardened" (Dickson 1974:5), these bricks are not identified as handmade or machine-made. The laying of electrical lines for outside lighting in 2002 exposed part of this foundation in a trench dug along the west side of the former Victorian porch. I examined the bricks and found them to be handmade, sand-struck bricks, well fired, probably in a stationary kiln at a brick factory. Such factories were not common in Knoxville until after the Civil War (Greene 1992). Since machine-made bricks were not made in these factories until the early 1880s (Greene 1992) and architectural historian Bernard Hermann believes this porch was built in the last quarter of the nineteenth century (personal communication 2004), it is likely it was built between 1865 and 1880.

While Dickson's excavation did not find indisputable evidence of the earliest porch, some comments in his report may have a bearing on the construction of this structure. Robert Van Deventer was interviewed during the 1973 excavation, and he suggested that the stones used for the pyramidal foundation and steps of the reconstructed portico or "stoop" porch were probably foundation stones from the first porch, some of which were found stored under the Victorian porch when it was razed in 1953 (Dickson 1974:9). Early twentieth-century photographs of the Victorian porch also show that rectangular blocks were used for the front steps of this later porch. Former property owner Sam Kreis said that these dressed rectangular limestone steps were once scattered around the yard, where they can still be seen today near the driveway entrance, and one of them, used as a step behind the visitor's center, is engraved "1797." Robert Van Deventer stated in an interview in 1985 that this was an original "date stone" of the porch steps. When the portico entrance was built in 1953, the stonemason described "zig-zag" marks on the wall leading down from the doorway to the ground, suggesting pyramidal stone steps. The stones found in the yard may have been used to reconstruct these steps, plainly visible in numerous photographs of the portico porch, some still being in place in the 1973 excavation (Dickson 1974:figures 2 and 6). It may also be significant that the Joseph C. Strong House, built in Knoxville in about 1814 and associated with Thomas Hope, had a portico entrance (Deaderick 1976).

Archaeological evidence indicates the Keeners and Watsons were the first residents of Swan Pond who also made substantial changes to the architecture of the east side yard. A major change was the moving of the original cabin, Structure 4, a few feet east, where it was designated Structure 3 in earlier field seasons. This also meant the dismantling of the board or palen fence C built by Alex Ramsey. A trench of one of the skid logs on which Structure 3 was slid was identified at the north end of the building. This trench, Feature 136, had been capped with sterile red clay and contained ceramics with a TPQ of 1860 and a window glass range of 1860–1880 (Faulkner 2001:17–18). The girder, remains of another log skid, was left in place after the move and chinked with rocks for additional stabilization of what by then was probably a sagging puncheon floor (Faulkner 2001:25). The latest median ceramic date for sherds under the girder is 1860. Forty-six window glass sherds under the girder have individual thickness dates from 1792.7 to 1876 (Faulkner 2003a:14–15).

In 1995 the recovery of horseshoes within the upper Structure 3 strata suggested this building functioned as a blacksmith shop after it was moved. By the end of the 2000 field season, 15 horse or mule shoes were found within the structure in addition to 15 horseshoe nails and 66 pieces of blacksmithing waste and iron bar stock (Faulkner 2001:27). These artifacts have a nonrandom distribution within the structure, with the majority of the horseshoes found at the south end of the building and the nails recovered at the north end, suggesting shoe removal and replacement took place in different areas in the building (Figure 36).

Most of the blacksmith waste was found near the center of Structure 3 over and around the girder. When excavation began on this structure in 1995, a fired area and ash deposit was uncovered on top of and around the girder at the west end of the building. While this did not appear to be a prepared hearth base, there was a heavier concentration of handmade bricks here than elsewhere in the building. Visual examination of these bricks reveal they are virtually identical to the bricks in the Victorian porch footers and the cistern. A large footer stone was also found under the girder in this location (Faulkner 2001:26). This feature has now been tentatively identified as the location of the hearth or forge of the shop. Besides the evidence of firing, the concentration of blacksmith waste would also be expected around this feature. While this feature had been disturbed, probably during or after Structure 3 was razed, the dating of ceramics, container glass, and window glass indicate the hearth/forge was destroyed sometime in the last quarter of the nineteenth century.

Further evidence that the Keeners may have been involved in blacksmithing at Swan Pond is the listing of a Joseph Keener, blacksmith, 39 years of age, in the 1900 U.S. census for the east Knox County area (United States Census 1900). This is probably the same Joseph Keener, one of Joseph Keener Sr.'s seven children recorded in 1879 as a 17-year-old "laborer" (United States Census 1880).

The large handmade brick-lined cistern adjacent to Structure 3 is believed to have been built to supply water to the smithy, since its separation from the kitchen where the rainwater conduit originated indicates it was not primarily constructed for domestic use. The bricks of the cistern walls are handmade and are very similar to bricks in what is believed to be the hearth/forge area

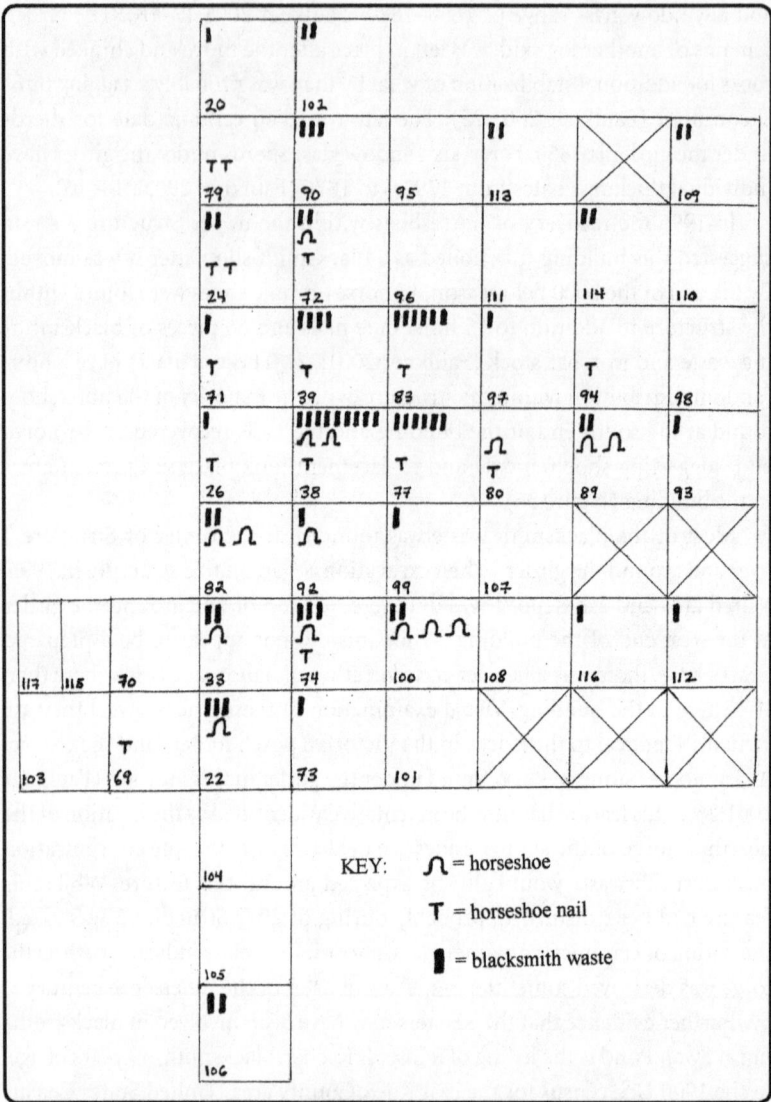

Figure 36. Distribution of horseshoes and blacksmith waste in Structure 3 area.

of Structure 3 and the foundation of the Victorian porch. Window glass in the red clay spoil dirt removed when the cistern was dug has a mean date of about 1875. This is compelling evidence that Structure 3 was moved and the adjacent cistern was built by the Keener family.

Another cistern was built in the nineteenth century at the corner of the house and kitchen near the west door of the latter structure. This cistern was described by Sam Kreis who later owned the house property and sold it to the APTA. Mr. Kreis said it was a domed structure with a chain and bucket pump. He removed the dome and backfilled the cavity during the renovation of the house (Carnes and Chapman 1984:8). A photograph by Robert Van Deventer shows the location of this cistern directly in front of the steps to the west door of the kitchen (Van Deventer 1975).

Unfortunately, we have no archaeological data as to when this cistern was built because the location has been further disturbed by installation of the air conditioning unit, underground telephone line, and drain from the kitchen sink, complicating any archaeological work that might be accomplished there (Carnes and Chapman 1984:8; Robert Van Deventer, personal communication 1985). It is believed, however, that this cistern was built at the same time as the east yard cistern, when the water table in the nearby well was getting low or perhaps polluted (Faulkner 1986).

Sweet sorghum cane from France, South Africa, and China was not introduced into the United States until the 1850s (American Agriculturalist 1880; Stewart 1867; Winberry 1980). The sorghum furnace excavated and identified in the 1995 and 1999 field seasons by the two heavily fired clay flues may have also been built by the Keeners, since the bricks found at one end of the flues are similar to those found in Structure 3, the east yard cistern, and the porch foundation. Although sorghum is not listed as a product from the Keener farm in the 1880 agricultural census, sorghum syrup could have been made periodically before or after that date.

In 1989, excavation around a construction area at the nineteenth century Matt Russell house in Farragut, Tennessee, exposed two heavily burned trenches. The major difference between the Swan Pond and Russell features is that the latter was not lined with clay. The location, form, and late-nineteenth-century artifacts associated with the Russell feature suggested that this was also a sorghum syrup furnace (Faulkner, ed. 1989).

Two types of pan evaporators were used on a rectangular sorghum furnace. The simpler devise was the batch pan, with the somewhat later continuous pan having a series of baffles through which the cooking syrup flowed (Walton et al. 1938; Winberry 1980). While the continuous boiler pan would require some control of the heat that could be maintained in a single flue, it is possible that the batch pan required two separate flues so that the boiling syrup could be primarily controlled by the heat rather than by the movement of the liquid through the pan.

Artifacts found in the large intrusive borrow pit on the west end of the sorghum furnace indicate it was dug around the turn of the century. These artifacts include a machine-pressed brick with a TPQ of about 1885 (Greene 1992) and a window glass sherd with a Moir formula date of 1888.7 (Moir 1987). It is interesting to note in this regard that by the beginning of the twentieth century sorghum syrup production went into a steady decline due to a failure of sorghum sugar production, the success of sugar beets, and the widespread production of glucose syrups (Winberry 1980).

Two years after Joseph K. Keener purchased the property in 1871, the Knox County tax list states that the farm was now worth $3,400, suggesting some improvements had been made (Knox County Tax List 1873). However, three years later, the value of the farm had dropped to $2,250, indicating that again it was going into a decline (Knox County Tax List 1876). Apparently Joseph Keener died shortly after 1878 when he sold the farm to William Keener (Knox County Administrator's Settlements 1881). By 1882, the Swan Pond acreage had been divided, apparently William Keener retaining 100 acres of the original Ramsey tract with the stone house, the property now valued at $1,500 (Knox County Tax List 1882).

The William Keeners sold the 100-acre Swan Pond farm on December 15, 1884, to John A. Watson for $2,000 (Knox County Deed Records 1884). John Watson's wife, Nancy Narcissa Keener Watson, was William Keener's sister (Faberson 2003). John Watson and his heirs owned the property until 1924. It was during this time that Swan Pond became known as the "Watson Place," a name still remembered by some of the older residents of the neighborhood (Faulkner 1986:52).

The earliest photographs of the Ramsey House were made during the John Watson ownership of the property. One photograph, taken in 1897 or 1898 from Thorngrove Pike, shows the facade of the house, the Victorian porch, and part of the east side yard (Figure 37). Ms. Edith Watson, granddaughter of John A. Watson, identified the three older Watson sons in the photograph: Sam Pitner Watson (b. 1882), John Keener Watson (b. 1885), and Carl Lee Watson (b. 1889) (Faulkner 1986:55). Persons in the background have not been identified, but the woman may be Nancy Watson. The 1900 Census lists John and Nancy Watson, the three boys, and their sister, Leona. In addition, the census indicates the Watson household may have included a niece, a servant, and boarders, the latter possibly wage laborers on the farm (Faberson 2003:44).

The Edith Watson photograph shows a well-cared-for house and yard. An important aspect of the photograph is what it does not show in the east side yard. A building can be seen at the extreme right of the photograph.

FIGURE 37. Photograph of Ramsey House made ca. 1897. Note the cantilever-roofed building to the extreme right of the photograph.

While it is close to the original location of the Ramsey cabin, its size indicates it is not this cabin or the later blacksmith shop. This indicates the moved cabin (smithy), Structure 3, was torn down by the Watsons between 1884 and 1897. When this photograph was first studied in 1985, it was believed that this was the Watson smokehouse because of the fact that it is very similar to the cantilever-roofed log smokehouses in East Tennessee (Rehder et al. 1979:77–79; Faulkner 1986:54). However, a careful study of the east side yard after the excavation in the later 1990s indicated this building appears to have stood over the cistern. Perhaps it was the early smokehouse that was moved to cover the cistern. Edith Watson said this was a woodshed and that the Watson smokehouse was behind the house and west of the kitchen (Faulkner 1986:57). This building might have been converted into a woodshed after the cistern was abandoned. Unfortunately, no definite foundation of this building was found in the units dug around the cistern, suggesting that ephemeral stone/brick footers or simply log sleepers supported this building. However, a gravel lens found in some units around this feature suggests a pavement of some sort surrounded it.

The earliest archival or archaeological evidence of a barn at Swan Pond dates only to the late nineteenth century, probably when the Watsons acquired the property. Informants who lived on the property in the early twentieth century remembered former farm buildings that stood in the rear peripheral yard (Area C) at that time and related that an earlier frame barn was struck by lightning and burned, a later twentieth century pole barn built in the same location (Faulkner 1986:64). This barn can barely be made out in an aerial

FIGURE 38. Aerial photograph of Swan Pond ca. 1920. Ramsey House is located in the cluster of trees near the center of the photograph. 1. Shed at the northeast corner of the house. 2. Barn. 3. Possible small structure south of the barn. Courtesy Tennessee Valley Authority.

photograph taken in the 1920s (Figure 38). The pole barn was still standing on the property when it was purchased by the APTA in 1952.

A concerted effort was made to find the archaeological remains of these barns in Area C. Testing in 1989 around the visitors center, a former cement block milking shed, produced only three nineteenth-century artifacts: two lead-glazed redware sherds and a cut nail (Faulkner and Young 1989a, 1989b). The area east of the visitors center parking lot was posthole-tested in 1994 (Faulkner 1994a), and in 1996 the area north of the parking lot was tested (Faulkner and Owens 1995). Except for two cut nails and two creamware sherds, all of the recovered artifacts date from the twentieth century.

During the 1997 season a 3-foot by 3-foot unit was placed over a possible footer detected in the 1996 testing of Area C. The supposed footer turned out to be a large piece of concrete block in a cluster of twentieth-century construction rubble, indicating that this area had been extensively disturbed during the destruction of the later barn after 1952. Besides the concrete block, datable artifacts included four wire nails and two window glass sherds (Faulkner and Owens 1995:16 and Table 3). Robert Van Deventer remembered that this area was bulldozed with barn rubble pushed over the nearby creek bank on the west side of the peninsula, where it is still visible today (personal communication, 1985). The scattered and disturbed nature of the artifacts in Area C bears this out.

Sixteen wire nails from the Area C testing assemblage suggest both barns were not built any earlier than about 1890, when wire nails replace cut nails in the Knoxville area. However, the sample is small and the location of the barns has now been either destroyed or disturbed by the visitors parking lot and bulldozing of the barnyard area. Nevertheless, the evidence at this time weighs toward the earlier barn in Area C being built by the Watsons.

The building of the barn in Area C may also be related to the lane that skirts the west side of the Ramsey House yard and can be seen in the 1920s aerial photograph leading to the barn. It is not known how long this lane has existed, but it is the most direct route from Thorngrove Pike to the rear peripheral farmyard. Robert Van Deventer (personal communication, 1985) said there was evidence of a stone retaining wall below and west of this lane, but testing in the area (Area A) did not reveal such a structure. However, such a wall might have been missed by the single transect of the posthole tests dug in 1994. Granting such a wall existed, it could mean this lane dates back to the early Ramsey period. However, if the borrow pit that intruded the sorghum furnace is connected to the building of the lane, it would have been constructed in the late nineteenth century.

If the Watsons built the large barn, what other improvements did they make when they purchased the property in 1884? Although the Keeners may have constructed the cisterns, tax records suggest they neglected the upkeep of the house, and shortly after the Watsons bought the farm in 1884 they made major improvements to the property. Improvements could have included building the Victorian porch, for example, since handmade bricks could still have been used during this transitional period of brick making in Knoxville (Greene 1992).

Two brick walkways are found in the east and front yards. The walkway from the kitchen, found in the posthole tests dug in 1964, is now completely covered with earth. The walkway from the front door to Thorngrove Pike is still functional. It is largely constructed of handmade bricks that are very similar to those used in the Victorian porch foundation and east yard cistern. Machine-made bricks are interspersed along the walkway, suggesting the recycling of bricks after 1880. This walkway might be visible in the 1897 photograph of the house (Figure 37). The walkway in the front yard also incorporates limestone blocks similar to those used in the early portico porch. If these were recycled after this porch was replaced, it suggests that this walkway may date from the Watson occupation of Swan Pond.

Tax lists for two years during the period the Watsons owned the property were also examined. Three years after they purchased the property its worth was listed at $1,800, $200 less than the sale price in 1884 (Knox County Tax List 1893). Five years later the property value was $2,500 (Knox County Tax List 1892). This suggests major improvements had been made by this time, including building the barn and possibly renovation of the house.

One improvement that can be directly tied to the Watson ownership is the final removal of the early Ramsey cabin. This is clearly evident in the 1897 photograph, which shows that a building matching the cabin's description is absent from the east side yard (Figure 37). This photograph also shows a fence behind the log cistern house/woodshed corresponding to Fence D in Figure 33, dated to the late nineteenth century and traversing the former location of the early cabin/blacksmith shop, Structure 3.

There is evidence that after Structure 3 was removed, the Watsons and later renters used the depression left by this building as a dumping area, filling it with cinders and other refuse from the nearby kitchen. The deposit of coal cinders over the Structure 3 area and portions of the rear yard is one of the most visible temporal horizons in the landscape history of the Ramsey house yard. This stratum ranges from as much as ½ foot thick over portions of Structure 3 to a thin continuous lens in other portions of the yard. Mean ceramic dates for this stratum average 1893, mean window glass dates average 1897, and two pennies in this deposit have dates of 1897 and 1899 (Faulkner 2001:6–7). This places it squarely within the Watson time frame.

The use of coal for heating and cooking in the Ramsey House in the last decade of the nineteenth century follows the pattern seen on other Knox County archaeological sites. This shift from wood to coal meant a major renovation of the fireplaces and stoves to accommodate this hotter burning fuel. It also identifies a major stratigraphic horizon (coal and cinder midden, Figure 15) seen in the east side yard.

The Watsons also constructed a large building in the east side yard over the former location of Structures 1 and 3. A photograph donated to the Ramsey House Association by Mrs. James Dean shows a couple, probably John and Nancy Watson, seated in an automobile in about 1910. A large building can be seen in the background in the east side yard. Since the building is not present in the 1897 photograph, it was built after that date and before about 1910. This is undoubtedly Structure 2, represented by the large limestone footers in the east side yard and visible in the 1920s aerial photograph (Figure 38). One of the footers of this 32-foot by 32-foot square building was superimposed over fence line D, further evidence for a post-1897 construction date. The function of this building during the Watson years is not known although the number of late-nineteenth- to early-twentieth-century machine parts in the area indicates possible automobile or farm equipment repair and storage.

That automobiles played an important part in activities in the east side yard after 1900 is indicated by the ca. 1910 photograph and a photograph made after 1927 in the east side yard showing an auto parked near the kitchen (Figure 39). Automobile parts found in the east side yard include spark plugs, a radiator hose clamp, rocker arm, iron and chrome taillight, chrome-plated antenna, gasoline tank cap, a Ford headlight part, windshield glass, and headlight glass.

In addition to modifying the heating and cooking facilities, other remodeling of the Ramsey House appears to have been done by the Watsons. During Robert Van Deventer's 1960 restoration of the kitchen, he discovered that a doorway in the center of the rear (north) wall of the kitchen had been opened from what had originally been a window (Van Deventer 1985). Evidence of a porch roof can also be seen over this former entrance in rafter pockets in the stone wall filled with bricks when the porch was later removed. It is not known when this porch was removed except that it was before 1952 when the APTA acquired the property.

A unit placed along the north wall of the kitchen addition during the 1997 field season revealed that the cinder stratum dated to the 1890s, probably deposited by dumping out of the recently built north door. Few artifacts were found below this, indicating such discard probably did not date earlier than the Watson occupation (Faulkner 1999:11). This suggests the doorway may have been constructed by the Watsons.

FIGURE 39. Photograph of east side yard ca. 1927.

It seems odd that the Watsons opened another exterior doorway in the kitchen when entrances already existed in the west and south walls of this building. However, a new entrance on the north side of the kitchen perhaps signals the shifting of agricultural and domestic activities from the east side yard to the rear active and peripheral yards. The barn was probably built by the Watsons, and Edith Watson related that the smokehouse was behind the house and west of the kitchen (Faulkner 1986:57). There is certainly considerable informant and archaeological evidence that such a shift had taken place in the later twentieth century before the APTA acquired the property.

Some details of life on the Watson farm were provided by Edith Watson. Miss Watson used to visit the farm with her father, Sam Pitner Watson, who told her stories about life at Ramsey House when he was a boy. In addition to the usual corn and stock, the Watsons also raised sweet potatoes and Irish potatoes that were stored in the house cellar. Strawberries were an important crop and were sold at the market in Knoxville. The kitchen garden was behind the house, probably in the same location as the Ramsey garden 100 years before. The Watsons also kept bees (Faulkner 1986:57).

MATERIAL CULTURE OF THE VICTORIAN PERIOD

The Victorian period at Swan Pond witnessed a proliferation of new arti-facts that appear at the end of the nineteenth century. This is due in large part to the economic recovery after the Civil War and the appearance of the mass-production of many artifact classes after 1870 including ceramics, glass containers, furniture, and other domestic products. Technology and styles changed so rapidly between 1866 and 1914 that it is difficult to specifically attribute many artifacts found in the Victorian strata to the Spurgin, Keener, or Watson families.

KITCHEN GROUP

Ceramics used during the Victorian period such as ironstone continued to grace the tables during this time, although this vitreous ware was eventu-ally replaced by a porcelaneous refined earthenware, which was thinner and whiter than the duller and thicker ironstone. Undecorated tablewares contin-ued to be popular for everyday meals, but transfer-printed ceramics are also present (Figure 40D), especially a new popular style called Japanesque. Flow blue table settings in a broad-painted style were also stylish (Figure 40E). Children's consumption and drinking vessels are also found, including a transfer-printed ABC plate and cup. While English refined earthenware con-tinued to be available to consumers, American-made refined ceramics are also found in the Victorian strata. Chinese hardpaste and English bone china no longer dominated the market, and high-fired, elegant porcelain ware from Germany, France, and Japan decorated with hand-painting and decaling (Fig-ure 40C) now graced formal meals. Gilting is also a common decoration on porcelain cups and saucers. At least one porcelain teapot is represented in the Victorian assemblage. The major development in refined tablewares was the invention in about 1890 of decal-decorated earthenwares and ironstone/ porcelains, a cheaper method of applying multicolored decoration on ceramic vessels. Many of these vessels were now manufactured in the United States (Figure 40A–B).

In addition to restyling in refined tablewares, utilitarian ceramics also witnessed significant changes. First made in the United States in about 1830, yellow ware appears in the ceramic assemblage of the Victorian period. Ves-sels of this type found at Swan Pond include bowls and pitchers (Figure 40H). Salt-glazed stoneware continued to be manufactured, represented by crocks and churns in the Victorian assemblage at Swan Pond. At least one of the salt-glazed crocks was manufactured at the Weaver pottery factory in Knoxville, dating from 1870 to 1888 (Faulkner 1981). A large cobalt-decorated 4-gallon

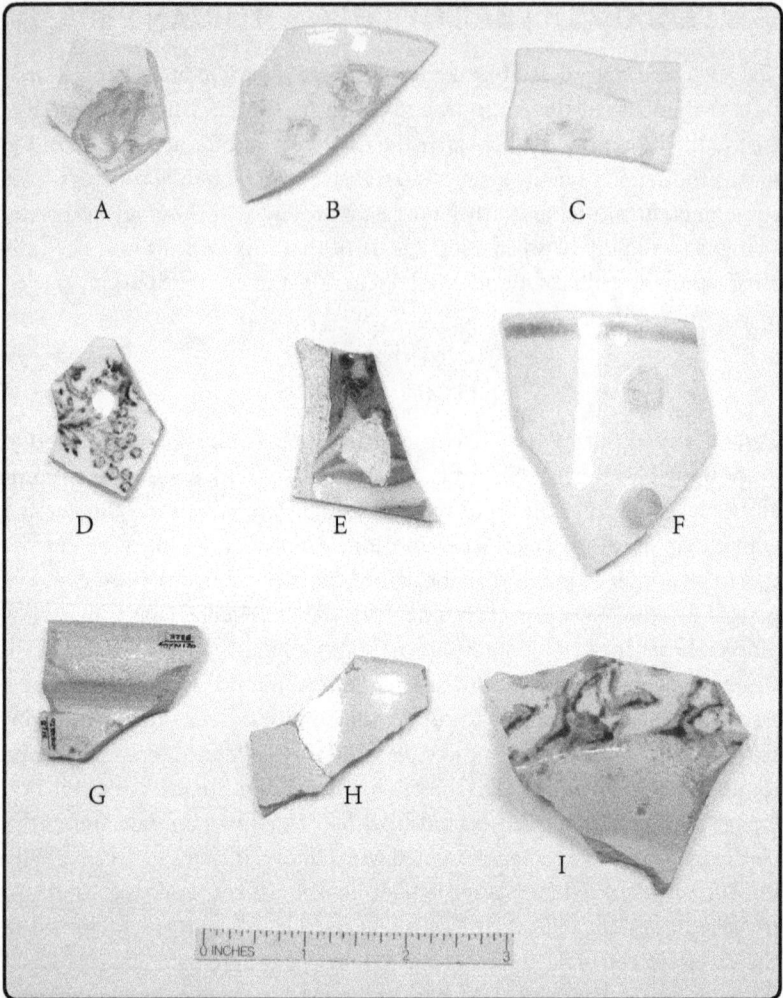

Figure 40. Victorian ceramics. A. Whiteware plate with decal decorations. B. Whiteware teacup with decal decorations. C. Porcelain plate, gilted and decal decorated. D. Whiteware saucer with blue transfer print. E. Whiteware plate with flow-blue transfer print. F. Porcelain mustache cup, gilted. G. Stoneware crock with Bristol glazing. H. Yellow ware bowl. I. Stoneware mixing bowl with blue sponge decorating.

churn was made by the Red Wing Stoneware or the Minnesota Stoneware company before 1900 (Faulkner 2001:11).

A new feldspatic glazing technique called Bristol glazing was developed in England in about 1890 (Figure 40G). At the same time, another dip-glazing technique called Albany slip-glazing, also found in the earlier nineteenth century, now became dominant, either covering the whole vessel or used in combination with Bristol glazing after the turn of the century. Both Bristol glazed and Albany slip-glazed crocks, jars, and jugs appear frequently in the late Victorian kitchen ceramic assemblage at Swan Pond. One distinctive Bristol-glazed vessel found in the Victorian strata is a cobalt blue–sponged mixing bowl (Figure 40I).

New metal kitchen appliances and metal utensils also appear on the site at this time. Several large fragments of a cast-iron cookstove were scattered over the east side yard. Metal enameled cookware also appears after the turn-of-the century. Bone-handled cutlery is replaced with wooden-handled (with metal insert) implements (Figure 41F). A French-pattern table knife was found with decorative bolsters and cocobolo handle. Silver-plated eating utensils including a tablespoon are also found in the Victorian strata.

Metal and glass food storage vessels become very common at Swan Pond during the Victorian period. The first evidence of tin cans at Swan Pond appears in the Victorian period. While the "hole-in-top" tin can was invented as early as about 1810, tin-canned foods did not become common until after the invention of the locked, double-sealed can in 1894. The metal key for opening sardine cans, invented in 1895, also appears on the site (Busch 1981).

The appearance of tin food cans indicates canned products were now being purchased at market. The home-canning of food, however, appears to have been the most important method of food preservation at Swan Pond, gradually replacing preserving vegetables and fruits by drying, pickling, or storing in the cool, dry Ramsey House cellar. Hundreds of sherds from glass canning jars and glass liners from zinc lids were found in the dumping areas under and around Structure 3 and in the overlying cinder stratum. Although the glass canning jar was invented in 1855, it was not until the invention of the zinc lid with milk-glass liner in 1879 did home canning become more safe and popular (Munsey 1970:146). Glass Mason canning jars are represented by earlier blow-back mold finishes (Figure 41E) and later fully machine-molded jars (Jones and Sullivan 1985:42).

The glass historical flask, popular during the first half of the nineteenth century, was replaced by undecorated flask-shaped whiskey bottles in pint and half-pint sizes in the latter part of the century. Several of these standardized bottles made of clear glass turned an amethyst color by the sun[1] were found in Victorian context.

1. From about 1880 to 1915, manganese was added to glass to decolorize it. When exposed to the sun's rays for a period of time, it turns an amethyst color.

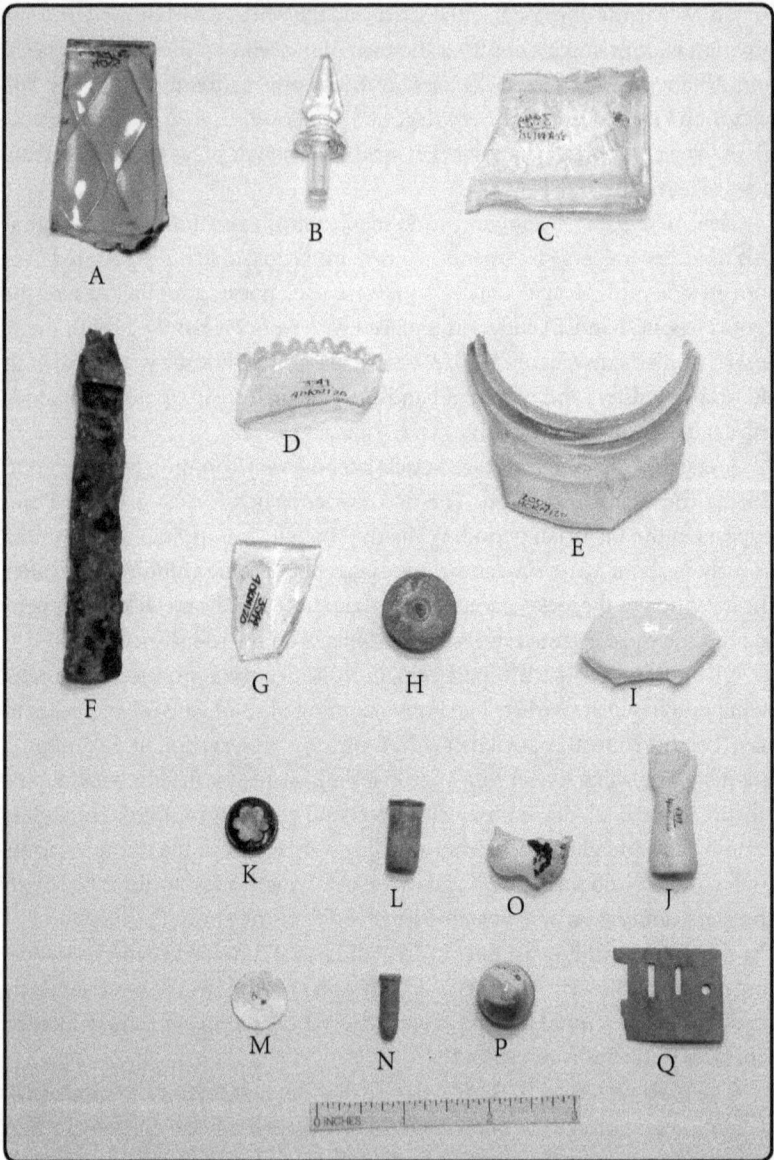

Figure 41. Victorian artifacts. A. Compote, pressed amethyst glass. B. Perfume bottle stopper. C. Medicine bottle embossed with the wording Albers, Knoxville, Tenn. D. Lamp chimney. E. Blowback-molded aqua glass canning jar. F. Iron fork handle with lead bolsters. G. Clear glass tumbler, optic molded. H. 12-gauge shotgun shell. I. Porcelain saucer from a child's tea set. J. Bisque porcelain doll arm. K. Black composition button. L. Brass .38-caliber cartridge. M. Shell button. N. Brass .22-caliber cartridge. O. White porcelain doll head. P. Glass marble. Q. Harmonica reed.

New, innovative glassware also appears at Swan Pond during the Victorian period. These include several sherds of milk-glass flatware, and a sherd from a pink/orange carnival glass dish. Carnival or taffeta glass dates from 1900 to 1920 (Kovel and Kovel 1980:95).

Glassware made earlier in the eighteenth and nineteenth centuries but appearing in the Victorian strata include drinking containers such as an optic molded tumbler (Figure 41G), a mold type invented in the eighteenth century but witnessing a revival in the late nineteenth– to early twentieth century (Jones and Sullivan 1985:32–33), enameled tumblers; and sherds of etched glassware and stemware. Pressed glass appears to be even more common, several sherds of an amethyst pressed compote (Figure 41A) and a clear bowl in the "sunburst" pattern (Lee 1946:338 and Plate 12) being recovered in the Victorian strata at Swan Pond.

Furniture Group

As in the earlier periods, furniture artifacts, except for lamp chimney glass, are rare in the Victorian period strata. In addition to the numerous lamp chimney glass sherds, fragments of a milk-glass lamp shade were also found. A good Victorian horizon dating marker is the "pie-crust" rimmed lamp chimney top (Figure 41D) that became popular in the 1870s (Woodhead et al. 1984:62). These kerosene or "coal oil" lighting fixtures are also represented by a clear pressed-glass lamp base and the brass stem of a lamp marked "P & A Manufacturing Company, Waterbury, Conn." Like the brass lamp stem, a brass coat hook probably dates from the Victorian period.

Clothing Group

Clothing styles continued to change rapidly, influenced by the materialism of the Victorian period. What is important for this study, as in earlier periods at Swan Pond, is what changes can be observed in the preserved accoutrements of the garments. In men's clothing, the few new garments that appeared were characterized by the trend of simplification. The jacket, waistcoat, and trousers of the suit made from the same fabric became popular after 1875 (Boucher 1967:402). In 1890, a patent was granted for the coat-styled shirt (Braclawski 1995:178–179). The most important invention in men's clothing, however, was probably denim trousers or jeans, patented by Levi Strauss in 1873 (Braclawski 1995:133).

For women, the continued development of the sewing machine meant full-blown forms with complicated trimming and overloaded ornament (Braclawski 1995:95; Boucher 1967:388). As an alternative to dresses, women were now wearing suits with contrasting blouses beneath (Braclawski 1995:95). For both men and women an important vogue in footgear was the laced shoe, replacing the popular boot.

How were these changes reflected in the archaeological assemblage? At Swan Pond they can be seen in the proliferation of the china button and the widespread use of freshwater shell buttons (Figure 41M) for shirts and blouses. Hard-rubber and composition buttons (Figure 41K) made from early organic plastics were used on suits worn by both men and women. Hard-rubber buttons marked "N.R. Company" with no patent date were manu-factured after 1870 (Poole 1982:286). Metal jeans buttons appear on the site during this period. Metal grommets from laced shoes also appear frequently in the Victorian strata.

PERSONAL/GROOMING/HEALTH GROUP

Five classes of artifacts are in this group: jewelry, medicine or pharmaceuti-cal bottles, coins, grooming devises, and sanitary vessels are found in the Victorian artifact assemblage. Jewelry dating to the late nineteenth to early twentieth century appears more commonly on the site. Some pieces of cos-tume jewelry such as a brooch and hair clasp with set synthetic stones have been recovered.

The pharmaceutical bottle class is represented by seven bottles. Two of these bottles were filled at a Knoxville drugstore. One body sherd is embossed "—— & Co. —— N St." This is probably a panel bottle from the W. W. Hall & Co. Drug Store, 822 Gay, Corner Main St., which was in business from 1902 to 1903. The other bottle is embossed "—— Albers, Knoxville, Tenn" (Figure 41C). This is from the drugstore of Logan and Albers, who bought the Hall business and was located at the same address on Gay Street from 1904 to 1905.

The other sherds with embossed names are from proprietary or patent medicine bottles usually dating after 1867 (Lorraine 1968:40). Two sherds are from embossed panels, one large enough to read the makers name, Cullen. This is from a bottle of Dr. C. C. Roc's Liver, Rheumatic, and Neuralgic Cure, Cullen and Newman, Knoxville, Tennessee, with two known dates, 1895 and 1910 (Fike 1987:105). The other has a partial embossed name, "——ell's," the size and color of the bottle indicating that it contained Dr. Bell's Pine-Tar-Honey for Coughs and Colds. This medicine was advertised in 1899 (Fike 1987:88). Another broken turn-of-the-century bottle is embossed "Fletcher's Castoria," which was "a vegetable preparation for assimilating the food and regulating stomach and bowels of infants and children" (Fike 1987:162). The only unbroken medicine bottle, associated with Structure 1, was embossed "J. R. Watkins." This Winona, Minnesota, company began making its products in 1868 and continued through 1986. Medicinal products manufactured by the Watkins Company included liniment, pain oil, and cough syrup (Fike 1987). A refitted solarized patent medicine bottle that would have had a paper label dates from between about 1880 and 1915. Recovery of these patent medicine bottles apparently dating from the Watson occupation indicates that although this family purchased medicine from a pharmacist, patent medicines were still considered important in combating illness.

Currency, specifically coins, first appeared in strata dating after the Civil War. There appears to have been a shortage of cash in East Tennessee before the war, and even after currency became more common after the opening of commercial banks, East Tennessee farmers often found money of uncertain value and negotiability. From the archaeological evidence at Swan Pond and other late-eighteenth to early-nineteenth-century historic sites, it appears most East Tennesseans conducted transactions through barter of goods and services or by credit at stores or IOUs.

Twenty-eight coins, including pennies, nickels, and dimes, were found in the east peripheral yard around the structures. Only two other coins, both dating from the 1960s, were found in other areas around the Ramsey House. The earliest dated coin is an Indian-head penny dated 1864 and associated with Structure 3. Based on the dates on the coins, two were minted during the Spurgin-Keener occupation and six during the Watson occupation although they could have been lost any time later than the minting date (TPQ). The importance of the dates and provenance of these coins is that only one pre-Victorian coin has been recovered on the site, and the earliest coins were found around the early east peripheral yard structures. This suggests that a cash economy was not solidified in East Tennessee until after the Civil War, and some kind of cash transactions may have been taking place around these structures.

Artifacts in the grooming category from this period include a broken celluloid comb and perfume or cosmetics containers. Celluloid was patented in the United States in 1870 (Poole 1987:Table V-9). A pressed glass solarized perfume bottle stopper dates from between 1880 and 1915 (Figure 41B). A milk-glass cosmetic jar containing facial cream was also dated from the Victorian period. Sanitary vessels are also represented by sherds of whiteware and ironstone chamber pots and slop jars from this period.

LEISURE/ENTERTAINMENT GROUP

The occurrence of 55.7 percent of the total number of olive glass sherds in the Victorian strata indicates consumption of wine and other alcoholic beverages reached a peak during this time. A new beverage also appears at Swan

Pond, this being the bottled soft drink. Bottles like the Hutchison stopper or blob-top bottle were patented as early as 1879, but the invention of the crown cap in 1897 and improved transportation made the carbonated soft drink or soda increasingly popular and available to the general public.

If transportation can be classified as leisure activity on a domestic site, then the invention of the automobile and its presence at Swan Pond based on the ca. 1910 photograph and the automobile parts associated with Structure 2 are noteworthy. A piece of bicycle chain found in the Victorian strata also indicates this vehicle was present at Swan Pond by the turn of the century.

New toys include several glass marbles (Figure 41P), which now replace the stone and clay marbles of the earlier nineteenth century. A considerable number of bisque doll parts are also present (Figure 41J). Bisque dolls are made of unglazed porcelain with flesh-tinted heads and limbs and painted features. White-glazed porcelain dolls also continued to be present (Figure 41O). Sherds of a porcelain child's tea set were also found (Figure 41I). Metal harmonica reeds (Figure 41Q) indicate the playing of this instrument during the Victorian period.

Hunting/Military Group

The extensive use of firearms is evidenced by the recovery of 81 brass rifle and pistol cartridges and 15 brass heads from paper shotgun shells. The manufacturers' backstamps and diameter of the former indicate that .22-caliber (68) (Figure 41N), .32-caliber (8), .38-caliber (4) (Figure 41L), and .25-caliber (1) weapons were used. Based on the manufacturer's backstamp, the mean date of 49 of these cartridges is 1908. The shotgun shells included 13 twelve-gauge (Figure 41H), 1 sixteen-gauge, and one .410-gauge. The backstamp on 11 of these shells gives a mean date of 1907. These mean dates suggest that firearm use was primarily during the Watson occupation at Swan Pond. The large number of cartridges, especially from small-caliber weapons, suggests that they were used for target practice and shooting varmints in the yard.

Chapter 6

THE MODERN PERIOD, 1914–1952

John A. Watson died on January 7, 1912 (*Knoxville Daily Journal and Tribune* 1912). After his death, his widow remained on the farm for only a short time, eventually moving to Knoxville. In 1925 Nancy Watson was living with her son Carl Pitner Watson on Glenwood Street (Knoxville City Directory 1925). Edith Watson believed the farm was rented to tenants until it was sold by the Watson heirs in 1924 to the Appalachian Marble Company (Faulkner 1986:57).

We do not know who lived at the farm from the time Nancy Watson moved to town until 1924. Possibly the first renter of the house from the Appalachian Marble Company was Alexander Nelson, who lived there from 1924 to 1928. Nelson's daughter, Pauline Nelson Hickman, provided a detailed account of the farm where she lived as a teenager with her parents and eight siblings (Faulkner 1986).

The Ramsey House was called the "old stone house" when the Nelsons lived there, and it was still a working farm. Pauline Hickman remembered the large barn in the rear peripheral yard and a shed at the northeast side of the house. A milk cow, two mules used for plowing, and chickens were housed in the barn. The shed in the east side yard was made of logs and was open on one side; there were no doors or windows. It was used to store tools. This was probably Structure 2, built by the Watsons. A privy was located at the rear of the shed. A photograph of the east side yard taken in the 1940s also shows a privy in that area. The cistern near the west kitchen door still provided drinking water (Faulkner 1986:60).

The Nelsons raised a number of vegetables including sweet potatoes in a garden where the site manager's cabin now stands and the heritage garden is located. Pauline Hickman remembered what she believed to be a brick sweet potato slip bed between the house and barn. This is the rectangular brick foundation found in the northwest rear yard in the 1985 unit excavation (Figure 42). Sweet potatoes, watermelons, and milk were placed in the middle of the house cellar floor, where the temperature was coolest. Other produce grown by the Nelsons in a large garden included corn, green beans, tomatoes, cucumbers, and cantaloupe (Faulkner 1986:60).

The next family to rent the Swan Pond farm was probably the James Combs family. An article in the April 5, 1931, *Knoxville News Sentinel* about the Ramsey House states, "The Ramsey House today is occupied by Jim Combs, his wife, and son [Walter], who have closed the upper part, as the house is quite

FIGURE 42. Sweet potato slip bed, Feature 3.

large." In 1985 I interviewed Mrs. Walter Combs, daughter-in-law of James Combs and widow of Walter Combs, who lived nearby on Thorngrove Pike, and her daughter Lora Combs Sands, who was born in the house in 1934.

A photograph was made of the Ramsey House in 1931 looking west toward the house when the Combs lived there (Figure 43). Parts of the east side and peripheral rear yards can clearly be seen; the earlier large barn and Structure 2, the shed remembered by Pauline Hickman, were gone by this time. Mrs. Combs remembered that a barn was struck by lightning and burned on the property. A barbed-wire fence can be seen in this photograph and is probably fence line E represented by postholes 134 and 135 in Figure 33. This barbed-wire fence separated the east side yard from the field to the east. These postholes are round (indicating the use of a posthole digger, which dates after the Civil War) and were spaced 15 feet apart, also indicating this was a barbed-wire fence. Barbed wire was invented after about 1875 (Washburn 1917).

Mrs. Walter Combs described the two cisterns in the house lot. The cistern at the west kitchen door was accessible from a porch, which at that time was enclosed by a framed-in room. There is a photograph of Mrs. Combs dipping water from this cistern in a UT Agriculture Extension Service publication (1946). Mrs. Combs also mentioned the cistern in the east side yard but did not indicate that it was used for drinking water (Faulkner 1986:61). The domestic refuse in the top of this feature indicates it was abandoned by this time, as does the absence of a conduit from the kitchen porch gutters and an above-ground cistern dome in earlier photographs of the east side yard (Figure 39).

FIGURE 43. Photograph of Ramsey House looking west, 1931.

The 1931 newspaper article about Ramsey House stated that the large stone chimneys had been closed up, indicating stoves were used for cooking and heating. Lora Combs Sands remembered a chicken house that stood in the northwest rear yard. It was described as a long, narrow frame building with a door on the south side and a fenced run on that side of the building. She thought it was torn down around 1940 when the Combs moved from the property (Faulkner 1986:61).

While Mrs. Combs related that the family grew considerable numbers of sweet potatoes when they lived at Ramsey House, producing 75 bushels in one season, she did not remember a brick slip bed. However, that the Combses were familiar with this type of permanent bed is indicated by the presence of two smaller brick slip beds constructed by her husband, Walter, behind their house on Thorngrove Pike (Faulkner 1986:64).

We do not specifically know who most of the people were who rented the Ramsey House after the Combs moved. That people continued to live there until about 1948 is indicated by a recently discovered photograph of the Charlie Hickman family taken about that time. It was also during this time that the concrete-block milking barn was built by Cas Cox, who also constructed the adjacent frame pole barn that stood on the property until 1966.

Based on photographs, informants, and archaeological evidence, all intensive domestic activity had ceased in the east inner yard and had shifted to the rear inner yard by about 1930. This is evidenced by the absence of outbuildings in the east side yard, the use of the cistern at the west doorway of the kitchen, the description of the chicken house in the northwest area of the rear inner yard, and the brick sweet potato slip bed in the same area. Dumping also shifted from the east inner side yard to around and behind Structure 2 while it was standing and thereafter, and to a sheet midden around the abandoned sweet potato slip bed, as well as directly into the bed. A large, shallow trash pit was also dug into the old sorghum furnace and filled with 1940s–1950s trash. When a drainage ditch was dug in the field east of the house in 2002, shallow refuse pits dating from the 1930s–1940s were exposed, indicating this field was no longer cultivated by this time and was used as a dumping area.

A neighbor, Lester Lane, remembered the house after the last renters had left, sometime between 1948 and 1950 (Lester Lane, personal communication, 2005). It stood empty, but he said the main part of the house was in remarkably good condition; the doors were always closed and the windows were not broken. The kitchen was in much poorer condition, and he remembered the floor was dirt. Drying racks hung from the ceiling. This may have been for drying corn, since the kitchen was said to have been used as a corn crib at that time.

Chapter 7

LOOKING BACK AT THE PAST
AND FORWARD TO THE FUTURE

All human culture is dynamic; that is, it is constantly transformed by new sociocultural experiences, it readapts to the changing environment, yet can also be characterized by unpredictable, idiosyncratic behavior. The archaeological remains, historic documentation, and oral traditions left by the Native Americans and historic Euro-Americans and African Americans at Swan Pond have provided a dynamic story about how they adapted to the unique natural environment and the complexities of the social/cultural interaction with their East Tennessee contemporaries. On the one hand, we can view the human experience at Swan Pond as a generalization of past lifeways in East Tennessee and the southern Appalachian area, yet on a more personal level it is the story of how individuals and families adapted to, and in turn made an indelible impression on, the natural landscape and social milieu that surrounded them.

Fortunately, we know what the prehistoric environment of Swan Pond was like thanks to detailed descriptions of the surrounding landscape when the Ramsey family settled the land. The shallow pond, covering hundreds of acres, had probably been in existence for several thousand years from the time prehistoric beavers first dammed Swan Pond Creek. The age of this pond may be indirectly established by prehistoric Native American artifacts that date as far back as 9,000 years ago.

The majority of these tools and weapons were used by Archaic hunters and gatherers who seasonally moved over the landscape and lived in small camps along the shore of Swan Pond. Later, more sedentary village Indians during the Woodland and Mississippian periods occasionally hunted at Swan Pond to exploit its wild bounty. Despite the fact that these native people lived here for thousands of years, there is no indication that their presence changed this pristine environment. Living close to nature, the native people depended upon the abundance of wildlife that the pond provided for their livelihood.

As was the case throughout North America, the settlement by Old World colonists caused major changes in the landscape of the continent. Shortly after Francis Alexander Ramsey settled at Swan Pond, he drained the pond for health and economic reasons. Unlike the occupants who preceded him, Francis Alexander viewed the pond as an impediment to intensively farming the land and a health hazard to his family. This action changed a major feature of the environment and had a major impact on the native vegetation and animal life around the area. Francis Alexander Ramsey's choice of a homestead site on a peninsula in the pond, however, suggests that health was not his main concern. This naturally defensive location and the archaeological remains of his fortlike compound here indicate that fear of Indian attack may have been uppermost in his mind. Although it would have taken a few years after draining the pond before it became tillable ground, it is clear in the recollections of his son J. G. M. Ramsey that Francis Alexander envisioned "the beauty of a Pennsylvania meadow, unsurpassed in the luxuriance of its grasses and the depth of its alluvial soil" (Hesseltine 1954:8–9). That it had already become a wet meadow that could be used for hay as early as 1802 is suggested by the statement of John Gamble, one of Francis Alexander's tutors, who on December 31 of that year mentioned in his diary an "afternoon ramble with Col. Ramsey over his excellent plantation [to] visit the laborers, sett [sic] fire to the dry bushes and leaves to clear the land" (Ramsey Papers, UT Special Collections Library, Knoxville). Francis Alexander's comment about cutting the meadow in 1815 indicates that hay could be cut from the meadow by that year (Ramsey Papers, University of Tennessee Special Collections Library, Knoxville). The map of the tracts inherited by Ramsey's four children shows what is believed to have been cleared or cultivated ground west and south of the stone house (see Figure 31). This also suggests that the former wet meadow may have been tillable by this time. Until parts of the pond could be cut and plowed, grain crops such as wheat and corn would have to be grown on the peninsula and the uplands around the house. This indicates a considerable acreage had been cleared of trees, not only to open the land for cultivation but to supply timber for constructing the house, outbuildings, and fences and for fuel for heating and cooking.

Archaeological remains of the original cabin site correspond almost exactly to the building described by Francis Alexander Ramsey's son J. G. M. Ramsey, who was born in this dwelling. The corner fireplace in this log structure indicates the Ramseys were influenced by the Fenno-Swedish architectural style when they built their first home at Swan Pond. Another architectural feature brought with them is the gable end fireplace in the early smokehouse, a design probably borrowed from their German neighbors in Pennsylvania.

While the Ramseys' home and smokehouse were apparently different from those of their southern Appalachian neighbors, the defensive fence around their compound was modeled after those protecting the fortified stations, in that domestic structures formed part of this barrier. The cabin anchored the southeast corner, with the smokehouse at the northeast corner. Artifacts found by posthole-testing the northwest rear yard suggest another domestic building stood here, possibly the slave quarters. Although we do not know how many enslaved African Americans the Ramseys brought with them to Swan Pond, we know they were present on the farm as early as 1804, and between 1810 and the year Francis Alexander died, the number of bondspersons at Swan Pond fluctuated between four and six individuals. The small number of enslaved persons and predominance of females suggest the Ramsey slaves were primarily domestics. All could have lived in one slave house. It is possible that some enslaved persons may have been quartered outside the compound at a later date, but this seems unlikely during the early years when the Indian threat was still paramount.

The next major modification of the natural environment of Swan Pond occurred when Francis Alexander Ramsey built the beautiful stone house in 1796–97. The hiring of Thomas Hope to design this house and a premier stonemason to construct it speaks to the fact that Francis Alexander spared no expense to build what has often been referred to as one of the most stately mansions in late-eighteenth-century Tennessee. Because of the exquisite Georgian styling, I once speculated that Francis Alexander was strongly influenced by this popular eighteenth-century style, which emphasized symmetry in architecture and landscape design (Faulkner 1986). On discovery of the continued presence of the defensive compound and the log house immediately adjacent to the stone house, however, it appears that aesthetics were not uppermost in the mind of the master of the house. This is also evident in the attachment of the kitchen block to the house, which not only ruined the Georgian symmetry of the structure but was also more poorly built.

Connected with the impact of the construction of the stone house on the Swan Pond peninsula was the quarrying of limestone/marble in the area across an arm of Swan Pond, an area still quarried for stone today. The transport of stone to the building site might also have implications for establishing the construction date of what is now Thorngrove Pike. It is obvious that this road, shown on an early-nineteenth-century map, could not have been built until the pond was drained after 1793. Original access to the peninsula must have been from the high ridge on the north end of the Ramsey House property, but the exact route through the property is not known. It is believed that at least a portion of what is now Thorngrove Pike was probably in place when the stone house was built, allowing the limestone/marble to be more easily transported to the peninsula. The road had to be filled in on the east side of the peninsula, the narrowness of the pond here indicating the fill could be from the road cut that is still obvious in front of the house. The orientation of the stone house in a slightly different direction than the cabin and parallel to the road is another indication that the road was present, under construction, or at least planned when the stone house was built.

The archaeological and historical evidence implies that Francis Alexander Ramsey, even during the earliest occupation of Swan Pond, could be called a "gentleman farmer" in the sense that farming was not his principal occupation. Nevertheless, the stock and farm equipment in his estate inventory indicate that he successfully competed in a frontier market economy. While we do not know how Francis Alexander's farm production compared to that of his peers, nor the extent of his domestic consumption, he grew a variety of crops, including corn, wheat, flax, and apples, and his 15 cattle and steers were probably a significant commodity in both local and distant markets. Francis Alexander apparently had an even larger cattle herd since there is a statement in his estate inventory that "Other sheep and cattle had died previous to the sale." Swan Pond would have been ideal for raising cattle after the drained pond became the grassy meadow mentioned by Francis Alexander in his 1815 letter to his sons. Some of the Ramsey's cattle may have been sold at a beef market in Knoxville that existed as early as 1794 (*Knoxville Gazette* 16 May 1794). In 1802, François Michaux reported that farmers in East Tennessee "rear a great number of cattle, which they take four or five hundred miles to the seaports belonging to the southern states" (Michaux 1805). Is this how Francis Alexander first became acquainted with Charleston and Thomas Hope?

While Francis Alexander Ramsey was obviously a successful farmer, he made his fortune as an attorney, a surveyor, clerk of the first senate of the State of Tennessee, and late in life as a bank president (Rothrock 1946:467–468). He started his political career as a young man, being named secretary of the State of Franklin Convention in 1783 when he was 19 years of age, and in June 1785, he was appointed clerk of the superior court of the Washington District (Ramsey 1853:278–296). His public service in Knox County included being named a trustee of Blount College in 1794, and he served the new state of Tennessee as clerk of the first state senate in 1796. His entrepreneurial activities included running a ferry at the forks of the Holston and French Broad rivers, his estate inventory stating that "At an hour that will be mentioned hereafter the sale will take place at the Fork for the purpose of selling the flat chain and the things belonging to the Ferry" (Knox County Administrator's Settlements 1821). An obviously learned man, Ramsey had approximately 138 books in his estate inventory, but only one dealt with farming.

Ramsey owned around 2,000 acres in the last decade of the eighteenth century, but his estate inventory contained less than 100 farm stock animals. The question is, what was he doing with such a large acreage (assuming, of course, that it was all around Swan Pond). There is evidence he was extensively cutting timber in that the map dating between 1816 and 1823 shows a sawmill at the confluence of Swan Pond and Cruze creeks north of the stone house (Figure 31). It is also interesting to note on this map that the cleared or cultivated lands shown as small rectangles or squares are widely dispersed, suggesting the growing of crops and raising of stock was diversified among several farms. Perhaps his barn or barns were on these other farms, explaining why we have yet to find archaeological remains of an eighteenth-century barn at Swan Pond. Most importantly, however, he was holding the land in trust for his children.

The small number of enslaved Africans could also mean an absence of extensive farming on the home place or that field labor was primarily in the hands of the Plumblee and the later Burnett families who appear to have been tenants on the Ramsey land (Faulkner 1986:30). Perhaps these were the "labourers" whom John Gamble encountered during his "ramble" over the Ramsey Plantation and who asked him, "What do you stare at Yankee. Why —— Jonathan we don't have such confounded winters and bet —— but what we can burn bushes and leaves even in December" (Francis Alexander Ramsey's Clerk's Diary, University of Tennessee Special Collections Library, Knoxville). Their manner of address to John Gamble suggests they were not enslaved Africans.

Several things about Francis Alexander Ramsey, the man, appear contradictory. On one hand, he seems to have been a stylish individual. His stone house, its magnificent architecture remarkable even to this day, was a showplace for his time. On the other hand, he allowed his log cabin, which some might call an eyesore, to stand almost touching his elegant stone house. Although this patrician seems to have drifted away from his pioneer roots, he apparently kept a symbol of those challenging times as did his contemporaries James White and John Sevier, who actually went a step further and continued to live in log houses until their deaths in 1821 and 1815, respectively.

The large amount of broken ceramics, especially tea wares, found around the log cabin indicates that even when they arrived on the frontier, the

Ramseys frequently entertained. Later, Bishop Asbury recounted that Ramsey "pursued us to the ferry, franked us over, and took us to his excellent mansion—a stone house. . . . We were kindly and comfortably entertained." In his autobiography, J. G. M. Ramsey said that his father lived at Swan Pond for 23 years, and "was up to the time of his death in November 1820 a center of generous hospitality, refined and elegant and not less sincere, unostentatious and cordial" (Hesseltine 1954:10).

Archaeological studies of eighteenth- and nineteenth-century household deposits indicate that the amount of broken ceramics is directly proportional to the number of people being served in the household (Dyson 1982; Smith 1984). Status and degree of entertainment is also indicated by the percentage of refined earthenware and porcelain, as is indicated from percentages of these ceramic wares in deposits at the homes of prominent Knoxville families such as the Blounts (92 percent) (Faulkner 1985:Table 2) and the Whites (87 percent) (Faulkner 1984:Table 6). This compares favorably with percentages of wares from Ramsey deposits dating from 1793 to 1820, in which 86 percent of the sherds are imported refined tablewares, 74 percent of these being tea ware sherds (Faulkner 2000b:164). Tea and its associated serving and consumption pieces and the ritual of drinking it called the "tea ceremony" was introduced from England and became an integral part of early American entertaining (Roth 1961).

In some ways Francis Alexander Ramsey also seems to have been a very conservative, private individual. While the Indian threat no longer hung over East Tennessee settlers by 1800, the substantial defensive fence remained in place long after Francis Alexander's death in 1820. Why such an imposing fence remained around the Ramsey house for so long is puzzling. Despite his progressive business dealings and political involvement, Francis Alexander Ramsey may have been uncomfortable with change in his surroundings and also used this fence to protect his privacy.

While the layout of Swan Pond does not seem to have been altered during Francis Alexander's lifetime, the function of the buildings and fence appears to have changed. Artifacts found in the vicinity of the early cabin indicate that this probably became Ramsey's office after he built the stone house. The defensive fence first served to protect his family against Indian attack during the first decade the Ramseys lived at Swan Pond. While there is no historical account that Francis Alexander Ramsey directly participated in the frontier warfare that raged during this time, he had firsthand knowledge of the danger to his family. In 1794 Francis Alexander aided neighbor Elizabeth Casteel, whose family had been massacred south of the French Broad River (Ramsey 1853:593). Later, when the frontier was no longer aflame, the defensive fence functioned as a privacy barrier. Nevertheless, the inner house yard continued to be work space, certainly devoid of the beautiful lawn that surrounds the house today, and was alive with the daily sounds and smells of household and farming activities.

One of the most important life events on a family farm was household succession, in which a son or daughter assumed control of the property when the parents retired or died. Such a transition can have a significant impact on the domestic landscape as the new owners assert their ideas on improvement of the property. When Francis Alexander Ramsey died, Swan Pond was inherited by his second-oldest son, William Baines Alexander Ramsey, who was living on the family farm at that time (*In Memoriam: Col. Wm. B. A. Ramsey,* Ramsey Papers, 1874, UT Special Collections Library, Knoxville; Hesseltine 1954; Knox County Court Records 1825). Based on the archaeological record, there is nothing that indicates that W. B. A. Ramsey substantially modified the Swan Pond landscape during his ownership of the property.

While it appears unusual that young "Billy" did not exercise his prerogatives even though the defensive fence was no longer needed and the outbuildings were probably in need of repair, there are two possible reasons the farm might have remained in its original state during W. B. A. Ramsey's tenure. In a study of seventeenth- and eighteenth-century family genealogy in Andover, Massachusetts, it was found that it was not until the third generation that sons were establishing independence from parental control (Greven 1970). Considering historical evidence, however, a more likely explanation seems to be that W. B. A. Ramsey did not live on this property for several years due to political and business involvement in Knoxville and out of state. More to the point, W. B. A. Ramsey was like his father, an entrepreneur who did not take up farming as his life's work. We do not have an agricultural census telling us what crops were grown and stock kept by W. B. A. Ramsey. However, as long as the farm supported itself and even stayed somewhat productive, William could probably see no reason to remodel or rebuild the premises. It is also likely that W. B. A. Ramsey still viewed the land as a sacred trust to keep the "old home place" within the family. This obligation, while not patrimony, can also be seen in his later sale of Swan Pond to his older brother, J. G. M. Ramsey.

At the death of their father, J. G. M. Ramsey inherited the 353-acre farm at the Forks of the River, his younger brother John M. A. Ramsey received the tract north of Swan Pond, and his sister, Eliza Ramsey, received the tract south of the home place. While such a division of Francis Alexander Ramsey's property seems equitable, a major problem with such partible inheritance in nineteenth-century rural America is that, as the population grew and family tracts became increasingly subdivided with each succeeding generation, eventually the land could no longer support individual farms (Salstrom 1991; Groover 2003).

It is believed that, like his father, W. B. A. Ramsey was deeply involved with business and political ventures at a relatively young age. William was 21 years old when his father died and he took control of the Swan Pond farm. Sometime between 1821 and 1828 when the first steamboat reached Knoxville, W. B. A. Ramsey and his brother J. G. M. arranged for the purchase of a low-draft steamboat to operate between Muscle Shoals, Alabama, and Knoxville, and in 1831 W. B. A. was president of the Knoxville Steamboat Company (Rothrock 1946:96–98). Continuing his interest in transportation, W. B. A. Ramsey was one of the backers of the Hiawassee Railroad Company, incorporated in 1836 to build a line from Knoxville south through Georgia (Rothrock 1946:103). In 1837 he became a co-owner of the *Knoxville Register* (Rothrock 1946:422). He also served as clerk and master of the chancery court after he sold Swan Pond to his brother J. G. M. in 1840.

Before he became secretary of state, William moved to Nashville, where he lived the remainder of his life, dying in 1874 in Edgefield, Tennessee. W. B. A. Ramsey probably moved to Nashville in 1842, when he married Susan P. Washington on May 8 of that year (Lucas and Sheffield 1981). After the death of his second wife, W. B. A. Ramsey married Charlotte Williams in 1860. Congenial relations between J. G. M. and W. B. A. Ramsey appear in several letters sent from the former to his brother in Nashville (McIver Collection, Tennessee State Library and Archives, Nashville).

How close these brothers were before W. B. A. moved to Nashville remains unclear. Nevertheless, W. B. A. seemed anxious for the home place to remain in the family, since he sold Swan Pond to his brother at least a couple of years before he moved to Nashville. That this sale may not have been entirely altruistic, however, is suggested by the fact that W. B. A. did not marry until 1834, and the children born to W. B. A. and his wife Eliza were not old enough to inherit the property in 1840, making partible inheritance impossible for many years. It is also clear that W. B. A. preferred business and politics over being a gentleman farmer.

There is now little doubt that the Ramseys were not living at Swan Pond between the early 1840s and the early 1850s; W. B. A. Ramsey was in Nashville during this time, and J. G. M. and his younger brother John M. A. Ramsey had their own farms. Shortly after W. B. A. Ramsey sold Swan Pond to his brother, the latter brought the Kinzel family from South Carolina to care for the place. When J. G. M.'s son Alex came of age, he was apparently put in charge of managing the farm. Trusted tenants like the Burnett family also seem to have been farming at Swan Pond during Alex Ramsey's absence in Kentucky. Like his father, J. G. M. Ramsey appears to have placed the welfare of Swan Pond in the care of kin and persons he trusted. In 1857 the farm was deeded to Alex Ramsey when he married Nancy Rebecca "Nannie" Presley in South Carolina and brought his new bride to Swan Pond.

Unlike his namesake grandfather, his father, J. G. M., and his uncle William, Alex was not a politician or a businessman but apparently made his living by farming. East Tennessee developed a diversified agriculture during the antebellum period, which had reached maturity by the outbreak of the Civil War (Winters 1994:179). While it is impossible to compare Alex's holdings found in the 1860 agricultural census to those of previous Ramseys who lived at Swan Pond, we can compare Alex Ramsey's farm production to a sample of 55 peers in his Knox County district. Corn was grown by all farmers in the sample, and data from the 1850 agricultural census from seven East Tennessee counties including Knox indicates a rank ordering of farm commodities as follows: corn, rye and oats, butter and cheese, potatoes, wheat, pork, wool, sheep, flax, cattle, tobacco, horses/asses/mules, and hay (Gray 1958). Francis Alexander, like his grandfather, practiced a diversified or mixed farming strategy by raising or producing corn, oats, butter, potatoes (both Irish and sweet), swine, sheep (wool), cattle, tobacco, horses, and hay (United States Census, Schedule 4 1860). Interestingly, he did not grow wheat like 36 of his neighbors. His production of corn (1500 bushels) greatly exceeded the average of 780 bushels for his peers. The number of horses (seven) and milk cows (four) that Alex Ramsey owned was also above the district average, and he was one of the top five cattle raisers in his district. He was the top producer of hay, with 80 tons, the average tonnage of this crop being 9 tons (United States Census, Schedule 4 1860). Not only was Alex Ramsey a very successful farmer, but he also followed in his grandfather's footsteps by utilizing the natural meadowland of Swan Pond to raise cattle.

Alex Ramsey was also the first Ramsey (third generation) that made "improvements" to the farm according to his father (Hesseltine 1954:137). This may be due in part to the fact that he was also the first in the male family line who was not born on the home place. It is also likely that the 70-year-old farm had not been personally cared for by family members, who had not lived there during the past decade. Archaeological evidence indicates that Alex removed the second large defensive fence and replaced it with a smaller board or palen fence. Alex may also have razed what may have been the original slave quarters at the northwest corner of the former defensive compound.

During the late Ramsey period, the east side yard probably continued to function as a work area and may have witnessed even more domestic activity, with the early cabin, Structure 4, now occupied by enslaved Africans. After

Alex Ramsey began living at Swan Pond and the defensive fence was removed, the inner yard became more open, enclosed by the lighter fence C, either a post-and-rail fence or perhaps a stout picket or palen fence. This fence continued to separate the inner house yard from the outer and peripheral yards and apparently continued to enclose the domestic-oriented outbuildings such as the smokehouse as well. By this time, we also know that the outer fields were enclosed with split-rail fencing, suggesting protection was needed from free-ranging stock.

According to a biography of Francis Frost Horlbeck Alexander Ramsey in *Ramsey of Swan Pond,* Alex enlisted as a sergeant for three years in Capt. W. C. Kain's Light Artillery of the Army of Tennessee in Chattanooga on May 24, 1862. He was with Kain in the skirmish at Bridgeport, Alabama, and the raid on Winchester, Tennessee (Eubanks 1965:289). In August 1862, he went into the field with Gen. Edmund Kirby Smith's division of the Army of Tennessee on the Kentucky campaign and was at Cumberland Gap in 1863. He was at Swan Pond in September 1863, just prior to the capture of Knoxville by the Union army under the command of Gen. Ambrose Burnside, and accompanied his father on their flight south to Confederate-held Georgia. J. G. M. Ramsey said Alex remained with Gen. Braxton Bragg's Army of Tennessee; however, elsewhere in his autobiography J. G. M. indicates that Alex continued to stay with the family in East Tennessee after Gen. James Longstreet's army retreated from the siege of Knoxville in early December (Hesseltine 1954). On June 5, 1864, Alex was captured at the battle of Piedmont, Virginia, in the Shenandoah Valley along with more than 1,000 Confederate soldiers and was held at Camp Morton, Indiana. At the conclusion of the conflict he returned to South Carolina and was reunited with his family (Ramsey 1982:206–212). Like his father, Alex was an exile from Tennessee, afraid to return to Swan Pond for fear of arrest or worse.

What made East Tennessee a particularly dangerous place after the Civil War was the fact that it had been a largely pro-Union island in a sea of Confederate gray, with Confederate supporters like the Ramseys being in the minority in many communities. At the beginning of the war when the Confederacy controlled East Tennessee the Unionists were persecuted, but after the summer of 1863 when the area was occupied by Federal forces, the tables were turned. This caused close friends and neighbors and even family members who supported opposing sides to become bitter enemies. That the vindictiveness spawned by the war continued to haunt the Ramsey family after the conflict is suggested by the sudden death Crozier Ramsey in Knoxville on January 1, 1869, while trying to win back the lost family property (Ramsey 1982:233). J. G. M. Ramsey believed that his son was murdered (Hesseltine 1954:253).

There is no record of who lived at Swan Pond from September 1863 until the property was purchased by the Spurgin family in 1866. It would be very surprising if this grand house stood vacant for three years, because the occupying Union forces billeted troops in many houses in the Knoxville area. If military personnel did live at Swan Pond, we have found little archaeological evidence of it, although the few military artifacts that have been recovered at the site suggest the Union army cavalry may have occupied the house for a short period of time. That the Ramsey farm was not destroyed like J. G. M. Ramsey's beloved Mecklenburg is a miracle.

Alex is the first Ramsey remembered by his descendants who were interviewed by Terry J. Faulkner in 1985 at the Ramsey family reunion at historic Ramsey House (Faulkner 1986:38–47). Francis Alexander Ramsey II, as he was later called, was 96 years old when he died and was remembered by his great-grandson Conrad Lam and his granddaughter Claudialea Ledger Watts. There is a photograph of Alex Ramsey and his wife "Nannie" taken in 1921 with other members of the Ramsey family (Jarnigan 1976).

According to his grandchildren, Alex was an outdoors person who loved the river and his father's house at Mecklenburg at the forks of the French Broad and Holston rivers. They said the war hurt him deeply but he lived through it and started a new life when the family moved to Texas. He was an avid reader and could read Greek. They also recalled he had second sight. Claudialea Watts fondly remembered that "my grandfather was the happiest person that I ever knew, he was very inspirational" (Faulkner 1986:47).

Alex sold Swan Pond while he was living in Georgia. In the years following the war, the Ramseys were a refugee family like so many southerners during those trying times. According to family letters Alex first went to live with his wife's parents, the Presleys, in Yorkville, South Carolina, and later moved to North Carolina to be with his father's family. In late 1865 he left North Carolina for Georgia where he bought a flour mill. According to his grandchildren, he lost money on this venture, returning to North Carolina, where he took in his parents. The exact date of this move is unclear (Faulkner 1986:47, Hesseltine 1954:249).

Alex's grandchildren recounted in the 1985 interview that in 1872 the family went by boat from Charleston to Galveston, Texas, and then on to Gatesville, a small town in central Texas (Faulkner 1986:39). Another Ramsey family story was that Alex's wife Nancy and their three children did not accompany Alex on the boat trip to Texas but went later by hack from Yorkville to Gatesville with a black man and woman and the milk cow (Faulkner 1986:41).

The condition of the Swan Pond farm when the Spurgins purchased it in 1866 was not recorded. An account from neighboring Blount County during the war states in part:

> By 1865 . . . the farms of the area were but lightly tilled for lack of
> men. Food long since had grown painfully scarce. The dirt of smoke-
> house floors was frequently dug up and boiled for salt . . . Bands of
> raiders almost daily terrorized the people [Tindell 1973:60].

Another historian wrote about the plight of the East Tennesseans:

> Northern soldiers who could not always distinguish a loyal Tennes-
> sean from a Rebel added to the woes of the beleaguered area. Their
> countryside stripped bare by both armies, the people of East Tennes-
> see discovered that friend and foe alike had robbed them [Seymour
> 1963:218].

While the Civil War had a significant impact on the lives of upper-class farmers such as the Ramseys, unlike the deep South where a plantation economy was based on such labor-intensive crops as cotton and rice, large East Tennessee farms were based on mixed farming (hogs, cattle, corn, and wheat), and some large farms soon continued to operate at practically the same economic level as before the war. Nevertheless, there were readjustments in farming after the war, including a decline in grain, hog, and sheep production and an increase in production of wheat and hay and dairying (Rothrock 1946:186–188).

A diminished value of Swan Pond from 1860 to 1870 indicates the farm was probably in a run-down condition when the Spurgins purchased it. Except for an increase in the number of sheep and bushels of oats and the addition of a wheat crop, farm production in 1870 was considerably less than during the previous Alex Ramsey occupation, another factor in the lowered value of the farm. The animals and crops raised by the Spurgins do not mirror the production trends in East Tennessee after the war and indicate the Spurgins were subsistence-level farmers who did not raise an appreciable surplus but produced only enough resources to meet their daily needs and acquire necessary consumer goods. Evidence of wild game consumption may also be associated with this immediate post–Civil War occupation. Another problem facing the Spurgins may have been the absence of older children in the household who could help on the farm. The 1870 agricultural census reveals the Spurgins paid $60 in wages for that year (United States Census, Schedule 4 1870).

Considering their economic status and evidence from the archaeological remains, it appears the Spurgins made few if any improvements to the Swan Pond farm. In 1871 the Spurgins sold Swan Pond to the Keeners for only $400 more than they had paid for it five years before. This is additional evidence that no major improvements were made during the Spurgin occupation on the farm. During the next 37 years, however, extensive modifications and improvements were made to the Swan Pond property.

The 13-year Keener occupation appears to have maintained the farm on a largely subsistence basis. However, by 1880, apple trees had been planted, which could have brought in additional income, and firewood or tanbark may have been sold, as a value of $50 was placed on forest products (United States Census, Schedule 4 1880). The approximate date for the moving of Structure 3 and its conversion to a blacksmith shop, the building of the east side yard cistern to serve this facility, and the fact that Structure 3 had been razed by 1897 by the Watson family suggest these facilities were built by the Keeners. That the Keeners paid $200 in wages on a subsistence-level farm also suggests they were paying persons to produce other commodities (such as iron goods or repairs) in order to "make a go" of the farm. In other words, Swan Pond could no longer be maintained by farm production on the property alone.

While patrimonial succession of the land was no longer possible at Swan Pond by the late nineteenth century, a lateral inheritance of sorts took place when the William Keeners sold the property to John Watson and his wife, Nancy Keener Watson, William Keener's sister, for only $2,000 in 1884.

A shift away from even basic subsistence farming may also be signaled by the purchase of the farm by John and Nancy Watson; in any case, it does not appear that the Watsons completely depended on farming for their livelihood, although some truck farming was done within the growing market economy of the late nineteenth century. This is indicated by Edith Watson's recollection that a major crop was strawberries, which were sold at market in Knoxville. Strawberry growing reached a peak in Knox County in the early 1900s with 876,000 quarts grown in 1909 (Rothrock 1946:206). In the 1900 census the Watsons' oldest son, Sam, was listed as a farm laborer, and the boarders living with the Watsons could also have been farm laborers. That an additional enterprise may have been started at the farm is indicated by the large building (Structure 2) constructed in the east side yard by 1910. This may have been for the repair of increasingly complex mechanized farm equipment.

It is also significant to note that John Watson was not a farmer for most of his life. According to his obituary in the *Knoxville Daily Journal and Tribune*, January 8, 1912, Watson was a schoolteacher educated at Carson-Newman College. His last teaching position may have been in Sevierville, and it is possible that shortly after he married Nancy Keener in 1881 at age 48, he retired to his country "estate" at Swan Pond. It is also evident that the Watsons were somewhat wealthy, perhaps even independently so. They had a house servant, drove an automobile in the early twentieth century, and the photographs of the house at this time indicate a well-kept yard, the old Ramsey cabin having finally been removed and household dumping taking place outside a fenced inner yard. The Watsons were the last owners who improved Swan Pond, and the property seems to have retained much of its original grandeur until they moved. They were also the last owners whose heirs or relatives did not continue to live on the property, even though they had three grown sons when they moved to town. Nancy and her sons Samuel and Carl lived at 208 Glenwood, Sam being the manager of the S. P. Watson Electric Company and Carl a clerk for Cowan, McClung & Company by 1910 (Knoxville City Directory 1910). Such moves to town and the pursuit of business careers were common among the younger generation at the turn of the century, leaving old family farms to renters or tenants. Today those who inherit family farms often sell their property to developers.

We do not know who lived at Swan Pond from 1914 to 1924. Apparently the farm was occupied by renters, as it was after the property was purchased by the Appalachian Marble Company. Although the house certainly suffered slow deterioration during the time it was occupied by renters, there is evidence that what is sometimes called "benign neglect" actually preserved much of the original eighteenth-century interior. Absentee landlords had no incentive to modernize the house, and renters rarely, if ever, would do this on their own. Thus, electricity and plumbing were not installed, so woodwork and floors remained intact. In 1934, the Historic American Building Survey report on the Ramsey House noted that the condition of the house was "good." The exterior photograph of the house taken in about 1931 also shows what still appears to be a fairly well-maintained structure and neat yard (Figure 39).

The nature of farming and the existence of support buildings at Swan Pond continued to undergo major change. While the tenants continued to practice some subsistence agriculture to meet basic needs, most if not all had other employment to earn a living. One informant from this period told me that her father walked to Knoxville to work (Faulkner 1986:60); jobs were also found in the nearby marble quarry. In time, most of the remaining acreage was taken over by the raising of cattle and cultivation right up to the back door of the house.

Any original outbuildings that may still have been standing from the previous century had now disappeared. In the 1920s aerial photograph the building constructed in the east side yard by the Watsons in the earlier years of the century still stood; by the 1930s it, too, was gone. A large late-nineteenth-century gambrel-roofed barn stood in the rear peripheral yard. This provided shelter and stored hay for the cattle herds that now grazed in the open pastures seen surrounding the house in the aerial photograph. The barn was later replaced by the more modern pole barn and a cement-block milking shed. The house remained basically unchanged.

Other farms and family homes have been archaeologically studied in East Tennessee, but often the focus has been only on the founders or prominent families who lived at these sites. While the archaeological project at Swan Pond began with the intent of locating the outbuildings associated with the Francis Alexander Ramsey occupation, and the current mission of the Knoxville Chapter, APTA is to focus on the Ramsey family, it is only fitting that this book cover the totality of human occupation at Swan Pond. Certainly the Ramseys deserve to be singled out as one of the first and most distinguished pioneer families on the East Tennessee frontier, but a comprehensive study of a cultural landscape can only be relevant if we include all those people who helped shape what we see today. One of the strengths of historical archaeology is that it allows us to examine all the remains of past lifeways on a site, if we so desire. Scientific archaeology does not sort through what we believe is important at any place or time, discarding the rest, to be lost forever. Historical archaeology at Swan Pond has not only fleshed out the complete history of one East Tennessee farm, but it also serves as a model for understanding the changing cultural patterns in this region over the past 10,000 years.

This archaeological study of Swan Pond also has implications for a better understanding of the social and economic history of East Tennessee. The southern Appalachian area has often been thought to have been inhabited during the past 250 years by people who tenaciously clung to outdated, conservative ways. This "backwardness" was attributed to the isolation of a mountain fastness, isolated from the "civilized" coastal cities since the time of earliest settlement, where hardy pioneers eked out a spartan existence in crude log cabins in an untamed wilderness. It is hoped that the excavations at Ramsey House and other frontier sites around Knoxville will put such unfounded characterizations to rest. The ingenuity and efficiency of the inhabitants' construction techniques, table settings, and clothing demonstrate that these sturdy folk enjoyed most of the same conveniences and fashions found on the Atlantic seaboard. Such amenities were not only found among the archaeological remains of the wealthy like the Ramseys but also among those of their neighbor yeoman farmers who settled this land (Faulkner 2000b:159).

It is also clear from the archaeological record that from the very beginning of the historic period East Tennesseans were drawn into a modern capitalist, market economy (Groover 2003). Francis Alexander Ramsey had over two dozen cattle and steers and 40 hogs in 1820 suggesting that while being called a "gentleman farmer" he was actively engaged in marketing his farm products. In the mid-nineteenth century the eastern Tennessee River valley was often called the "breadbasket of the South," one of several reasons both the Confederate and Union forces fought so hard over this area. The market economy is evident in the agricultural census during Alex Ramsey's ownership of the property and even in postwar times when, despite the devastation of the Civil War, Swan Pond farmers were still producing goods for sale. As occurred in other parts of the country, however, Swan Pond was caught in continuing partitioning of the land, making it increasingly difficult for the individual small-acreage farmer to survive on the sale of farm products alone; other outside revenue sources such as blacksmithing were often necessary for survival. The absence of currency in the archaeological record at Swan Pond until after the Civil War indicates barter was still prevalent until that time. When the land could no longer sustain this traditional rural economy, it was sold to absentee landlords who no longer tilled the soil. The history of Swan Pond serves as a microcosm of the economic and social changes in rural southern Appalachia during the past 200 years.

One human trait that did endure at Swan Pond for thousands of years was the respect for the land and a close tie to kin. We do not know what kind of kinship system the prehistoric people who lived on this land had, but we do know from their living descendants that they honored and preserved the natural bounty of the environment. In spite of being enslaved, the African Americans who lived at Swan Pond created their own culture, and through an enduring kinship system proudly passed their heritage down to the present day. While the Ramseys changed the natural environment, they preserved their kin ties to the land through patrimony, preserving those architectural vestiges of their lives at Swan Pond until they were forced to leave. Awareness of family relationships and pride in ones earliest ancestors is alive and well in southern Appalachia to this day.

A photograph of the rear of the Ramsey House taken in 1952 when the APTA purchased the acre of ground on which it stood poignantly shows an empty building on the edge of a plowed field, a fate suffered by too many of our historic farm sites in East Tennessee. Due to the foresight of the APTA, Ramsey House was saved, restored to its former splendor, and 100 acres of the former Ramsey land around it have been purchased and are now protected from encroaching development. And after 140 years the descendants of Francis Alexander Ramsey have come back to honor their ancestors at family reunions. As part of the restoration of this significant historical landscape, the Knoxville Chapter of the APTA began the scientific archaeology program at Swan Pond in 1985. This revival of the story of Swan Pond has just begun, however. One of the truths of archaeological excavation is that the more one digs, the more one discovers, and the more questions about past lifeways are raised. Considering that the story of life at Swan Pond has taken thousands of years to unfold, we must be patient as it continues to give up its secrets.

REFERENCES CITED

ADAMSON, JUNE
1976   The Communications Media. In *Heart of the Valley: A History of Knoxville, Tennessee,* edited by Lucile Deaderick, pp. 273–336. East Tennessee Historical Society, Knoxville, Tennessee.

ALBERT, LILLIAN S., AND JANE F. ADAMS
1970   Essential Data Concerning China Buttons. In *Guidelines for Collecting China Buttons.* Boyertown Publishing, Boyertown, Pennsylvania.

AMERICAN AGRICULTURALIST
1880   Sorghum in America—Its Introduction. *American Agriculturalist* 39(3):116.

AVERY, PAUL G., TIMOTHY E. BAUMANN, AND CHARLES H. FAULKNER
1998   *1996 Testing at the Ramsey House: Final Report.* Report prepared for the Tennessee Historical Commission and the Association for the Preservation of Tennessee Antiquities, Knoxville Chapter. Department of Anthropology, University of Tennessee, Knoxville.

BALL, DONALD B.
2005   Personal communication.

BAUMANN, PAUL
1970   *Collecting Antique Marbles.* Mid-America Book, Leon, Iowa.

BEALER, ALEX W., AND JOHN O. ELLIS
1979   *The Log Cabin: Homes of the North American Wilderness.* Barre Publishing, Barre, Massachusetts.

BIVINS, JOHN, JR.
1972   *The Moravian Potters in North Carolina.* Published for Old Salem, Inc., Winston-Salem, North Carolina by the University of North Carolina Press, Chapel Hill.

BIVINS, WILLIE R. H.
1987   *The Family of Reynolds Ramsey, Revolutionary Soldier.* Oklahoma City, Oklahoma.

BOUCHER, FRANÇOIS
1967   *A History of Costume in the West.* Translated by John Ross. Thames and Hudson, London.

BOWMAN, ELIZABETH S., AND STANLEY J. FOLMSBEE
1965   The Ramsey House: Home of Francis Alexander Ramsey. *Tennessee Historical Quarterly* 24(3):203–218.

BRACLAWSKI, KAREN
1995   *The Guide to Historic Costume.* B. T. Batsford, London.

BUSCH, JANE
1981   An Introduction to the Tin Can. *Historical Archaeology* 5(1):95–104.

CARNES, LINDA F., AND JEFFERSON CHAPMAN
1984   An Assessment of the Potential for Archaeological Resources at the Ramsey House Property. Report submitted to the Association for the Preservation of Tennessee Antiquities, Knoxville Chapter.

CASE, LYNN M.
ca. 1969 *A Swedish Log Cabin: Three Centuries of History on Darby Creek.* Privately printed.

CASHION, JIM, ZACK CARNEY, AND JEAN CRESWELL
1980   Swan Pond. Unpublished report by the School of Architecture, University of Tennessee, Knoxville, for the Association for the Preservation of Tennessee Antiquities, Knoxville Chapter.

CHAPEL, CHARLES E.
1960   *The Complete Book of Gun Collecting.* Coward-McCann, New York.

CHAPMAN, JEFFERSON
1985   *Tellico Archaeology: 12,000 Years of Native American History.* Tennessee Valley Authority, Knoxville.

CONTINENTAL MONTHLY
1862   *The Continental Monthly.* 2, July–December, 1862.

COUGHLIN, SEAN P.
1996   Research on Ramsey House: Dating the Kitchen Addition. Research paper on file, Department of Anthropology, University of Tennessee, Knoxville.

DEADERICK, LUCILE (EDITOR)
1976   *Heart of the Valley: A History of Knoxville, Tennessee.* East Tennessee
        Historical Society, Knoxville.

DICKSON, D. BRUCE
1974   Archaeological Test Excavations at Ramsey House, Knoxville Tennessee,
        September 1973. Report submitted to the Association for the Preservation
        of Tennessee Antiquities, Knoxville Chapter. Department of Anthropology,
        University of Tennessee, Knoxville.

DIDEROT, DENIS
1959   *A Diderot Pictorial Encyclopedia of Trades and Industries.* Vol. 2. Dover
        Publications, New York.

DYSON, STEPHEN L.
1982   Material Culture, Social Structure, and Changing Cultural Values: The
        Ceramics of Eighteenth- and Nineteenth-Century Middletown, Connecti-
        cut. In *Archaeology of Urban America: The Search for Pattern and Process,*
        edited by Roy S. Dickens Jr., pp. 361–380. Academic Press, New York.

EUBANKS, DAVID L.
1965   Dr. J. G. M. Ramsey of East Tennessee: A Career of Public Service.
        Unpublished Ph.D. dissertation, Department of History, University of
        Tennessee, Knoxville.

FABERSON, TANYA A.
2003   Yeoman Farmers in Turn-of-the Century Knox County: A Ceramic
        Distribution Comparison between Marble Springs (40KN125) and
        Ramsey House. In *Archaeological Excavations at Marble Springs, Summer
        2002,* edited by Tanya A. Faberson and Charles H. Faulkner, pp. 43–65.
        Department of Anthropology, University of Tennessee, Knoxville.

FAIRBANKS, CHARLES H.
1977   Backyard Archaeology as a Research Strategy. *Conference on Historic Sites
        Archaeology Papers* 11:133–139.

FAULKNER, CHARLES H.
1984   *An Archaeological and Historical Study of the James White Second Home
        Site.* University of Tennessee, Department of Anthropology, Report of
        Investigations No. 28. Knoxville.
1985   A Final Report on Archaeological Testing in the Garden of Blount Mansion,
        Knoxville, Tennessee. Department of Anthropology, University of Ten-
        nessee, Knoxville.
1986   *A History of the Ramsey House and Its Occupants, 1797–1952.* Department
        of Anthropology, University of Tennessee, Knoxville.
1989   Field Notes, Matt Russell House, Knox County, Tennessee.

1993 Archaeology at Blount Mansion: Architectural Metamorphosis of a Frontier Landmark. Paper presented at the 11th Annual Symposium on Ohio Valley Urban and Historical Archaeology, Giant City State Park, Illinois, March 13, 1993.

1994a 1994 Testing for the Ramsey Barn. Report prepared for the Association for the Preservation of Tennessee Antiquities, Knoxville Chapter.

1994b 1994 Archaeological Investigations in the Ramsey House Cellar. Report prepared for the Association for the Preservation of Tennessee Antiquities, Knoxville Chapter.

1995 *Archaeological Testing at Ramsey House: Fall 1994.* Report prepared for the Tennessee Historical Commission and the Association for the Preservation of Tennessee Antiquities, Knoxville Chapter. Department of Anthropology, University of Tennessee, Knoxville.

1996a *Archaeological Testing at Ramsey House: 1995 Season.* Report prepared for the Tennessee Historical Commission and the Association for the Preservation of Tennessee Antiquities, Knoxville Chapter. Department of Anthropology, University of Tennessee, Knoxville.

1996b An Archaeological and Architectural Study of Small Outbuildings in East Tennessee. *Ohio Valley Historical Archaeology* 11:41–47.

1999 *Archaeological Excavations at Ramsey House: 1997 Season.* Report prepared for the Tennessee Historical Commission and the Association for the Preservation of Tennessee Antiquities, Knoxville Chapter. Department of Anthropology, University of Tennessee, Knoxville.

2000a *Archaeological Excavations at Ramsey House: 1999 Season.* Report prepared for the Tennessee Historical Commission and the Association for the Preservation of Tennessee Antiquities, Knoxville Chapter. Department of Anthropology, University of Tennessee, Knoxville.

2000b Knoxville and the Southern Appalachian Frontier: An Archaeological Perspective. *Tennessee Historical Quarterly* 59(3):158–173.

2001 *Archaeological Excavations at Ramsey House: 2000 Season.* Report prepared for the Tennessee Historical Commission and the Association for the Preservation of Tennessee Antiquities, Knoxville Chapter. Department of Anthropology, University of Tennessee, Knoxville.

2002 A Nineteenth-Century Stoneware Pottery Manufacturing Site in Knoxville, Tennessee. *Ohio Valley Historical Archaeology* 17:108–113.

2003a *Archaeological Excavations at Ramsey House: 2001 Season.* Report prepared for the Tennessee Historical Commission and the Association for the Preservation of Tennessee Antiquities, Knoxville Chapter. Department of Anthropology, University of Tennessee, Knoxville.

2003b Archaeological Excavation at Marble Springs: Summer 2002. In *Archaeological Excavations at Marble Springs: Summer 2002,* edited by Tanya A. Faberson and Charles H. Faulkner, pp. 14–29. Department of Anthropology, University of Tennessee, Knoxville.

FAULKNER, CHARLES H. (EDITOR)

1981   *The Weaver Pottery Site: Industrial Archaeology in Knoxville, Tennessee.*
       Department of Anthropology, University of Tennessee, Knoxville.

FAULKNER, CHARLES H., AND DALFORD DEAN OWENS JR.

1995   *Archaeological Testing of the Ramsey House Barnyard.* Report prepared
       for the Tennessee Historical Commission and the Association for the
       Preservation of Tennessee Antiquities, Knoxville Chapter. Department
       of Anthropology, University of Tennessee, Knoxville.

FAULKNER, CHARLES H., AND AMY L. YOUNG

1989a Archaeological Testing of the Expansion Area of the Ramsey House Visitor's
       Center. Report prepared for the Association for the Preservation of Tennes-
       see Antiquities, Knoxville Chapter.

1989b Archaeological Testing of the East Expansion Area of the Ramsey House
       Visitors Center. Report prepared for the Association for the Preservation
       of Tennessee Antiquities, Knoxville Chapter.

FAY, ROBERT P.

1986   *Archaeological Investigations at Liberty Hall, Frankfort, Kentucky.* Kentucky
       Heritage Council, Frankfort, Kentucky.

FIKE, RICHARD E.

1987   *The Bottle Book: A Comprehensive Guide to Historic, Embossed, Medicine
       Bottles.* Peregrine Smith Books, Salt Lake City, Utah.

FINK, PAUL M.

1989   *Jonesborough: The First Century of Tennessee's First Town, 1776–1876.* The
       Overmountain Press, Johnson City, Tennessee.

GLASSIE, HENRY H., III

1965   Southern Mountain Houses: A Study of American Folk Culture. Unpub-
       lished Master's thesis, Cooperstown Graduate Program, State University of
       New York College at Oneonta.

GOODSPEED PUBLISHING

1974   *Goodspeed's History of Hamilton, Knox, and Shelby Counties of Tennessee.*
       Reprinted. Charles and Randy Elder Booksellers, Nashville. Originally
       published 1887, Goodspeed Brothers, Nashville.

GRAY, LEWIS C.

1958   *History of Agriculture in the Southern United States to 1860.* Vol. 2. Peter
       Smith, New York.

GREENE, LANCE K.

1992   The Penfield Is Mightier Than the Sword: Machine-Made Bricks in Knox-
       ville and Knox County, Tennessee. In *Proceedings of the Tenth Symposium*

on Ohio Valley Urban and Historic Archaeology, edited by Amy L. Young and Charles H. Faulkner, pp. 74–91. Tennessee Anthropological Association, Miscellaneous Paper No. 16. Knoxville.

GREVEN, PHILIP J.
1970   *Four Generations: Population, Land, and Family in Colonial Andover, Massachusetts.* Cornell University Press, Ithaca, New York.

GROOVER, MARK D.
2003   *An Archaeological Study of Rural Capitalism and Material Life.* Kluwer Academic/Plenum Publishers, New York.

HAMBY, E. BROOKE
1999   An Archaeological and Historical Investigation of the Blount Mansion Slave Quarters. Unpublished Master's thesis, Department of Anthropology, University of Tennessee, Knoxville.

HESSELTINE, WILLIAM B. (EDITOR)
1954   *Dr. J. G. M. Ramsey, Autobiography and Letters.* Tennessee Historical Commission, Nashville.

HILLIARD, SAM B.
1972   *Hog Meat and Hoecake: Food Supply in the Old South, 1840–1860.* Southern Illinois University Press, Carbondale.

HILLIER, MARY
1968   *Dolls and Doll-makers.* Putnam, New York.

HISTORIC AMERICAN BUILDINGS SURVEY
1936   J. G. M. Ramsey House, History and Architecture. Historic American Buildings Survey/Historic American Engineering Record. Library of Congress, Washington, D.C.

HOWELL, ALICE L.
1986   Tennessee Biography: John Craighead. *Tennessee Ancestors* 2(3):161–165.

HUGHES, ELIZABETH, AND MARION LESTER
1981   *The Big Book of Buttons.* Boyertown Publishing, Boyertown, Pennsylvania.

JACOBSON, JODI A.
2000   Faunal Analysis of the 1999 Ramsey House Excavation: Historic Archaeology Term Paper. On file, Department of Anthropology, University of Tennessee, Knoxville.

JARNIGAN, WILLIAM S.
1976   *A Genealogical Chart of the Alexander-Ramsay-Ramsey Family of Scotland & America.* Walden Press, Concord, Massachusetts.

Jones, Olive, and Catherine Sullivan

1985   *The Parks Canada Glass Glossary for the Description of Containers, Tableware, Flat Glass, and Closures.* National Historic Parks and Sites Branch, Parks Canada, Environment Canada, Ottawa.

Jordan, Terry G., and Matti Kaups

1989   *The American Backwoods Frontier: An Ethnic and Ecological Interpretation.* Johns Hopkins University Press, Baltimore.

Kaups, Matti

1986   Finns. In *America's Architectural Roots: Ethnic Groups That Built America,* edited by Dell Upton, pp. 124–129. Preservation Press, New York.

Knox County Administrator's Settlements

1821   Estate Inventory of Francis Alexander Ramsey, 21 October. Knox County Archives, Knoxville, Tennessee.

1881   Estate Inventory of Joseph Keener. Knox County Archives, Knoxville, Tennessee.

Knox County Court Records

1825   Minutes of the Knox County Court for 1825. Knox County Archives, Knoxville, Tennessee.

Knox County Deed Records

1804   Bill of Sale. Register of Deeds, City-County Building, Knoxville, Tennessee.

1810   Deed of Trust. BS N1, p. 413. Register of Deeds, City-County Building, Knoxville, Tennessee.

1811a   Bill of Sale. BS 01, p. 226. Register of Deeds, City-County Building, Knoxville, Tennessee.

1811b   Bill of Sale. BS 01, p. 226. Register of Deeds, City-County Building, Knoxville, Tennessee.

1822   Deeds of Trust. BS T1, pp. 129–130. Register of Deeds, City-County Building, Knoxville, Tennessee.

1840   Warranty Deed. D2, p. 306. Register of Deeds, City-County Building, Knoxville, Tennessee.

1844   Warranty Deed, J2, p. 125. Register of Deeds, City-County Building, Knoxville, Tennessee.

1857   Warranty Deed. W2, p. 503. Register of Deeds, City-County Building, Knoxville, Tennessee.

1866   Warranty Deed. D3, p. 542. Register of Deeds, City-County Building, Knoxville, Tennessee.

1871   Warranty Deed. J3, p. 236. Register of Deeds, City-County Building, Knoxville, Tennessee.

1878   Warranty Deed. R3, p. 163. Register of Deeds, City-County Building, Knoxville, Tennessee.

1884 Warranty Deed. B4, p. 555. Register of Deeds, City-County Building, Knoxville, Tennessee.

KNOX COUNTY TAX LIST
1867 Knox County Tax List for 1867. Knox County Archives, Knoxville, Tennessee.
1872 Knox County Tax List for 1872. Knox County Archives, Knoxville, Tennessee.
1873 Knox County Tax List for 1873. Knox County Archives, Knoxville, Tennessee.
1876 Knox County Tax List for 1876. Knox County Archives, Knoxville, Tennessee.
1877 Knox County Tax List for 1877. Knox County Archives, Knoxville, Tennessee.
1882 Knox County Tax List for 1882. Knox County Archives, Knoxville, Tennessee.
1887 Knox County Tax List for 1887. Knox County Archives, Knoxville, Tennessee.
1892 Knox County Tax List for 1892. Knox County Archives, Knoxville, Tennessee.
1893 Knox County Tax List for 1893. Knox County Archives, Knoxville, Tennessee.

KNOXVILLE CITY DIRECTORY
1910 *City Directory of Knoxville, Tennessee, 1910.*
1925 *City Directory of Knoxville, Tennessee, 1925.*

KNOXVILLE DAILY JOURNAL AND TRIBUNE
1912 Deaths and Funerals. *Knoxville Daily Journal and Tribune,* 8 January.

KNOXVILLE GAZETTE
1794 John Chisholm, Knoxville, May 16. *Knoxville Gazette,* 16 May.

KNOXVILLE JOURNAL
1931 *Knoxville Journal,* 7 June.

KNOXVILLE NEWS SENTINEL
1931 Knoxville's Forgotten Landmarks. *Knoxville News Sentinel,* 5 April.

KOVEL, RALPH, AND TERRY KOVEL
1980 *The Kovel's Antiques Price List.* Crown Publishers, New York.

LEE, RUTH
1946 *Early American Pressed Glass.* Lee Publications, Wellesley Hills, Massachusetts.

LONG, AMOS, JR.
1972   *The Pennsylvania German Family Farm: A Regional Architectural and Folk Cultural Study of an American Agricultural Community.* Vol. 6. Pennsylvania German Society, Breinigsville, Pennsylvania.

LORRAINE, DESSAMAE
1968   An Archaeologist's Guide to Nineteenth Century American Glass. *Historical Archaeology* 2:35–44.

LUCAS, SILAS E., JR., AND ELLA F. SHEFFIELD (EDITORS)
1981   *Tennessee Marriage Records and Bonds, 1783–1870.* Southern Historical Press, Easly, South Carolina.

MCKEARIN, GEORGE S., AND HELEN MCKEARIN
1941   *American Glass.* Crown, New York.

MCKEE, W. REID, AND M. E. MASON
1995   *Civil War Projectiles II: Small Arms & Field Artillery with Supplement.* Reprinted. Publisher's Press, Orange, Virginia. Originally published 1980 by the authors.

MCKELWAY, HENRY S.
2000   *Slaves and Master in the Upland South: Data Recovery at the Mabry Site (40KN86), Knox County, Tennessee.* Publications in Archaeology, No. 6. Tennessee Department of Transportation, Nashville.

MARTIN, CHARLES E.
1984   *Hollybush: Folk Building and Social Change in an Appalachian Community.* University of Tennessee Press, Knoxville.

MICHAUX, FRANÇOIS A.
1805   *Travels to the West of the Alleghany Mountains, in the States of Ohio, Kentucky, and Tennessee, and Back to Charleston, by the Upper Carolinas . . . Undertaken in the Year 1802.* 2nd ed. D. N. Shury, London.

MOIR, RANDALL W.
1987   Socioeconomic and Chronometric Patterning of Window Glass. In *Historic Buildings, Material Culture, and the People of the Prairie Margin,* edited by David H. Jurney and Randall W. Moir, pp. 83–96. Institute for the Study of Earth and Man, Archaeology Research Program, Richland Creek Technical Series, Vol. 5, Southern Methodist University, Dallas.

MORGAN, JOHN
1990   *The Log House in East Tennessee.* University of Tennessee Press, Knoxville.

MUNSEY, CECIL
1970   *The Illustrated Guide to Collecting Bottles.* Hawthorn Books, New York.

NOEL-HUME, IVOR
1970   *Guide to the Artifacts of Colonial America.* Alfred A. Knopf, New York.

PALMQVIST, LENA A.
1986   Swedes. In *America's Architectural Roots: Ethnic Groups That Built America,* edited by Dell Upton, pp. 154–159. Preservation Press, New York.

PATRICK, JAMES
1981   *Architecture in Tennessee, 1768–1897.* University of Tennessee Press, Knoxville.

PATTERSON, JUDY A.
1998   Dietary Patterning at an Upland South Plantation: The Ramsey House Site (40KN120), Knox County, Tennessee. Unpublished Master's thesis, Department of Anthropology, University of Tennessee, Knoxville.

PETROSKI, HENRY
1989   *The Pencil: A History of Design and Circumstance.* Alfred A. Knopf, New York.

POLHEMUS, RICHARD R.
1977   *Archaeological Investigation of the Tellico Blockhouse.* University of Tennessee, Department of Anthropology, Report of Investigations No. 26 and Tennessee Valley Authority, Reports in Anthropology No. 16. Knoxville.

POOLE, JULIANN C.
1982   Fanthorp Inn: A Study of Nineteenth- and Twentieth-Century Buttons. Appendix V in *Archaeological Excavation at Fanthorp Inn State Historic Site (41GM79), Grimes County, Texas, Spring and Fall, 1982.* Texas Parks and Wildlife Department, Historic Sites and Restoration Branch, Austin.

RAMSEY, FREDERIC R.
1982   *Ramsey of Swan Pond.* Fiddler Doubleday, Inc., Kalamazoo, Michigan.

RAMSEY, JAMES GETTYS McGREADY
1853   *The Annals of Tennessee to the End of the Eighteenth Century.* Walker and James, Charleston, South Carolina.
1868   Autobiographical and Historical Remarks of His Own Family By J. G. M. Ramsey of Mecklenburg, Tennessee Written in Exiles Retreat, North Carolina. University of Tennessee Special Collections.
1918   *History of the Lebanon Presbyterian Church.* Knoxville.

RAMSEY, MARGARET C.
1865–   Journal of Mrs. J. G. M. Ramsey. Typed copy in the McClung 1876
1876   Collection, Lawson-McGhee Library, Knoxville.

RANDALL, MARK E.
1971   Early Marbles. *Historical Archaeology* 5:102–105.

REHDER, JOHN B., JOHN MORGAN, AND JOY L. MEDFORD
1979   The Decline of Smokehouses in Grainger County, Tennessee. *Studies in the Social Sciences* 18:75–83.

ROBERTS, WAYNE D.
1986   *Archaeological Investigations at the Historic Ramsey House, Knox County, Tennessee.* Report prepared for the Association for the Preservation of Tennessee Antiquities, Knoxville Chapter. Department of Anthropology, University of Tennessee, Knoxville.

ROENKE, KARL G.
1978   *Flat Glass: Its Use as a Dating Tool for Nineteenth-Century Archaeological Sites in the Pacific Northwest and Elsewhere.* Northwest Anthropological Research Notes, Memoir No.4 (Vol. 12, No. 2, Pt. 2). Moscow, Idaho.

ROTH, RODRIS
1961   Tea Drinking in 18th-Century America: Its Etiquette and Equipage. In *Contributions from the Museum of History and Technology,* pp. 63–91. United States National Museum, Bulletin 255. Washington, D.C.

ROTHROCK, MARY U. (EDITOR)
1946   *The French Broad–Holston Country: A History of Knox County, Tennessee.* East Tennessee Historical Society, Knoxville.

SALSTROM, PAUL
1991   Origins of Economic Dependency, 1840–1880. In *Appalachian Frontiers: Settlement, Society, and Development in the Pre-Industrial Era,* edited by Robert D. Mitchell, pp. 261–337. University Press of Kentucky, Lexington.

SEYMOUR, DIGBY
1982   *Divided Loyalties: Fort Sanders and the Civil War in East Tennessee.* University of Tennessee Press, Knoxville.

SMITH, SAMUEL D.
1984   Excavation of a Mid-Nineteenth-Century Trash Pit, Wynnewood State Historic Site, Sumner County, Tennessee. *Tennessee Anthropologist* 7(2):133–181.

SMITH, SAMUEL D., AND STEPHEN T. ROGERS
1979   *A Survey of Historic Pottery Making in Tennessee.* Tennessee Department of Conservation, Division of Archaeology, Research Series No. 3, Nashville.

SOUTH, STANLEY A.
1977   *Method and Theory in Historical Archaeology.* Academic Press, New York.

SOUTH CAROLINA MARRIAGE RECORDS

1823– York County, South Carolina, Marriage Records. Yorkville, South
1865   Carolina.

STEWART, F. L.

1867   *Sorghum and Its Products.* J. B. Lippincott, Philadelphia.

STILGOE, JOHN W.

1982   *Common Landscapes of America, 1580–1845.* Yale University Press, New
       Haven.

STINE, LINDA S., MELANIE A. CABAK, AND MARK D. GROOVER

1996   Blue Beads as African-American Cultural Symbols. *Historical Archaeology*
       30(3):49–75.

TATE, SUSAN D.

1972   Thomas Hope of Tennessee, c. 1757–1820, House Carpenter and Joiner.
       Master's thesis, Department of History. University of Tennessee, Knoxville.

TENNESSEE ANCESTORS

1986   Knox County, Tennessee, Tax List, 1812. *Tennessee Ancestors* 2(1):4–15.

TINDELL, TED

1973   *Blount County: Communities We Live In.* Brazos Press, Maryville, Tennessee.

TOWNSEND, ALEX H.

1976   *Archaeological Excavations at Ramsey House, Knoxville, Tennessee, March 1976.*
       Report prepared for the Association for the Preservation of Tennessee Antiq-
       uities, Knoxville Chapter. National Heritage, West Chester, Pennsylvania.

UNITED STATES CENSUS

1830   Census of Knox County, Tennessee, 1830. Special Collections, University of
       Tennessee, Knoxville.
1840   Census of Knox County, Tennessee, 1840. Special Collections, University of
       Tennessee, Knoxville.
1850   Census of Knox County, Tennessee, 1850. Special Collections, University of
       Tennessee, Knoxville.
1860   Census of Knox County, Tennessee, 1860. Special Collections, University of
       Tennessee, Knoxville.
1870   Census of Knox County, Tennessee, 1870. Special Collections, University of
       Tennessee, Knoxville.
1880   Census of Knox County, Tennessee, 1880. Special Collections, University of
       Tennessee, Knoxville.
1900   Census of Knox County, Tennessee, 1900. Special Collections, University of
       Tennessee, Knoxville.

UNITED STATES CENSUS, SCHEDULE 4
1860   United States Census, Schedule 4, Production of Agriculture. Special
         Collections, University of Tennessee, Knoxville.
1870   United States Census, Schedule 4, Production of Agriculture. Special
         Collections, University of Tennessee, Knoxville.
1880   United States Census, Schedule 4, Production of Agriculture. Special
         Collections, University of Tennessee, Knoxville.

UNITED STATES CENSUS, SLAVE SCHEDULE
1840   United States Census, Slave Schedule for 1840. Special Collections,
         University of Tennessee, Knoxville.
1860   United States Census, Slave Schedule for 1860. Special Collections,
         University of Tennessee, Knoxville.

UNIVERSITY OF TENNESSEE AGRICULTURE EXTENSION SERVICE
1946   *Electric Water Systems, Water Systems for the Farm.* University of Tennessee
         Agricultural Extension Service, Publication 260. Knoxville, Tennessee.

VAN DEVENTER, ROBERT
1960   Notes on the Restoration of the Ramsey House Kitchen. McClung
         Collection, Lawson McGhee Library, Knoxville, Tennessee.
ca. 1965 Papers, Resources, and Correspondence. McClung Collection, Lawson
         McGhee Library, Knoxville, Tennessee.
1975   Ramsey House and Garden: A Pictorial History. On file, Ramsey House
         library.
1985   Tape recording about Ramsey House. In possession of the author.

WALTON, C. F., E. K. VENTRE, AND S. BYALL
1938   Farm Production of Sorgo Syrup. *Farmer's Bulletin* No. 1791. U.S. Depart-
         ment of Agriculture, Office of Information, Division of Publications, Wash-
         ington, D.C.

WASHBURN, CHARLES G.
1917   *Industrial Worchester.* Davis Press, Worchester, Massachusetts.

WESLAGER, C. A.
1969   *The Log Cabin in America from Pioneer Days to the Present.* Rutgers Univer-
         sity Press, New Brunswick, New Jersey.

WETHERBEE, JEAN
1996   *White Ironstone: A Collector's Guide.* Antique Trader Books, Dubuque, Iowa.

WILKIE, LAURIE
1997   Secret and Sacred: Contextualizing the Artifacts of African-American Magic
         and Religion. *Historical Archaeology* 31(4):81–106.

WILLIAMS, SAMUEL C., EDITOR
1928   *Early Travels in the Tennessee Country, 1540–1800.* Watauga Press, Johnson City, Tennessee.

WINBERRY, JOHN J.
1980   The Sorghum Syrup Industry. *Agricultural History* 54(2):343–352.

WINDHAM, R. JEANNINE
2002   Faunal Remains Recovered from the 2000 Field Season at Ramsey House. Term paper on file, Department of Anthropology, University of Tennessee, Knoxville.

WINTERS, DONALD L.
1994   *Tennessee Farming, Tennessee Farmers: Antebellum Agriculture in the Upper South.* University of Tennessee Press, Knoxville.

WOODHEAD, E. I., C. SULLIVAN, AND G. GUSSET
1984   *Lighting Devises in the National Reference Collection.* Studies in Archaeology, Architecture and History. National Historic Parks and Sites Branch, Parks Canada, Environment Canada, Ottawa..

WYCKOFF, MARTIN A.
1984   *United States Military Buttons of the Land Services, 1787–1902.* McLean County Historical Society, Bloomington, Illinois.

INDEX

Association for the Preservation of
Tennessee Antiquities (APTA):
begins archaeology program, 6,
146; grants from, 7; mission of, 145;
purchase of Swan Pond (Ramsey
House), 5, 7, 56, 61, 111, 115,
117, 118. *See also* Ramsey House
Association
Atwell, Margaret, 90
automobile artifacts, 117
AXUM computer program, 12

Big Limestone Creek, TN, 39, 40, 68
blacksmith/stable artifacts, 109,
110; horseshoe nails, 109, 110;
horseshoes, 17, 109, 110; iron bar
stock/waste, 109
blockhouse, 47, 49–50
Blount College, 134
Blount County, TN, 141
Blount, Gov. William, 40, 50, 75;
mansion of, 50, 77, 84
Breck, Daniel, Jr., 89
bricks: cistern construction 109, 111;
hand-made, 102, 109, 116; machine-
made, 108; porch foundation,
107–8, 111; sorghum furnace, 111;
walkways, 116
Brownlow, Parson William G., 90, 91
Brunswick pattern, 53
Buck House, DE, 61
Burnette, Jesse, 87, 88
Burnette, Joseph, 87–88
butchering, 72, 93, 95, 105, 106

California gold fields, 88, 89, 90. *See also*
Ramsey, Francis A. F. H.
Carson Newman College, TN, 143
Casteel, Elizabeth, 136
Cavett's Station, TN, 50

ceramic wares, historic: creamware, 49,
73, **74**, 75; ironstone, white, 96, 97,
98; pearlware, 73, **74**, 75, 97, **98**;
porcelain (china), **74**, 75, 96, **98**
119, **120**,136; porcelaneous refined
earthenware, 119; redware, **74**, 75,
77, 96; stoneware, **74**, 75, 80, 96, **98**,
119, **120**; tea wares, **74**, 75, 96, 119,
120, 135, 136; tin-glazed (Delph),
74, 75; whiteware, 28, 96, 97, **98**;
yellow ware, 119, **120**. *See also*
kitchen wares
Chattanooga, TN, 103
Charleston, SC, 53, 87
Chandler pottery, Edgefield District, SC,
96, **98**
Cincinnati, OH, 83
Civil War: artifacts, **99**, 102; Army of
Tennessee, 103, 140; Bridgeport, AL,
skirmish at, 140; General Braxton
Bragg, 140; General Amos Burnside,
140; Camp Morton, IN (P.O.W.
camp), 103, 140; Confederate army,
102–3, 145; Confederate government, 104, 140; devastation of, 3,
146; economic recovery after, 119;
Capt. W. C. Kain, light artillery,
103, 140; Kentucky campaign, 140;
General James Longstreet, 140;
Knoxville (Fort Sanders), battle of,
103; Knoxville, siege of, 140; outbreak of, 139; Piedmont, VA, battle
of, 103; 140; Brig. General James M.
Shackleford, 103; General Edmund
Kirby Smith, 140; Union army, 102,
103, 140, 141, 145; Unionists, 140
clothing, historic: bale seal, cloth; 78;
buttons, **76**, 78, 80, 99, 100, 101,
122, 124 ; hook and eye, 78, 100;
grommets, 124; scissors, iron, 78;
suspender buckle, **99**, 100, 101;
thimble, brass, 78; straight pins,
78, 100

Combs, James, 128
Combs, Walter, 128, 130
Combs, Mrs. Walter, 129
Coughlin, Sean, 63
Cowan, McClung and Company, 144
Cox, Cas, 130
Craighead, James P. N., 84
Craighead, John, 84
Craighead, Robert, 84
Craighead, Temperance Nelson, 84
crops, historic: apples, 71, 134, 143;
    beans, 94, 128; cantaloupe, 128;
    corn, 71, 94, 101, 118, 132, 134,
    139, 142; cotton, 142; cucumbers,
    128; flax, 70, 134; grapes (wine),
    94, 101–2; hay, 71, 94, 95, 139, 142,
    144; oats, 94, 105, 139, 142; peas, 94;
    potatoes, Irish (white), 94, 105, 118;
    potatoes, sweet, 94, 118, 130; rye,
    139; sorghum, 111; strawberries,
    118, 143; tobacco, 94, 139; tomatoes,
    128; watermelons, 128; wheat, 71,
    132, 134, 139, 142
Crozier, C. W., 83
Crozier, John, 68
Cumberland Gap, TN, 140

Dandridge, TN, 55, 56
Davenport, William, 68
Dean, Mrs. James, 117
Delaware County, PA, 46
Delaware River Valley, 46, 47
de Soto, Hernando, 35
Diderot, Denis, 57
Dixon, D. Bruce, 56, 107, 108
Dutch (Holland), 47, 75

English (England), 47, 49, 73, 75, 80,
    96, 120
Edgefield District, SC, 96

Farragut, TN, 111
Faulkner, Terry J., 141
Fenno-Scandinavians (Swedes and
    Finns): cabins of, 41, 46, 47; settle-
    ment of, 39, 41
fences, 16, 22, **23**, 25, 30, 54–**55**, **92**;
    barbed wire, 129; board, 92–93,
    108, 139; defensive, 19, **23**, 25, 30,
    49, **50**, **51**, **52**, 91, 92–93, 94, 133,
    136, 139; gate in, 51, 54; osage
    orange, 54; palen, 92–93, 139, 140;
    picket, 140; post and rail, 140; split
    rail, 88–89, 140
fire-cracked rock, 12, 16, 35
Forks of the River, 56, 86, 137, 141. *See
    also* Ramsey, J. G. M.
Frankfort, KY, 89
Franklin, state of, 40, 134
French (France), 75, 80, 119, 121
French Broad River, 135, 136, 141
furniture artifacts, historic: castor 100;
    coat hook, brass, 123; lamp chimney
    glass, 100, **122**, 123; lighting fixtures
    123; mirrors, 77, 100

Gamble, John Naylor, 65, 132, 135
Galveston, TX, 141
Gatesville, TX, 141
Georgia, 141
Germans (Germany), 47, 48, 61, 62, 77,
    87, 119, 133
Gettysburg, PA, 41, 65, 68
Gillespie House, TN, 54
Gilliam, Deverous, 67
Gilliam's Station, TN, 34
Great Smoky Mountains, 35
Greene County, TN, 39, 40
girder (log skid), **21**, 25, **29**, 30, 86, 109.
    See also Ramsey log cabin
Graves pottery, Corryton, TN, 96

HABS report, 107, 144
Hawthorne, Mrs., 69
Hepplewhite furniture, 77
Hermann, Bernard, 108
Hiawassee Railroad Company, 138
Hickman, Charlie, 130
Hickman, Pauline (Nelson), 127, 129
Holston River, 40, 135, 141
Hooper, James, 60
Hope, Thomas: construction of stone
    Ramsey House, 53, 54, 65; M.A.
    thesis on, 60; children of, 64; builds
    Joseph C. Strong House, 53; builds
    "Statesview," 64; lives at Swan Pond,
    69; knows John Adam Horlbeck, Sr.,
    87; moves to Knoxville, 53
Horlbeck, John Adam, Sr., 87
Horlbeck, John Adam, Jr., 87
Humphreys, Lyle, 65

Ice Age, 34, 35
I-house, Federal period, 107
Indians, American: artifacts of, 35, **36**
    37, 131; Cherokee, 35, 37, 50; Creek,
    50; frontier warfare, 136; historic,
    35; prehistory, 2, 34–37, 146

Jamestown, VA, 2
Japanese (Japan), 119
Jarnigan, William Spencer, 39
Jefferson County, TN, 40
Jonesborough, TN, 54

Keener, Esther, 106
Keener, Joseph, 109
Keener, Joseph L., 106, 109, 112
Keener, Leroy S., 106
Keener, Mary, 106
Keener, William A, 106
Kentucky River, 89

Kinzel, Edward John, 87
Kinzel, Jacob John, 87
Kinzel, John C., 87
Kinzel, Anna, 87
kitchen (foodways) artifacts: bottles,
    glass, 73, **74**, 77, 92; carnival glass,
    123; compote, glass, **122**, 123;
    cordial, glass, **99**; flasks, whiskey
    97, **99**, 121; jars, glass, 121, **122**;
    glassware, table, 70, 73, 75, 97, **99**,
    123; kettles (cast iron), 77; milk
    glass, 121, 123; table (flat) ware, **76**,
    77, 121, **122**; tin cans, 121; tumbler,
    glass, 73, 97, **99**, 122
Knoxville, TN: brick factories in, 108;
    farm market in, 143; mercantile
    stores in, 73; intended Indian attack
    on, 50; early road to, 56; visited by
    Bishop Asbury, 70; elite families in,
    75, 77; J. G. M. Ramsey returns to,
    104; W. B. A. Ramsey mayor of, 83
Knox County, TN, 5, early judicial
    district in, 40; I-houses in, 54; John
    Kinzel acquires land in, 87; listing of
    taxpayers in, 68
Kreis, Sam, 111

Lam, Conrad, 141
Lane, Lester, 130
lateral inheritance, 143
leisure artifacts, historic: alcoholic bev-
    erage bottles, **76**, 101–2; soft-drink
    bottles, 126; bicycle, 126; dolls,
    bisque, **122**, 126; dolls, porcelain,
    99, 102, **122**, 126; musical instru-
    ments, 102, **122**, 126; pipes, tobacco,
    76, 101; marbles, **76**, 99, 102, **122**,
    126; tea set, child's, **122**, 126
Limestone, TN, 71
Little Tennessee River, 35, 40
Lones, John, 94
Love, Robert, 39

Mabry, TN, site, 86
Marble Springs, TN, 71. *See also* Sevier, Governor John
Marsh Creek, PA, 39
McClung, Charles, 53, 64, 67
mean ceramic dating, 28, 43, 45, 48, 93, 116
Mecklenburg, NC, 40, 81
medicinal artifacts: medicine bottles, **76**, 79, 99, 101, **122**, 124; phials, 79
Michaux, Francois, 134
midden: sealed 49, 52, sheet, 52, 130
military/hunting artifacts, historic: cartridge, brass, **99**, 102, **122** 126; gun flints, **76**, 79, 80; percussion cap, brass, 102; shells, shotgun, **122**, 126; shot, spherical, 79, 80; shot, conical (bullet) **99**, 102; sprue, lead, 79; trigger, 79. *See also* Civil War: artifacts
Moravian, NC potters, 79
Moreton, Hannah, 69
Muncell color chart, 27

nails: cut, 45, 115; finishing, 45; machine cut, early, 49; machine cut, late, 63; wire, 45 115; wrought, 45, 49, 63, 64, 73
Nashville, TN, 86
New Castle, DE, 39
Nelson, Alexander, 127

Patrick, James, 53, 54
patrimonial succession, 3, 143, 146
personal artifacts, historic: bottle, perfume, **99**, 101, 125; chamber pot, **99**, 101, 125; cosmetic jar, 125; coins, 29, 116, 125; comb, 101; jewelry, **99**, 101; knife, clasp, **76**
Pickel, James, 33
Plumblee, Harvey, 88

prehistoric periods: Archaic, 34–36, 131; Mississippian, 132; Paleo-Indian, 34; Woodland, 36–37, 132. *See also* Indians, American

Rader, Ike, 53
Ramsey House Association, 146. *See also* Association for the Preservation of Tennessee Antiquities
Ramsey, Arthur Crozier, 90
Ramsey, Charlotte Barton, 90
Ramsey, Eliza, 41, 81, 82, 137
Ramsey, Eliza C. White, 83, 84, 138. *See also* Ramsey, W. B. A.
Ramsey, Elizabeth (Lizzie), 91, 104
Ramsey, Francis Alexander: abstinence of, 70, 77, 94; ancestors, 39; birth of, 39; construction of log house, 46–47, 135; construction of stone house, 5, 54; death of, 66, 69, 81, 84, 93, 137; death of Margaret "Peggy" Alexander, 65; estate divided between children, 81, 82; estate (probate) inventory, 65, 66, 69, 70, 71, 72, 73, 75, 77, 135, 145; "gentleman" farmer, 134; letters to his children, 3, 71; marries Margaret "Peggy" Alexander, 40; marries Ann Agnew Fleming, 65; marries Margaret (Russell) Cowan Humes, 81; names farm Swan Pond, 33; office, 43, 65; privacy, 136; public service, 40, 134–35; purchase and sale of slaves, 67–68; will of, 82
Ramsey, Francis Alexander (Frank), 81
Ramsey, Francis Alexander Frost Horlbeck (Alex/Elick), 94, 103, 146; birth of, 88; captured by Union army, 103; Colonel in local militia, 91; improvements to Swan Pond farm, 91, 139; leaves Swan Pond during Civil War, 103; letter from

Ramsey, Francis Alexander Frost (cont.)
father about care of Swan Pond,
88–89; living in Kentucky 138; marries Nancy (Nannie) R. Presley, 89,
139; moves to Chattooga County,
Georgia, 104, 141; moves to Texas,
141; photograph with wife "Nannie,"
141; purchases mill in Georgia, 104;
raising cattle on Swan Pond meadowland, 139; rebuilds defensive
fence, 91–92; receives Swan Pond,
83, 88, 89, 90, 139; removes defensive fence, 92, 138; sale of Swan
Pond after Civil War, 104; travel to
California goldfields, 88; Ramsey,
James McKnit, 90
Ramsey, James Gettys McCready, 71, 87,
94; acquires additional farms, 90;
believes son Crozier murdered, 140;
burning of Mecklenburg, 103, 141;
describes original Ramsey cabin, 30,
41, 43, 45, 132–33; describes father's
move to Tennessee, 39; describes
father's move from Limestone to
Swan Pond, 40; describes father's life
at Swan Pond, 136; describes former
Swan Pond, 33; description of
yard and grounds around Ramsey
House, 70; discusses relatives living
at Swan Pond, 69; exile in North
Carolina, 104; father drains Swan
Pond, 41; hiring of father's clerks,
65; inheritance of Forks of River
tract (lives at), 81, 82, 86, 37, 138;
letter about Daniel Breck, 89; letter
to wife about care of Swan Pond,
88; letter to Francis A. F. H. Ramsey,
88; letter to W. B. A. Ramsey about
tenants and return of Alexander,
87; 88; Mecklenburg home, 82, 103,
141; mentions "Road to Dandridge",
55; return to Knoxville after Civil

War, 104; Swan Pond transformed
into meadow, 132
Ramsey, John Crozier, 90, 104, 140
Ramsey, John McKnitt Alexander, 41,
82, 137, 138
Ramsey, John McKnitt, 40
Ramsey, Margaret (Russell) Cowan
Humes, 81. *See also* Ramsey, Francis
Alexander
Ramsey, Margaret (Peggy) Alexander,
40, 41, 65, 75, 81. *See also* Ramsey,
Francis Alexander
Ramsey, Margaret Crozier, 90. *See also*
Ramsey, J. G. M.
Ramsey, Naomi (Nancy or Nannie)
Pressley, 89, 91, 96. *See also* Ramsey,
F. H. A.
Ramsey, Reynolds, 39, 47
Ramsey, Robert McCready, 90
Ramsey, Samuel, 41
Ramsey, Susan Alexander, 90
Ramsey, Susan P. Washington, 86. *See
also* Ramsey, W. B. A.
Ramsey, William Baines Alexander:
daughters of, 84, 138; first wife Eliza
dies, 83; inheritance of Ramsey House
and farm, 81, 82, 137, 138; lives in
Knoxville, 86; marries Eliza C. White,
138; marries Susan P. Washington,
86, 138; marries Charlotte Williams,
138; mayor of Knoxville, 83; letter
from father, 71; memorial for, 84, 86;
moves to Nashville, 86, 138; public
service, 83, 86, 138; sells homeplace to
J. G. M. Ramsey, 86, 137; steamboat
enterprize/navigation, 83, 138 (see
also steamboat, *The Knoxville*); at
Swan Pond (homeplace), 81, 83, 93,
137; Tennessee Secretary of State, 86
Ramsey, William, 39, 87
Ramsey, William B., 40
Ramsey, William S., 87

Smith, William, 65
South, Stanley, 72
Spurgin (Spurgeon), Dorcas, 105
Spurgin (Spurgeon), John R., 105
Spurgin (Spurgeon), Mary T., 105
Spurgin (Spurgeon), Narcissa, 105
Spurgin (Spurgeon), William C., 105
"Statesview" (house), TN (also see
    Charles McClung), 53, 64
steamboat, *The Knoxville*, 138
Strawberry Plains Pike, 33
Strong House, TN, 53, 108
SURFER computer program, 49
Swan Pond, body of water, 2, 40, 54,
    68, 71; creek, 82, 135; description
    of, 131; draining of, 41, 51, 55, 132;
    location of, 33; peninsula in, 9,
    33–34, 35, 41, 49, 56, 58, 59, 132,
    134; prehistoric use of, 35–37

"tea ceremony" (also see tea wares), 96, 136
Tellico Blockhouse, TN, 80
tenant farmers (renters), 3, 87, 127, 144
Tennessee Historical Commission, 7
Tennessee River Valley, 35, 40
Tennessee Valley Authority, 34
Terminus post quem TPQ (dating), 92,
    125; bricks, 112; ceramics, 81, 108;
    window glass, 91
Territory of the U.S. South of the River
    Ohio, 40, 50
Thorngrove Pike, TN: construction of,
    51, 54, 55, 59, 133, 134; early cabin
    on, 69; farm lane to, 115; road to
    Dandridge, 56, 69, 115, 116, 130;
    walkway to, 116
Townsend, Alex H., 56, 107

UT Department of Anthropology,
    archaeological field school, 6, 19,
    21, 25, 29

UT School of Architecture, 61, 62
UT Special Collections Library, 81, 90
Upper Darby Creek, PA, 46

Van Deventer, Robert: on cellar cabinet,
    60; date stone on porch step, 108;
    restoration of kitchen, 62, 63, 64, 69,
    117; on master mason of Ramsey
    House; 54; on early outbuilding,
    10–12; on stone retaining wall,
    115

Washington College, TN, 71, 81
Washington County, NC, 39, 40
Washington County, TN, 105
Watson, Carl L., 112, 144
Watson, Edith, 61, 112, 127, 143
Watson, John A., 112, 117, 127, 143
Watson, John K., 112
Watson, Leona, 112
Watson, Nancy Keener, 112, 117, 127,
    143, 144
Watson, Sam P., 61, 112, 118, 127, 143,
    144
Watts, Claudialea Ledger, 93, 141
Weaver pottery factory, Knoxville, 119
West Chester, PA, 56
White, James, 39, 75, 135
window glass, 27, 28, 30, 73; dating of,
    28, 46, 64, 91, 93, 109, 110, 112, 116;
    distribution of, 46, 60
Williamsburg, VA, 2
writing implements, (office): ink bottle,
    66, **67**, 80, 103; ink well, 22, 66, **67**,
    80; pencil, slate, 22, 66, **67**, 80, 103;
    pencil, wood, 103; slate, writing, 66,
    67, 80, 103

York County, PA, 39
Yorkville, (York County) SC, 89, 103